Horatius Bonar

Family Sermons

Horatius Bonar

Family Sermons

ISBN/EAN: 9783337116699

Printed in Europe, USA, Canada, Australia, Japan

Cover: Foto ©Lupo / pixelio.de

More available books at **www.hansebooks.com**

Family Sermons.

BOOKS

BY THE

REV. HORATIUS BONAR, D.D.

	Cts.
THE NIGHT OF WEEPING	40
THE MORNING OF JOY	50
THE STORY OF GRACE	40
TRUTH AND ERROR	50
MAN, HIS RELIGION AND HIS WORLD	50
THE ETERNAL DAY	60
THE BIBLE HYMN BOOK	60
THE DESERT OF SINAI	1.00
THE LAND OF PROMISE	1.25
HYMNS OF FAITH AND HOPE, 1st *Series*	1.00
DO. DO. DO. 2d *Series*	1.00
GOD'S WAY OF PEACE	50
FAMILY SERMONS	1.50

ROBERT CARTER & BROTHERS, NEW YORK.

FAMILY SERMONS.

BY

HORATIUS BONAR, D. D.,
KELSO.

NEW YORK:
ROBERT CARTER AND BROTHERS,
No. 530 BROADWAY.
1863.

PREFACE.

These Sermons are short; and will, on that account, be found the more suitable for family reading. They are fifty-two in number, in order to furnish one for every Sabbath in the year. They are not upon family duties; but are rather meant as statements of the glorious gospel in some of its manifold aspects, as "the gospel of the grace of God."

Kelso, *Dec.* 19. 1862.

CONTENTS.

I.
BETHLEHEM AND ITS GOOD NEWS.
John i. 14.—" The Word was made flesh." . . . 1

II.
NAZARETH AND ITS GOOD NEWS.
Luke iv. 19.—" The acceptable year of the Lord." . . . 11

III.
THE MANIFESTED LIFE.
1 John i. 2.—" The Life was manifested." 20

IV.
THE MANIFESTED LIFE.
1 John i. 2.—" The Life was manifested." . . 26

V.
DIVINE PHILOSOPHY.
1 Cor. i. 24.—" Christ . . the wisdom of God." . . . 88

VI.
DIVINE PHILOSOPHY.
Cor. i. 24.—" Christ . . the wisdom of God." . . . 41

VII.
THE BANISHED ONE BEARING OUR BANISHMENT.
John x. 23.—" Jesus walked in the temple, in Solomon's porch." . 48

VIII.
THE BANISHED ONE BEARING OUR BANISHMENT.
John x. 23.—" Jesus walked in the temple, in Solomon's porch." . 56

IX.
THE SERVANT OF SINNERS.
Luke xxii. 27.—" I am among you, as he that serveth." . . 64

X.
THE SERVANT OF SINNERS.
Luke xxii. 27.—" I am among you, as he that serveth." . . 70

XI.
CHRIST THE HEALER.
Matt. ix. 21.—" If I may but touch his garment, I shall be whole." 79

XII.
CHRIST THE CLEANSER.
John xiii. 10.—" He that is washed needeth not, save to wash his feet, but is clean every whit." 87

XIII.
THE SURETY'S BAPTISM.
Luke xii. 50.—" I have a baptism to be baptized with ; and how am I straitened till it be accomplished !" . . . 96

XIV.

THE SURETY'S BAPTISM.

LUKE xii. 50.—"I have a baptism to be baptized with; and how am I straitened till it be accomplished!" . . . 102

XV.

THE SURETY'S SORROW.

JOHN xii. 27.—"Now is my soul troubled." 108

XVI.

THE SURETY'S THIRST.

JOHN xix. 28.—"Jesus saith, I thirst." 119

XVII.

THE SURETY'S THIRST.

JOHN xix. 28.—"Jesus said, I thirst." 125

XVIII.

THE SURETY'S THIRST.

JOHN xix. 28.—"Jesus said, I thirst." 132

XIX.

THE SURETY'S CROSS.

GAL. vi. 14.—"The cross of our Lord Jesus Christ." . . 138

XX.

THE SURETY'S CROSS.

GAL. vi. 14.—"The cross of our Lord Jesus Christ." . . 148

XXI.

THE CROSS THE EXPRESSION OF MAN'S UNBELIEF.

LUKE xxiii. 21.—"They cried, saying, Crucify him! crucify him!" 157

XXII.

LIFE AND FRUITFULNESS THROUGH DEATH.

JOHN xii. 24.—" Verily, verily, I say unto you, Except a corn of wheat fall into the ground and die, it abideth alone: but if it die, it bringeth forth much fruit." 168

XXIII.

LIFE AND FRUITFULNESS THROUGH DEATH.

JOHN xii. 24.—" Verily, verily, I say unto you, Except a corn of wheat fall into the ground and die, it abideth alone: but if it die, it bringeth forth much fruit." . . . 175

XXIV.

THE RISEN CHRIST AND THE THINGS ABOVE.

COL. iii. 1.—" If ye then be risen with Christ, seek those things which are above, where Christ sitteth on the right hand of God." 185

XXV.

THE RISEN CHRIST AND THE THINGS ABOVE.

COL. iii. 1.—" If ye then be risen with Christ, seek those things which are above, where Christ sitteth on the right hand of God." 194

XXVI.

FAITH IN AN UNSEEN CHRIST.

JOHN xx. 9.—" Blessed are they that have not seen, and yet have believed." 202

XXVII.

CONSECRATION BY BLOOD.

LEV. viii. 22, 23.—" And he brought the other ram, the ram of consecration: and Aaron and his sons laid their hands upon the head of the ram. And he slew it; and Moses took of the blood of it, and put it upon the tip of Aaron's right ear, and upon the thumb of his right hand, and upon the great toe of his right foot." 212

XXVIII.

A PRESENT SAVIOUR.

JOHN xx. 14.—"And knew not that it was Jesus." . . . 224

XXIX.

SELF OR CHRIST; WHICH IS IT?

ROM. xiv. 7–9.—"For none of us liveth to himself, and no man dieth to himself. For whether we live, we live unto the Lord; and whether we die, we die unto the Lord: whether we live therefore, or die, we are the Lord's. For to this end Christ both died, and rose, and **revived**, that he might be Lord both of the dead and living." 235

XXX.

PRIMITIVE DOUBTINGS, AND THEIR CURE.

LUKE xxiv. 40.—"When the Lord had thus spoken, he shewed them his hands and his feet." 249

XXXI.

PRIMITIVE DOUBTINGS, AND THEIR CURE.

LUKE xxiv. 40,—"When the Lord had thus spoken, he shewed them his hands and his feet." 255

XXXII.

CHRIST AND THE WORLD.

2 COR. vi. 14.—"What fellowship hath righteousness with unrighteousness?"
JAS. iv. 4.—"The friendship of the world is enmity with God." . 263

XXXIII.

THE GOD OF GRACE.

EPH. ii. 7.—"That in the ages to come he might shew the exceeding riches of his grace, in his kindness toward us through Christ Jesus." 273

XXXIV.

THE GOD OF GRACE.

Eph. ii. 7.—" That in the ages to come he might shew the exceeding riches of his grace, in his kindness toward us through Christ Jesus." 282

XXXV.

THE SINCERITY OF THE DIVINE COMPASSION.

Gen. vi. 6.—" It repented the Lord that he had made man on the earth, and it grieved him at his heart." . . . 293

XXXVI.

THE SINCERITY OF THE DIVINE COMPASSION.

Gen. vi. 6.—" It repented the Lord that he had made man on the earth, and it grieved him at his heart." . . . 302

XXXVII.

THE SINCERITY OF DIVINE EXPOSTULATIONS.

Ezek. xxxiii. 10, 11.—" Therefore, O thou son of man, speak unto the house of Israel, Thus ye speak, saying, If our transgressions and our sins be upon us, and we pine away in them, how should we then live? Say unto them, As I live, saith the Lord God, I have no pleasure in the death of the wicked; but that the wicked turn from his way and live: turn ye, turn ye, from your evil ways; for why will ye die, O house of Israel?" . . 311

XXXVIII.

THE SINCERITY OF DIVINE EXPOSTULATIONS.

Ezek. xxxiii. 10, 11.—" Therefore, O thou son of man, speak unto the house of Israel, Thus ye speak, saying, If our transgressions and our sins be upon us, and we pine away in them, how should we then live? Say unto them, As I live, saith the Lord God, I have no pleasure in the death of the wicked; but that the wicked turn from his way and live: turn ye, turn ye, from your evil ways; for why will ye die, O house of Israel?" . . 319

XXXIX.

THE SIN AGAINST THE HOLY GHOST.

MARK iii. 28–30.—" Verily I say unto you, All sins shall be forgiven unto the sons of men, and blasphemies wherewith soever they shall blaspheme; but he that shall blaspheme against the Holy Ghost hath never forgiveness, but is in danger of eternal damnation: because they said, He hath an unclean spirit." . 330

XL.

THE SIN UNTO DEATH.

1 JOHN v. 16, 17.—" If any man see his brother sin a sin which is not unto death, he shall ask, and he shall give him life for them that sin not unto death. There is a sin unto death; I do not say that he shall pray for it. All unrighteousness is sin; and there is a sin not unto death." 340

XLI.

THE THREE WITNESSES.

1 JOHN v. 5, 6.—" Who is he that overcometh the world, but he that believeth that Jesus is the Son of God? This is he that came by water and blood, even Jesus Christ: not by water only, but by water and blood. And it is the Spirit that beareth witness, because the Spirit is truth." 348

XLII.

THE DIVINE BANQUET.

LEV. xxi. 22.—" He shall eat the bread of his God, both of the most holy, and of the holy." 358

XLIII.

BETHANY AND ITS FEAST.

JOHN xii. 1–3.—" Then Jesus, six days before the passover, came to Bethany, where Lazarus was which had been dead, whom he raised from the dead. There they made him a supper; and Martha served: but Lazarus was one of them that sat at the table with him. Then took Mary a pound of ointment of spikenard, very costly, and anointed the feet of Jesus, and wiped his feet with her hair: and the house was filled with the odour of the ointment." 368

XLIV.
THE CHURCH'S WIDOWHOOD.
LUKE xviii. 3.—" And there was a widow in that city; and she came unto him, saying, Avenge me of mine adversary." . 376

XLV.
THE CHURCH'S WIDOWHOOD.
LUKE xviii. 3.—" And there was a widow in that city: and she came unto him, saying, Avenge me of mine adversary." . 285

XLVI.
THE WORLD'S ORACLES.
ZECH. x. 2.—" The idols have spoken vanity." . 394

XLVII.
THE VAIN WISH.
NUM. xxiii. 10.—" Let me die the death of the righteous, and let my last end be like his." . 408

XLVIII.
THE MORTAL AND THE IMMORTAL.
LUKE xx. 36.—" Neither can they die any more." . **416**

XLIX.
LONGINGS FOR THE LAND.
DEUT. iii. 23-29.—" And I besought the Lord at that time, saying, O Lord God, thou hast begun to shew thy servant thy greatness, and thy mighty hand; for what God is there in heaven or in earth, that can do according to thy works, and according to thy might? I pray thee, let me go over, and see the good land that is beyond Jordan, that goodly mountain, and Lebanon. But the Lord was wroth with me for your sakes, and would not hear me: and the Lord said unto me, Let it suffice thee; speak no more unto me of this matter. Get thee up into the top of Pisgah, and lift up thine eyes westward, and northward, and southward, and eastward, and behold it with thine eyes: for thou shalt not go over this Jordan. But charge Joshua, and encourage him, and strengthen him: for he shall go over before this people, and he shall cause them to inherit the land which thou shalt see. So we abode in the valley over against Beth-peor." . 424

L.
CHRIST AND THE NEW CREATION.

2 Cor. v. 17.—" If any man (one) be in Christ, he is a new creature (there is a new creation to him); old things are passed away; behold, all things are become new." . . . 435

LI.
APOSTOLIC SIGHS.

1 Cor. iv. 8.—" I would to God ye did reign, that we also might reign with you." 448

LII.
THE CHURCH'S AMEN.

Rev. xxii. 20, 21.—" He which testifieth these things saith, Surely I come quickly: Amen. Even so, come, Lord Jesus. The grace of our Lord Jesus Christ be with you all. Amen." . . 456

SERMON I.

BETHLEHEM AND ITS GOOD NEWS.

"The Word was made flesh."—JOHN i. 14.

THERE was nothing great about Bethlehem. It was "little among the thousands of Judah" (Mic. v. 2); perhaps but a shepherd-village or small market-town; yet there the great purpose of God became a *fact;* "The Word was made flesh."

It is in *facts* that God's purposes come to us, that we may take hold of them as real things. It is into *facts* that God translates his truth, that it may be visible, audible, tangible. It is in *facts* (as in so many seeds) that God embodies his good news, that a little child may grasp them in his hand. So was it with the miracle of our text. God took his eternal purpose and dropped it over Bethlehem in the form of a fact, a little fragment of human history. Over earth, the first promise had been hovering, for four thousand years, till at last it rested over Bethlehem, as if it said, "This is my rest; here will I dwell."

The city is poor rather than rich. It is not without its attractions; but these are of the more homely kind. Its scenes are not stately; its hills are not lofty; its plains are not wide; its slopes are rocky; it is not like the city of the Great King, beautiful for situation, the joy of the whole earth. Yet there "the Word was made flesh."

It has no palace nor temple; only an inn for the travellers passing between Hebron and Jerusalem; its dwellers are not priests nor princes; it is not a sacred city, and is but little noted in history. Yet there, not at Jerusalem, "the Word was made flesh."

But its lowliness makes it more suitable as the birthplace of Him who, though he was rich, for our sakes became poor. And all about it seems to suit him too. It is "the house of bread," fit dwelling for him who is "the bread of God." Its old name was Ephratah, "the fruitful," as if pointing to the fruitful one. At its gate is the well of David; and not far off are the pools of Solomon, which pour their water into Jerusalem, telling us of the living water, and the river whose streams make glad the city of our God. The gardens of Solomon are also hard by, speaking to us not only of "the garden of the Lord," and the second Adam, and the tree of life, but giving us the earthly scenes (which are the patterns of the heavenly) which the "Song of songs" describes. (Song of Sol. ii. 12, 13.)

In walking through its streets, or wandering over its heights, one seems to read text after text, written, not with an iron, but a golden pen, upon its hills and rocks. "Unto us a Child is born," seems inscribed on one ; " Unto us a Son is given," on another; "Unto you is born a Saviour," on a third ; "Glory to God in the highest," on a fourth ; the name of JESUS upon all. The city is not now what it was, yet there it sits upon the northern face of its old height ; the one town in Palestine still possessed exclusively by those who call themselves by the name of Christ.

Bethlehem is not named in our text ; but you cannot read the verse without being transported to that city. "In the beginning was the Word," carries you up into heaven, and back into past infinity. "The Word was made flesh," brings you down to earth and the finite things of time; to the manger, and the stable, and "the young Child." The shepherds are gone ; the wise men have departed to their own country ; the glory has passed up again into heaven ; the angels have left; the song of the plain has ceased ; the star has disappeared,—the star of which Balaam spoke, as yet to sparkle somewhere in these eastern heavens, and which Micah may be said to have fixed and hung over the city, when he named the name of Bethlehem as the birthplace of the coming King,—but the city itself is still there, rooted to its old spot; not, like Rachel's tomb hard by, a memorial of death and sorrow, but a remembrancer of joy and peace, a witness of the everlasting life which came down from heaven.

At Bethlehem our world's history begins. All

before and after the birth of the young child takes its colour from that event. As the tree, rising from a small root or seed, spreads its branches, and with them its leaves, its blossoms, its fruit, its shade, north, south, east, and west; so has this obscure birth influenced all history, sacred and secular, before and behind. That history is an infinite coil of events, interwoven in endless intricacies, apparently with a thousand broken ends; now upward, now downward, now backward, now forward; but the ravelled coil is *one*, and its centre is Bethlehem. The young Child there is the interpreter of all its mysteries. As He is "the beginning of the creation of God," the "first-begotten of the dead," so is he the beginning and ending, the centre and circumference of human history. "Christ is all and in all;" and as such, from the manger to the throne, he is the incarnation of Jehovah's purposes, the interpretation of the divine actings, and the revelation of the heavenly mysteries.

Few statements contain in them such a world of truth as this of our text. Let us see (I.) what it is, (II.) what it teaches.

I. *What it is.*—The "Word" is the eternal name for the young Child of Bethlehem. He is so called because he is the revealer of the Father, the exponent of Godhead. He is so now; he was so in the days of his flesh; he has been so from eternity. The names *Christ, Immanuel, Jesus,* are his earthly ones; his names in time, connected with his incarnate condition ; but the names "Word" and "Son" are expressive of his eternal standing, his eternal relationship to the Father. What he was in time and on earth, that same he has been in heaven and from eternity. The glory which he had "before the world was" (John xvii. 5), and of which he "emptied himself" (Phil. ii. 7, see Greek), was the glory of the eternal Word, the everlasting Son. As the eternal revealer of Godhead, the "brightness of Jehovah's glory, and the express image of his person," his name ever was THE WORD; as the declarer of the mind of God to man, his name is no less THE WORD, with this addition, " the Word *made flesh.*"

" In the beginning was the Word," is the divine, or heavenly, or upper portion of the mystery; "the Word was made flesh," is the human, the earthly, the lower. It is this latter that so specially concerns us; for without it the former was nothing to us. God *manifest in flesh* is the "great mystery of godliness," which links together the creature and the Creator; which brings down to the sinner's side the waters of the eternal well. It is this that makes the inaccessible and unapproachable Godhead accessible and approachable ; the unseen becoming the seen,—nay, the most seen of all ; the far-off becoming the near,—nay, the nearest of all ; the incomprehensible becoming comprehensible,— nay, the most comprehensible of all, a little child, —a child of poverty and weakness, suckled at a woman's breast, and resting upon a woman's knee.

The Word was made flesh! He became truly man;—man all over, within and without, in body, soul, and spirit; in everything but sin. All the nations of the earth God hath made of *one blood*, and of that *one blood* was the Word made partaker, becoming bone of our bone and flesh of our flesh; his soul truly human, not superhuman nor celestial; his body of the very substance of the Virgin,—true, real, yet holy flesh; the holiness not making him less truly flesh, and the flesh not making him less truly holy.

Thus Bethlehem becomes the link between heaven and earth. God and man meet there, and look each other in the face. In the young child man sees God, and God sees man. There is joy in heaven, there is joy on earth, and the same song suits both,—"Glory to God in the highest; on earth peace and good-will towards men." Jacob's ladder is now firmly planted on the earth. God is coming down; man is going up; angels are in attendance upon both. The seed of the woman has come. God has taken man's side against the old serpent. He has not only knocked at man's door, but he has come in. The winter is past; the rain is over and gone; the day has broken; the shadows have fled away!

II. *What it teaches.*—The angel was the first to interpret it,—"Behold, I bring you good tidings of great joy." Yes, tidings of peace and good-will; tidings of God's free love; tidings of his design to pitch once more his tabernacle here, and to take up his abode with the sons of men.

It teaches us God's thoughts of peace; for incarnation means this at least, that God's desire is to bless us, not to curse; to save, not to destroy. He seeks reconciliation with us; nay, he has brought about the reconciliation. He has not merely made proposals of peace, and sent them to us by the hand of an ambassador; but he has himself come to us bearing his own message, and presenting himself to us, in our nature, as his own ambassador. Incarnation is not, indeed, the whole, but it is much. It is the voice of love, the message of peace. God himself is both the *speaker* and the *maker* of peace.

The message that comes to us from Bethlehem is a very decided one. It is not a finished one; it was only finished at the cross; but, so far as it goes, it is quite explicit; quite unambiguous. It means love, peace, pardon, eternal life. The lesson taught us at Bethlehem is the lesson of grace; the grace of God, the grace of the Father and of the Son. We may learn much, indeed, as to the way of life, from Bethlehem. It must not, indeed, stand alone; you must associate it with Jerusalem; you must bring the cradle and the cross together. But still it teaches us the first part of the great lesson of peace. It says, though not so fully as Golgotha, God is love. The beginning is not the end, but still it is the beginning. The dawn is not the noon, but still it is the dawn. Bethlehem is not Jerusalem, but still it is Bethlehem. And the Prince of peace is there. The God of salvation is there. The manifested life is there.

Do not despise Bethlehem. Do not pass it by. Come; see the place where the young child lay. Look at the manger : there is the Lamb for the burnt-offering, the Lamb of God that taketh away the sin of the world. These little tender hands shall yet be torn ; these feet, that have not yet trod this rough earth, shall be nailed to the tree. That side shall yet be pierced by a Roman spear ; that back shall be scourged ; that cheek shall be buffeted and spit upon ; that brow shall be crowned with thorns ;—and all for you ! Is not this love ? Is it not the great love of God ? And in this love is there not life ? And in this life is there not salvation, and a kingdom, and a throne ?

At Bethlehem, the fountain of love was opened, and its waters have gushed out in their fulness. The well of David has overflowed the earth, and the nations now may drink. The good news have gone forth from the city of David, and all the ends of the earth have seen the salvation of our God.

Would you learn the way to God ? Go to Bethlehem. See yon infant : It is God; the Word made flesh. He is " the Way." No man cometh to the Father but by him. Go and deal with him. So shall Bethlehem be to you the gate of heaven.

Would you learn the vanity of earth. Go to

yon manger where the Lord of glory lies. That is reality; all else is hollow. What a vain world is this of ours! Yon manger contains the only thing on earth of which it cannot be said, "Vanity of vanities; all is vanity."

Would you have a safeguard against worldliness, and sin, and error, and the snares of the last days? Choose and keep the young Child's companionship. Wherever you go, be like Joseph and Mary, when they fled into Egypt; take the young Child with you. Is it into the world's business? Take the young Child with you. Is it into its philosophy and literature? Take the young Child with you. Is it into its relaxations and amusements? Take the young Child with you. If you take Him, all is right. If you forget to do so, or find you cannot, all is wrong.

Would you learn to be humble? Go to Bethlehem. There the highest is the lowest; the eternal Word a babe; the King of kings has not where to lay his head; the Creator of the universe sleeps in a woman's arms. How low he has become; how poor! Where shall we learn humility if not here? All earthly pride is here rebuked and put to shame. Be not proud, says yon Bethlehem manger. Be clothed with humility, say the swaddling-bands of yon helpless Child.

Would you learn to be self-denied? Go to Bethlehem. See the Word made flesh. He "pleased not himself." Where shall we find such self-denial as at the cradle and the cross? Where shall we read a lesson of self-sacrifice, such as we have in him who made himself of no reputation; who chose not Jerusalem, but Bethlehem, for his birthplace; not a palace nor a temple, but a stable for his first earthly home? Shall we not be followers of his lowly love? Shall we not deny self? Shall we not stoop for others as he has stooped for us?

SERMON II.

NAZARETH AND ITS GOOD NEWS.

"The acceptable year of the Lord."—LUKE iv. 19.

It is as a "preacher of the gospel" that the Lord here announces himself. He was sent of the Father, that he might "testify the gospel of the grace of God." Both in that which he *spoke*, and in that which he *did*, he shewed himself the Revealer of the free-love of God.

Not to *create* that love, nor to *call it forth*, but to *reveal* it; not to *buy* it, but to *make a way* for its reaching us, did the Son of God take flesh, and live, and die. It was as the messenger of peace between God and man, that he came from the Father, and "dwelt among us." It was as the bringer of good news, that he was born at Bethlehem, and died on Golgotha; and it is as such that he "stands up to read" in the synagogue of Nazareth.

This Nazareth, to which he brought his first message of grace, had no claim for such favour and honour. It was not one of the holy or famous cities of the Old Testament. It was neither a city of refuge nor a Levitical city. It had no name in

Israel in former days, and, when the Lord made it his dwelling, it was noted for its evil, not for its good.

Certainly it is "beautiful for situation," nestling in the heart of the mountains of Galilee, far above the broad plains on either hand, yet girt in with hills on all sides as with a curtain, which shuts out everything of earth, and leaves nothing for its dwellers to gaze upon, but the blue sky above. Even as it now stands, it looks fair, though its slopes are bare, and its olives, and fig-trees, and sycamores are few. From its heights how exquisite the prospect around us,—Hermon, Tabor, Carmel, the hills of Gilead, the plain of Esdraelon, with the blue of the Great Sea filling up the bay of Acre, into which the Kishon is pouring its ancient waters.

Yet fair as it lay in the seclusion of its mountain-dell, it was full of sin; nor did it present any attraction to the Son of God, save that which the sick man does to the physician, when "the whole head is sick, and the whole heart is faint."

But where sin abounded, there grace did much more abound; and it was this abounding grace that now visited this home of abounding sin. The Son of man came to seek and to save that which was lost; and on these hills of Zebulon we find the good Shepherd pursuing his stray sheep, bent upon their recovery, as if they had been the choicest of his flock.

It is, then, to Nazareth-sinners that the first words of grace are spoken; and the speaker is the

Son of God himself. The gracious words at which the synagogue wondered, are the words of "the only begotten of the Father;" and they to whom they are addressed are not the best, but the worst specimens of Israel, the inhabitants of a city where there was no loveableness to attract the Saviour's love, no worth to invite the favour, and no fitness to qualify for the honour conferred.

The Lord here, quoting Isaiah, states his mission to be the preaching of the acceptable year of Jehovah. Let us inquire what the acceptable year of the Lord is, and how he preached it.

I. *The acceptable year of the Lord.* This expression corresponds to that of Paul, " the accepted time," " the day of salvation" (2 Cor. vi. 2) ; and means that there is a time when God accepts or shews favour to the sinner. It is what Ezekiel calls " the time of love ; " what our Lord calls "the time of visitation" (Luke xix. 44) ; and what we usually call " the day of grace." It does not refer to the lifetime of an individual, or to any portion of that lifetime, but to the whole period during which God is exercising mercy upon earth, a period which, no doubt, began when the first promise announced mercy to man, but which might be said to have received its great visible commencement or start, when " the Word was made flesh ; " or, still more definitely, when he went forth as " the sent" of the Father, to proclaim to men the " exceeding riches of the grace of God." Then the new age or era of grace began; Jehovah's "acceptable year" commenced running its course.

It is sometimes called a *day*, sometimes a *year*, sometimes a *time*; implying a considerable period; but, at the same time, intimating that this season *has an end*. The mercy that marks it will not always last. At the appointed time the long-suffering will cease, and the grace be transformed into vengeance, vengeance as true and as terrible as has been the grace.

Jehovah's acceptable year is the season during which he is revealing himself as the "Lord God, merciful and gracious, long-suffering, and abundant in goodness and truth, keeping mercy for thousands, forgiving iniquity, and transgression, and sin." It is the season during which he is shewing himself able to save to the uttermost, and to quicken the dead in sin with an everlasting life. It is the season during which he is giving bread to the hungry, and water to the thirsty, and health to the sick, and clothing to the naked, and riches to the poor, and abundance to the needy; during which he is forgiving sin, cleansing guilt, loosing chains, opening prisons, finding lost ones, welcoming prodigals, receiving sinners, stretching out his hand all the day to a disobedient and gainsaying people.

Every era has its character, and the character of this is "grace." In it the long-suffering of God gets full vent to itself, and his almighty love is pouring itself down upon an unworthy world. He has thrown wide open both his home and heart, that the men who have forsaken both may return and be blest.

If, then, the special characteristic or mark of this era be that of God's "receiving sinners," who can hesitate to come, or doubt as to his own personal welcome? The gracious character of this era continues to the very last. It began in love, and it ends in love; and, not the less so, because it is to be succeeded by vengeance and wrath. There is no diminution of the blessing; no drying up of the blessed stream; no narrowing of the heart out of which the gracious wonders come. Nay, as rivers grow fuller and deeper in passing downward, and as they are widest at their entrance on the great ocean, so does this acceptable year preserve its character to the last, and the free-love which marks it seems to increase and enlarge, as the time of the end draws nigh. The last messages of grace which the Bible contains, and which are specially meant for the last days, are the fullest and the largest of all;—"Whosoever will, let him take of the water of life freely." Peter, at the close of his second epistle, brings out this blessed truth, when he tells us the reason of the Lord's delay,—"Account the long-suffering of our Lord, salvation;" and never did words more expressively proclaim the yearning, the compassion, the unabated and unchanging fulness of divine tenderness to sinners, than when they announced through the lips of that apostle, that "the Lord is not slack concerning his promise, as some men count slackness; but is long-suffering to us-ward, not willing that any should perish, but that all should come to repentance" (2 Peter iii. 9).

How truly are all the parts of this era in keeping with each other! And is not this a fitting close to such a long, long day of grace, a noble summing-up of the loving-kindnesses and tender mercies that have been unfolding themselves during the "acceptable year of the Lord."

> "The setting sun and music at the close,
> As the last taste of sweets, is sweetest last."

And here, at the close of this day of salvation, we have the brightness of bright sunset made brighter by the heavenly music and the last long peal of the silver trumpet, proclaiming pardon, and life, and favour to the guiltiest; bidding, in the name of the long-suffering Jehovah, each wanderer welcome home!

II. *How Christ preached this acceptable year.*—This preaching of the acceptable year was to run through his whole life and ministry. It was to be their sum and their burden; their beginning and their ending; their first and their last.

In his *person* he preached it; for his mere presence upon earth among sinful men was an announcement of it. Grace and truth came by Jesus Christ; grace and truth shone out from him; so that every one who saw him, or heard of him, could not but know that this was the acceptable year of the Lord. So long as the Son of God, the only-begotten of the Father, full of grace and truth, was upon earth,—so long men might understand that God was receiving sinners; for they that saw him saw the Father.

He preached it by what he did. He went about healing all manner of sicknesses, and all manner of diseases. He raised the dead; he cast out devils; he opened the eyes of the blind; he unstopped the ears of the deaf; he gave feet to the lame; he fed the multitudes; he forgave sins and received sinners; he sought and found the lost. Each one of these acts spoke of the divine free-love that was now richly going forth towards the sons of men; not condemning, but pardoning; not destroying, but saving; not repelling, but welcoming the wanderer. Each one of these acts preached the acceptable year of the Lord, and said, not only in the name of the Son, but of the Father too,—" Him that cometh to me, I will in no wise cast out."

He preached it by what he did *not* do. He did no deeds of terror, and wrought no miracles of wrath or woe. He was greater than Elijah, yet he called down no fire from heaven; he smote the land with no famine; he was the song of the drunkard, the object of reviling, yet not one stroke of vengeance came from his hand. Was not this the intimation of the gracious errand on which he had come? Did it not say,—I have not come to destroy men's lives, but to save them? And even when Peter took up the sword in his behalf, and smote off the ear of Malchus, did he not heal the wounded man; as if to confirm this grace to the last, not only by abstinence from self-vindication, but by returning love for hatred; thus declaring that no amount of sin in man, or wrong done to Himself, could alter the character of this "day of salvation," or make it less "the acceptable year of the Lord?"

He preached it by what he said. His words were all of grace; and even the sharp rebukes against Scribes and Pharisees were the warnings of grace, not of wrath. Never man spake like this man; crowds hung upon him to hear his discourses; and men wondered at the gracious words which proceeded out of his mouth. When he said, "I am come, a light into the world, that whosoever believeth on me should not abide in darkness," he was preaching the acceptable year of the Lord, and saying, This is the time when God is receiving sinners; so that all who are in darkness are welcome to this light. When he said, "Her sins, which are many, are forgiven;" and again, "Neither do I condemn thee;" he was preaching the acceptable year of the Lord, and saying, Now is the season for pardon; so that the most guilty of men may go at once to God, with the certainty that their condemnation shall be taken away. When he said, "I am the bread of life, he that cometh to me shall never hunger, and he that believeth on me shall never thirst," he was preaching the acceptable year of the Lord; so that the hungriest and thirstiest of the sons of men might know that the bread of God is provided for them, and the living water flowing out to quench their thirst. And when, upon the cross, he cried, "Father, forgive them," and again, "It is finished," he was still preaching to the last the acceptable year of the Lord, and announcing the consummation of that sacrifice, by means of which grace had been identified with righteousness, and righteousness with grace.

It is still the acceptable year of the Lord, and Christ still preaches it. The season of God's free love is not yet over; and the Son of God, now seated at the Father's right hand, is to us the evidence and seal of this. His sitting on the mercy-seat, his continuing on the throne of grace, tells us that God is still receiving sinners. And this is the good news which we bring; this is the burden of our message, and the object of our embassy.

It is on this foundation of free love that, as saints, we stand, and rejoice in hope of the glory of God. It is this air of free-love which we breathe, and which is the very health of our souls. It is with this light of free-love that we are compassed about, and so made partakers of the heavenly joy. We entered on this liberty, when we received Christ's testimony to the acceptable year; and we continue in it, by continuing to believe that same testimony to the end. Embosomed in his grace, encircled with his free-love, we pass onward to the kingdom, in the expectation of receiving yet larger measures of love,—" the grace that is to be brought to us at the revelation of Jesus Christ" (1 Pet. i. 13).

SERMON IV.

THE MANIFESTED LIFE.

"The Life was manifested."—1 JOHN i. 2.

THIS word "life" was one which the Son of God took up when here, and held it forth, in many forms, and under many figures. He speaks of himself as "the Life," as the *bread* of life, as the *water* of life, as the *light* of life. All that life can mean or embody is deposited in him, personified in him, dispensed by him. All that God calls life is in him. The fulness of the eternal life is contained in this divine vessel, this heavenly well-spring; for in him we have the well of water springing up into everlasting life. He is the eternal Life; he is the Prince of life; he is the tree of life; he is the living stone, and the living way.

Surely there is no lack of life for us. But what if it be all untasted by us? What if it be rejected and despised? Here is life *for* you; but is it *in* you? Here is life come down to earth; but has it quickened *you*? Here is life knocking at the door of death; have you admitted it, or has it knocked in vain? For, as it was with the world at large, so is it with individual souls. It is the death that is in grace, or principle on which God's actings of free-love proceed, is what man would call the law of unfitness, and unworthiness, and unlikeness.

Well for us that it is so! What would have been our hope, had it been otherwise?

In God's dealings with man, it is the *unlike* that we see uniting. What more unlike than God and the sinner? yet they have come together! What more dissimilar than heaven and earth? yet they have come together! The mutual attraction has been the mutual *unlikeness*. Want of resemblance has been the knitting bond. The evil has drawn out the good; the darkness has attracted the light; the unrighteousness has awakened the righteousness: the death has brought down the life; the grave has called up resurrection. Where sin has abounded, grace has abounded much more.

The Life has been manifested! This is our gospel. It is not, "the Life *is*," but "the Life" has come forth from its eternal mystery; "the Life" has been MANIFESTED; so as to be seen, and heard, and handled. In the Word was life; nay, the Word was *the* Life. "In Him was life, and the life was the light of men" (John i. 4). The "light of the world" is the Word made flesh, the manifested life of God. The Life was manifested, and we beheld his glory,—the glory as of the only-begotten of the Father, full of grace and truth. In the light we have the life, and in the life we have the light.

The Life has been manifested! But what has drawn it out? What has given it opportunity to come forth? Death! It is not life that has attracted life; nor light that has given occasion for the outshining of light. No; but death and darkness; utter death, absolute darkness.

Thus God, the God of all grace, has spoken out, and revealed to us the breadth and length of his infinite love. Thus we learn the true meaning, and discover the essence of that grace which has been proclaimed to us by the lips, and embodied in the person of the incarnate Son. It is the *total unlikeness* between the lover and the loved one that brings out the real nature of grace. Love to the unloveable and unloving is its very essence. Apart from this it has no meaning, no reality, no suitableness. Introduce one element of resemblance, one fragment or feature of loveableness, and grace is gone.

It was the manifestation of *death* on earth that called forth this manifestation of *life* from heaven. Man's utter death has drawn out the fulness of the life of God. The entrance of death was the signal for the entrance of life. Life, in its boundless fulness, seemed on the watch to enter in and take possession of earth. But it could not do so till death had come. As it needs darkness to bring out the glory of the starry heavens, so it needed death to shew forth the life,—life such as had not been possessed before, nor could be, by man unfallen, or upon a sinless earth. Hence the deep significance of the Lord's words, "I am come that they might have life, and that they might have it more abundantly" (John x. 10).

Thus and then the Life entered! Not like a monarch, to take possession of a fitting palace; but like a physician, to take possession of an hospital; like spring, coming to take possession of a wintry earth; like day-spring, coming to take possession of the darkened skies. What an entrance! Not invited by kindred life, still lingering among men; but uninvited, nay, repelled. It is the absence of life here, that is the cause of its manifestation from on high. The reign of death is the herald of the reign of life, as midnight is the herald of the morn.

A manifestation such as this, in heaven, where all is life, would not have seemed so marvellous; for man's rule is, "like draws to like." But it is passing wonderful that it should have been here, in the land of death. Yet this is only the more like that God from whom the manifestation came. For his thoughts are not our thoughts, nor his ways ours. His love is not our love, nor his pity ours. As he sends his rain and his sunshine, just *where* they are needed, and *when* they are needed, and *because* they are needed, not because they are there already; so is it with his grace and its revelation; with life and its manifestation. That grace and life came to us simply because we needed them, and because God needed sin and death like ours, for the display of his fulness. He needs midnight that he may say, "Let there be light;" he needs the storm that he may say, "Peace, be still;" he needs the creature's emptiness for the display of the Creator's strength; he needs the sinner's evil to furnish a sphere for the forthcoming of the good in himself, which, but for this, had been pent up and hidden. He allows man to fall that he may shew how he can love and lift up the fallen. He lets Eden become a wilderness, that he may shew how he can make the desert rejoice and blossom as the rose. So he takes the dried-up well, and fills it; he takes the broken harp, and draws out from it the full compass of his heavenly music; he takes the quenched star, and lights it up into a more resplendent and everlasting sun.

It was the blind man that was the object of attraction to the Son of God; and Jesus needed him as truly as he needed Jesus. The *tomb* of Lazarus was to Him more attractive than the *house* of Lazarus; for at the house he was the receiver, at the tomb he was the giver. The leper drew near to him, and he to the leper, as by some mutual fitness, by some irresistible necessity; he needing the leper, and the leper needing him. The publican and he were daily meeting, finding each other out, attracted by their mutual need; the righteous and the unrighteous recognising, in each other, an object exactly suited to that which they severally possessed. The sick one and the healer had a link between them which no other knew, and with which a stranger could not intermeddle. It was the *lost* one that attracted the seeker; the *lost* sheep that made the shepherd's journey a necessity; the *lost* piece of silver that made the woman light her candle; and the *lost* son that brought the father to the door, to watch, in longing love, for the wanderer's return.

The Life was manifested! And we have seen it! Life in the realms of the dead; light in the land of darkness; God manifest in flesh;—this is what our eyes have seen. Yes; and these things are written for us, that our joy may be full; for in that *life* is *love*.

Go to Bethlehem; look into yon cradle; what is that? It is the manifested Life. Climb the hills of Galilee, and enter Nazareth; see yon boy, so like, yet so unlike all others; he is the manifested Life. Pass over Olivet, and visit Bethany; stand by yon tomb, where a dead man has lain four days; hear the voice which in a moment empties the grave, and recalls the dead; what is that? It is the manifested Life. Look at Golgotha; mark yon cross. Is it death, or is it life? It is both. It is death conquering life, and life overcoming death. The manifested Life is yonder; nay, in that very death there is the fullest manifestation of life. Look once more at yon empty grave, from which the stone has been rolled away. Who is it that early in the morning, while it is yet dark, comes forth from its rocky gloom? It is the manifested Life; the risen Son of God; the Resurrection and the Life; he who says, "I am he who liveth and was dead." Yes; at the cradle, and the cross, and the tomb, the Life has been manifested! Blessed manifestation for us, the dead in sin! The Life has come; and because he liveth, we shall live also; for he that hath the Son hath life.

SERMON III.

THE MANIFESTED LIFE.

"The Life was manifested."—1 John i. 2.

"Like draws to like," is man's maxim, and man's principle of action. The things that resemble, attract each other; the things that differ, repel. Love attracts love; the loving and the loveable knit themselves together. Life attracts life; and the living cleave to the living. Things congenial discover their mutual congenialities, and find their way to each other, as by some magnetic virtue; things uncongenial keep far asunder. Life and death have no brotherhood; and what communion has light with darkness?

Such is the law of earth! Such is the action of human hearts; such the extent of the circle, within which, even at their widest stretch, they revolve; such the measure of the depths to which their loves and sympathies can descend. Likeness, and fitness, and worthiness, are necessary elements in all earthly affinities.

But such is not the heavenly law. The principle of divine action, the regulating power of the infinite heart above, is the reverse of this. The law of each that attracts the heavenly life; not some lurking remains of life, nor the possession, however slender, of some goodness, but the entire absence of both life and goodness. It is to the *dead* that the life comes; it is to the *unloveable* that the love comes; it is to the *lost* that the salvation comes. That which qualifies us for life, for healing, for riches, for deliverance, is our death, our sickness, our poverty, and our bondage.

The Life has been manifested! The Christ has come. For us the Word took flesh. For us he fought the great battle with death, and won the eternal victory; passing through death that he might destroy death, and convey to us the everlasting life. Never before was life so fully embodied, and revealed, and made accessible. Never before was death so terribly manifested. The two extremities of being were exhibited in him; all that God calls life, which is the highest and fullest form of being, and all that God calls death, which is its lowest and emptiest. Never had life seemed so real, and so glorious, as when the Life was manifested; never had death seemed so real, and so awful, as when the Prince of Life died. Yet this death is our life, for, only through death, could life reach us and fill us. Life died, that death might live. Immortality went down into the tomb, to bring up thence for us immortality and incorruption. Thus death became the destroyer of death, and the grave the spoiler of the grave.

Life for the dead! This is our message to the

sons of men. This is our gospel ; a gospel for the dead, not for the living. It is the gospel of the "manifested life."

You say, perhaps, that it is just your state of death that makes this no gospel to you. Your consciousness of death leads to despondency ; and you say, Were I not *so* dead, I should not despair. Ah! were you not so dead you would not need the life, and would present fewer attractions, as well as fewer necessities, to the living One ; there would be less in you to call out the life. You seem to be searching for some sparks of life within you, to attract the life from above. But in so doing you are repelling the very life that you are seeking. You are mistaking the real attraction to the life, and substituting one of your own. You act on man's maxim, "Like draws to like," instead of upon God's, "Where sin abounded, grace did much more abound;" "He hath concluded all in unbelief, that he might have mercy upon all."

The truth is, you did not know how complete was the death in which you lay. You thought there was a little life remaining, and that remnant was your hope ; but now that you have become conscious of your total death, that hope has left you. It is well; for it was a false hope, as all hope must ever be, that is founded upon the good, and not on the evil that is in you. But now that this vain confidence has perished, and the last prop of self-righteousness been struck from under you, are you so foolish as to despair ? Despair, when hope, true hope, is dawning? Despair, when the only thing that repelled the Life has been taken from you? It is not your *death* that repels the Life; it is your fancying that you are not dead! Know what you are; truly dead; and the repulsion ceases, the attraction begins. I am too dead to be quickened, you say. Nay, you are not. The Life goes down to the lowest depths of death, and there is no region of the soul's dark tomb to which this Life cannot reach, or into which it has not already entered. The danger lies, not in your being too dead, but in your not knowing how thoroughly dead you are. So long as there is the unconsciousness of death, there is a barrier, a non-conducting medium between you and the Life. The Holy Spirit, in revealing to you your true condition of utter death, is throwing down that barrier, and substituting a conducting for a non-conducting medium, that the Life, long shut out, not by the death, but by your refusal to acknowledge that death, may pour in, in its glad fulness, to all the regions of your being; transforming corruption into incorruption, and death into life.

"Ye will not come to me that ye might have life," said this Life, when manifested here. And what do these words mean, but just this, "Ye will not acknowledge the death that is in yourselves, and the life that is in me." This acknowledgment, this two-fold recognition of the death and the Life, would at once bring you into contact with the living One.

"I am the Way, and the Truth, and the *Life.*" Yes; he *lives;* he gives *life;* nay, he is *Life, the Life,* the *Life* that was manifested. All this fulness of manifested *life* is for the sinner,—for you! Recognise him as *the Life,* and straightway his fulness passes over to you; and because he *lives* you *live* also.

"This is the record, that God hath given to us eternal *life,* and this *life* is in his Son." His Son is the "manifested *life,*" the "resurrection and the *life,*" and "he that hath the Son hath *life.*" What say you to this manifested life? Is it *nothing* to you, or is it *all?* What have you found in it? What have you extracted from it? Have you read in it the love of God? Have you obtained from it the life of your soul; the supply of your eternal need? Or are you still as much in want of life as if the Life had never been manifested, as if the Word had never been made flesh, as if the Son of God had never come?

But the manifestation of this Life is not yet over. The Life has, as it were, retired for a season, and gone within the veil; but this same Jesus, who came the first time, as the Life, shall come, *as such,* the second time also; and that day of *his* manifestation shall be the day of ours as well. "When Christ, who is our life, shall *appear* (lit., 'be manifested,') then shall ye also *appear* (be manifested) with him in glory;" for that is "the day of the *manifestation* of the sons of God." The resurrection of the just is the great day of his revelation, and of ours. Then shall we know the "power of his resurrection," the resurrection of him who is "the resurrection and the life;" for all the fulness of "the Life" shall not be known, till he comes to be glorified in his saints, and to be admired in all them that believe. The "resurrection unto life" shall be the completion of the great manifestation. As his first coming was its alpha, or beginning, so shall his second coming be its omega, or end. For he comes as the living One, to die no more! He comes to give his church the full benefit of the manifested life. He comes to avenge us of death, to spoil the grave, and to bring up to light his long-buried jewels.

And which of us has not some tie to the tomb? something which makes us long to be avenged of death? I do not mean merely the mortality of these vile bodies, in which death and life are at daily warfare. I mean the dear ones that death has torn from us, and the grave devoured; a parent, a child, a brother, a sister, a beloved friend. The last enemy came to them, and we were powerless. He struck, and we could not ward off the blow. We grudged him his triumph, yet we could not resist. He carried off his prize, our precious ones, in spite of us, before our eyes. But ever since, oh how we have longed for the day of vengeance, when the spoiler shall be spoiled, the grave rifled, and death swallowed up of life. For life, not death, must triumph in the end. The Life is hastening back to us from the heaven where it now is, at the Father's right hand; and at its return the reign of death is over. Life shall be manifested in a way, and to an extent, unknown before. Expelling death alike from soul and body; emptying the grave of each fragment of mortality; glorifying the church with the robe of incorruption and beauty; overflowing creation with its blessed waters; it shall bring to pass the saying that is written, "Death is swallowed up in victory;" it shall realise the long-predicted triumph, " I will ransom them from the power of the grave; I will redeem them from death; oh death, I will be thy plagues; oh grave, I will be thy destruction; repentance shall be hid from mine eyes" (Hos. xiii. 14).

SERMON V.

DIVINE PHILOSOPHY.

"Christ .. the wisdom of God."—1 Cor. i. 24.

Our age is eager in its pursuit of knowledge. It professes to be a truth-loving, and a truth-seeking age. It is quite awake to science, and thoroughly in love with its marvels and mysteries. It has obtained a far insight into the dark processes of that which is called "nature." It has witnessed one substance, and another, and another, yielding up their hidden wonders; it has seen earth, and sea, and air giving out their treasures; and, by patient inquiry, it has wrung the deepest secrets from every region of being. It has taken possession of unreclaimed territory all over space, and covered the waste places of former days with verdure, and fragrance, and beauty.

Its fields of discovery lie all around us, near and far. Wherever it has turned its steps, it has found stores of truth. What a profundity of miracle there is contained in every ray of light, every drop of dew, every pebble of the brook, every fragment of rock, every blade of grass; what an exemplification of order and law there is revealed in every natural process,—the motion of earth, and sun, and stars, the shock of earthquakes, the flow of tides, the rush of the breeze, the braiding of the rainbow on the cloud, the change of seasons, the springing, growth, blossoming, and fruit-bearing of flower, and shrub, and tree!

These are the works of God, the laws of God, the daily miracles of God. In all of them *wisdom* is seen; divine wisdom; wisdom as profound as it is perfect, as incomprehensible as it is glorious, as magnificent in its minuteness as in its vastness, in the grain of sand as in the mighty mountain, in the blush of the unnoticed desert-flower as in the splendour of a new-lighted star.

In all this there is wisdom; wisdom which we do well to study. Yet all these are but parts,— mere fragments; and, even when gathered together, they still form but the minutest portion of a whole, whose dimensions are vaster than the created universe,—a whole, of which nothing less than the infinity of Godhead is the measure. There is some proportion between the fragments of the split planet, that astronomy has detected in their wanderings, and the planet itself, of which they are the broken parts; there is some proportion between a drop and the ocean, between the stream and the fountain, between a beam and the sun, between a moment and a million of ages; but there is no proportion between the fragments of wisdom that lie scattered over creation and the great whole, which can be contained in no treasure-house save that which is infinite and divine.

Hence it is that, while, in all the regions and departments of creation, may be seen portions of this wisdom, only in the Son of God,—in Christ Jesus, the incarnate Word.—is the mighty WHOLE contained. He, and he only, is "*the* Wisdom of God."

By the expression, "the Wisdom of God," thus applied to Christ, is not merely meant that he is *wise*, infinitely wise, but something much more comprehensive. To say that he is infinitely wise is one thing, but to say that he is *the* wisdom of God is another. We say of the Father, he is infinitely wise; but we cannot say of him, he is the wisdom of God. Of the Son alone, the Christ of God, can this be said. Both things are true of him. He is infinitely wise, and he is the wisdom of God. Only of him can we affirm that he *has*, and he *is*, "the wisdom of God." Suppose we have an able architect, and a goodly palace planned and built by him, into which he has thrown his whole mind, and skill, and genius; we say of himself, he is skilful, but we say of his work, *there* is his skill, *there* is the outward personification of all that is in him, and without which you could not have known what is in him. Of other buildings erected by him, we may say there is some skill; but only of his chief work, his masterpiece, should we say that it is *the* skill or *the* wisdom of the man. Suppose we have the poet, and the poem into which he has poured his whole soul; we say of him, he is the poet, of his work, this is the poetry; of him we say he *has* genius, of his poem, it *is* genius; it is the full embodiment, in the most perfect form of speech, of all the soul, the mind, the thought, the fancy, the fire, the love, the power, that were wrapt up in him.

Thus is it with regard to Christ. He is *the* wisdom of God. All that is in God, all that can come forth out of God, is contained in him. He is the full representative of the invisible and incomprehensible Jehovah. He is the brightness of Jehovah's glory, and the express image of his person. In the works of creation God has displayed fragments or portions of his wisdom: but in Christ he has summed up and put forth THE WHOLE of it; so that it can be said of this Christ, he is *the* wisdom of God. Hence it is that the knowledge of Christ not only transcends all other knowledge, but includes them all; the study of this wondrous embodiment of all that is in God is not only superior to, but actually embraces, all other studies. Here we cannot fathom this; hereafter we may. Here we cannot see how a discovered Christ should be the discovery of all other things, all science, all nature, all things in heaven and earth; hereafter we shall find it so.

Wisdom is one of the last things which we are in the habit of connecting with the name of Christ. We connect with it salvation, pardon, life, righteousness, love, but not *wisdom*. Yet it is *wisdom* that God so especially associates with Christ. "He, of God, is made unto us *wisdom*." "In him are hid all the treasures of *wisdom* and knowledge." When God looks at him, that which he especially sees in him is wisdom. When he bids us look at Him and admire him, it is because he is the Wisdom. He is the perfection of all perfection; but specially the perfection of wisdom; so that, while *each* perfection is in him, it is in him in such a way as to manifest the wisdom of God. Holiness is in him; but then, it is in him in such a way, and manifests itself in such a way, as to shew forth not only itself, but wisdom as well. Each perfection becomes thus not merely a display of *itself*, but an illustration, or embodiment, of *wisdom*.

It is of this Wisdom that the "wise man" speaks in the Proverbs so frequently. It is this Wisdom which utters its voice, and says, "The Lord possessed me in the beginning of his way, before his works of old. I was set up from everlasting, from the beginning, or ever the earth was." Sometimes the name given is the "Wisdom of God;" sometimes it is the "Word of God."

The subject is a very wide one; we take up here only that section of it which relates to *the Person of the Christ*.

In this there are two parts, the divine and the human, the heavenly and the earthly, the invisible and the visible, the infinite and the finite, the uncreated and the created; and these, both in themselves and in their union, distinction, adjustment, co-operation, harmony, make up that glorious Person, Son of God and Son of Man, of whom it is affirmed that he is the "Wisdom of God." The whole Creator is in him, and the whole creature is in him; yet both retaining their properties distinct and unchanged by the union.

On the subject of the divine and the human, philosophy, and mysticism, and metaphysics, and theology, have speculated. Various and strange have been the ideas which man has held regarding himself and God. Sometimes he would spiritualize all matter, as if the created and the human were mere ideas, or shadows projected from the Godhead; sometimes he would materialize all spirit, not only making the soul of man a mere part of his body, but bringing down the Godhead to the level and form of creaturehood, as if the Creator and the creation were one; every part of nature, animate and inanimate, being fragments of Godhead. Such is human wisdom. It cannot comprehend either the earthly or the heavenly, either the nature of man or God, nor adjust the connection between them, without destroying and confounding both.

God takes another way; a way which not merely preserves, unchanged and distinct, both natures, while uniting them in one, but which brings forth to view, in glorious fulness, the true properties of each. In man is seen God, very God; in God is seen man, very man. All that is glorious in the Godhead, and all that is excellent in manhood, is gathered into one person, and fully exhibited in him. The Word is made flesh; yet the Word is still the Word, and flesh is still flesh. The heavenly becomes earthly; yet both are preserved; nor is the one lost in the other. The Creator becomes the creature; yet Creator and creature, though conjoined in one person, remain still distinct. The Eternal becomes a Being of time, yet continuing Eternal. The Infinite becomes finite, yet abiding Infinite. The Immortal becomes mortal, yet continuing Immortal. The Omnipotent becomes the helpless child of clay, yet remaining Omnipotent still. The Prince of Life becomes the heir of death, yet abides still, the Prince of Life, the Living One, the life of the boundless universe!

Thus the two parts of the great universe are brought together, yet kept distinct. Thus they are linked to each other by a new tie, closer than that of creation; for the union which creation produces is not half so close or dear as that which is brought about by incarnation and redemption. By this union these two parts are revealed to each other; heaven is revealed to earth, and earth is revealed to heaven. Earth now knows what Godhead is, by its coming down and dwelling here; heaven knows what manhood is, by the human nature being taken up to sit at God's right hand, in the person of *the Christ*.

It seems to be union only at a single point; for it is with *one* body and *one* soul that the Godhead is united. But that single point is enough; that one link unites the nature. In order to moor a ship we do not require a thousand cables, each fastened to a separate plank or spar; *one* strong cable, fixed at *one* point, makes fast the whole, and connects the entire vessel with its anchor. So the incarnation of Christ, whereby Godhead took into union with itself a human soul and body, is the fastening or mooring of the whole nature to the throne of the universe,—to the great fountain-head of life and being.

Nor was it with one particular *stage* of our being that this union was formed; but with all; from the first moment of conception in the womb to death and the grave. Had the Son of God united himself with manhood in its maturity, there would have been no union and no sympathy with the different stages of human life and growth. But he enters the Virgin's womb and begins life just where we begin it, thus joining himself to us at the very commencement of human existence; taking the first small invisible thread of mortal life and weaving it into his own Godhead. He is made of a woman; and that links him to woman, and woman to him, in everlasting bonds. He is a man; and that links him to man, and man to him, in eternal union. He was an infant; and that links infancy to him, and him to infancy. He was a child, a boy, a youth; and that links childhood, boyhood, youth to him, and him to them. He passed through all the stages of humanity, uniting himself to us at these different points, and consecrating these steps of human development.

What a marvel of wisdom is here! What treasures of knowledge are thus spread out before heaven and earth! Truly he is "THE wisdom of God!"

SERMON VI.

DIVINE PHILOSOPHY.

"Christ . . the wisdom of God."—1 Cor. i. 24.

But why did He not become man till after man had sinned, and human nature had become vile and mortal? Why did He not unite himself with the unfallen Adam, and with an unfallen creation, thereby upholding our nature, and preventing that fall which has been so terrible, so disastrous? For many reasons; too many to be here enumerated. But this at least we may say, that it was needful that the creature should be abased, emptied, laid prostrate, ere it could be lifted up to a height so glorious as that of union with Godhead. It must be shewn that this was no natural process, no law of the creature's own being, whereby, after a certain time, it could rise from the human to the divine. It must be shewn that it was from no desert of the creature, no necessity of being or of righteousness, no claim which the finite can have on the infinite. Every possibility of boasting or pride must be cut off; hence sin, death, corruption, must be allowed to enter it ere it can be safe for itself, or honourable for God so to uplift and glorify it. Till it has been brought to its lowest depths; till it is seen to be the most abject, degraded, undeserving of beings; till the curse of God, pronounced over it, has declared it totally unworthy of anything but consuming wrath; till this has been accomplished, it could not be *trusted* with such an elevation, such a glory. Till it had sunk down to the lowest, it was not fit to be raised to the highest; till it had reduced itself to a condition rendering it only fit to be swept out of God's presence for ever, it was not in a condition to receive the destined honour; till it hung over hell, ready to drop into the devouring fire, it could not be trusted with personal affinity to Godhead, with the crown of heaven, or with the throne of the universe.

Nay, it was not in a condition fully to set forth the wisdom of God, till it had become sinful. As man's wisdom is not fully seen in prosperous, peaceful days, nor has opportunity to develop itself till everything is disordered, complicated, broken, and its resources are taxed to the very uttermost, so was it respecting the wisdom of God. There was needed a condition of creaturehood disturbed, accursed, ruined; a condition which, by its entanglements, its conflicting demands, its desperate wreck of law, and righteousness, and goodness, should tax wisdom's resources to their utmost. Till such had become the condition of the creature, there was comparatively little scope for the development of wisdom. Just as the fall was needed to let loose the boundless fountains of hidden love in God, so was it needed to disclose the treasures of his infinite wisdom. Just as this free-love of God could not rightly sing its song, in all the rich breadth of its harmony, over unfallen man, but needed that fall in order to get down to the lowest notes of the wondrous music, which are the deepest, the fullest, and the sweetest; so the wisdom of God could not half unfold itself, nor shew its breadth and length, its height and depth, over an unfallen race.

Thus, then, we see in Christ the God-man, the Wisdom of God. In the constitution of his person; in the incarnation itself; in the time and circumstances of the incarnation; in the purposes for which that incarnation was devised; in the way in which it has carried out these purposes;—in all these we see "Christ, the Wisdom of God;" Christ the great embodiment of divine wisdom; Christ not only the possessor of this wisdom, but the revealer, the exhibitor, the teacher of its mysteries.

What, then, must be the guilt of undervaluing this incarnation of wisdom! What the evil of errors as to the *person* of the Christ! This is the object which God so specially holds up to view, claiming for it our admiration, our reverence, our love. Above all objects of nature upon earth, in which science has discovered such wonders of wisdom, God has set his Son as the centre and summation of all wisdom. Woe be to the man who slights this, who prefers other objects to this, who finds other centres than this.

Here lies one of the crowning sins of Rome. She

has degraded the Son of God, and has done what she could to nullify the great objects of incarnation, as well as the great end of blood-shedding. She has exalted the human above the divine; she has seated a woman upon the throne of God; she has made the glory of the incarnation to centre in Mary, not in Mary's son; she has made, not Christ, but Mary, the wisdom of God; not Christ, but Mary, the power of God; not Christ, but Mary, the link between the earthly and the heavenly; not Christ, but Mary, the point of union between the human and the divine!

But the question which, from all this, is most closely brought home to us is, "What think *ye* of Christ?" Is he to you *wisdom?* Is he to you *the* wisdom of God? In him centres all that God counts excellent, and true, and perfect, and glorious, and wise. Does all that *you* esteem excellent, and true, and perfect, and glorious, and wise, centre also in him? He is the object of divine admiration; is he also the object of yours? He is the beloved of the Father, in whom *He* is well pleased; is he also your beloved, in whom *you* are well pleased? Do you see in him wisdom? Not merely salvation, forgiveness, life, but *wisdom*,—wisdom the highest, truest, noblest, ever tasted by man?

Or have you some other Christ, some object whom you admire more than him, in which you see more truth, more wisdom, more beauty, more attractiveness, than in him? Is pleasure your Christ? But will pleasure make you wise unto salvation? Will pleasure bring you into the everlasting kingdom? Is gold your Christ? But will gold make you wise, or be an introduction into the presence of God? Is the world your Christ? But will the world make you wise, or deliver you from the eternal darkness? Is sin your Christ? But will sin make you wise? Will sin save and bless you? Is literature your Christ? But will all earth's widest range of literature make you truly wise, or fill the void of your heart, or gladden you with abiding joy? Is science your Christ? But will science make you wise,—wise for eternity? Are poetry and romance your Christ? Will they heal your spirit's wounds? Will they minister to a mind diseased? Will they pluck from your memory the rooted sorrow? Will they raze out the written troubles of the brain? Will they fill you with the "joy unspeakable and full of glory?"

Christ is the wisdom of God; and in the knowledge of this Christ there is wisdom for you; nor wisdom only, but life, forgiveness, peace, glory, and an endless kingdom! Study him! Acquaint thyself with him! Whatever you are ignorant of, be not ignorant of him: whatever you overlook, overlook not him: whatever you lose, lose not him. To gain him is to gain eternal life, to gain a kingdom, to gain everlasting blessedness. To lose him is to lose your soul, to lose God, to lose God's favour, to lose God's heaven, to lose the eternal crown! O my friend and fellow-man, I charge thee, and again I charge thee, whatsoever thou losest, lose not him. Thou canst not afford such a loss; such an infinite, eternal loss; a loss for which there can be no compensation, here or hereafter. Other losses may be heavy, but they are light compared with this ; only the loss of a grain of sand when compared with a mine of gold. Other losses may be protracted for years, but this is for ever. Other losses may make thee poor for this life, but this impoverishes thee to all eternity. And it is the loss, too, of that very thing which thousands in our day are seeking, each in his own way,—the loss of wisdom ! It is not merely the loss of righteousness, the loss of pardon, the loss of gladness, the loss of heaven ; but it is the loss of wisdom ; that which God calls wisdom ; that which would make thy soul wise for ever and for ever! Remember that "the *wise* shall inherit glory;" that "they that be *wise* shall shine as the brightness of the firmament."

Young man, wouldst thou not be wise? Even though thou couldst save thy soul and gain heaven without it, would it not be better to have this wisdom, than to live and die without it? That cannot be of mean importance respecting which God has uttered this longing, this compassionate yearning, "O that they were *wise !*"

And where shall wisdom be found, and where is the place of understanding? The depth saith, It is not in me ; and the sea saith, It is not in me ; and the river saith, It is not in me ; and the cloud saith, It is not in me ; and the flower saith, It is not in me ; and the star saith, It is not in me ; and the light saith, It is not in me ; and the darkness saith, It is not in me. It is only in Him in whom are hid all the treasures of wisdom and knowledge. He is the Wisdom of God.

And what price shall we pay for it? "It cannot be gotten for gold, neither shall silver be weighed for the price thereof. It cannot be valued with the gold of Ophir, with the precious onyx or the sapphire ; the gold and the crystal cannot equal it, and the exchange of it shall not be for jewels of fine gold." But, just because it is *beyond* price, it is *without* price ; and that which is most precious is to be gotten at least cost ; nay, it is altogether free !

And how shall it be had ? "If any man lack wisdom, let him ask of God, who giveth to all men liberally, and upbraideth not, and it shall be given him." Take him who is wisdom, and thou hast it all. "He that hath the Son hath life ;" so he that hath the Son hath wisdom. The good tidings concerning this wisdom are the same good tidings that are made known respecting the Son of God. The Father's testimony to his Christ is his testimony to the wisdom. He who receives that testimony receives the Christ ; and he who receives the Christ, receives the wisdom ; and, in that wisdom, everlasting life and an inheritance of glory.

SERMON VII.

THE BANISHED ONE BEARING OUR BANISHMENT.

"Jesus walked in the temple, in Solomon's porch."—John x. 23.

The places which Jesus chiefly resorted to, during his life on earth, are unknown in Old Testament history. Bethany, and Nazareth, and Capernaum, and Nain, and Emmaus, are not mentioned in the lives of the saints before his coming. Their names rise up newly to the reader, and they have no sacred memories of any kind attached to them. They were not consecrated spots in any sense. Yet to these the Lord betook himself.

The chief places known, in the story of Israel's ancient saints, are passed by, in New Testament history. Hebron, the city of Abraham; Beersheba, the dwelling of Isaac; Bethel, the sanctuary of Jacob; Gilgal and Shiloh, old seats of worship, seem as if avoided; and even Bethlehem itself appears not to have been visited by the Lord during his ministry. The places that Israel counted holy he turned aside from; and even Jerusalem he only visited during the day, retiring from it at night to Bethany, like one cast out, and not allowed the shelter of its roofs.

For this there might be many reasons. It was

the Father's will. He chose, in his sovereign wisdom, the places for his Son to visit and to dwell in. And it was according to this will that the Son of God ever acted. "Not my will, but thine be done." In choosing these unknown places for his Son, He shewed that it was not former privileges, nor ancient sanctity, nor a venerable name, that could avail anything with him, or attract his favour. Christ was not born in Jerusalem; he was not sent to Bethel, because there Jacob had been, and there the heavens had been opened above him; nor to Shiloh, because for ages God himself had dwelt there. But he was sent to new places, where, so far as we know, the foot of patriarch, judge, prophet, king, had never been; shewing that no city was to be so favoured as to exclude others, and that all cities, as well as all souls, had a share in his divine regards. Nor were they the better and more reputable cities that were chosen for his abode; for Nazareth was one of the worst. Thus was it seen that he came not to call the righteous, but sinners, to repentance.

But specially do we see in this avoidance of what might be called the "holy cities," the actings of One who was "despised and rejected of men," treated by man as an outcast, and by God as one who was bearing our sin, and therefore, like the leper, kept apart from what was either ritually or traditionally holy. Our reproach was on Him, in life as well as in death. He was not to be allowed to die within Jerusalem, but must suffer without the gate; so He

D

was kept apart from all these places which had special sanctity connected with their names.

He visited Jerusalem indeed, but he did not dwell there. He frequented the temple; but never entered either the holy place or the most holy. It is only in the outer court, or in some of the great porches connected with it, that we find him. Beyond these he went not at any time. In the verse before us, we find him in Solomon's porch. This porch was at the eastern side of the temple, erected by Solomon, and fortunate in escaping the ruin which had once and again overtaken the other parts of the building. It was "winter" at this time. It was just the very middle of December; for the feast of the Dedication was celebrated on the 15th of that month. The inclemency of mid-winter,—its rains, and perhaps its snows,—had led the Lord to seek the shelter of this porch; for, as a true man, he felt earth's heat and cold, needing a shadow from the former and a covering from the latter, just as we do. Under this spacious porch he was walking to and fro,—perhaps to increase the vital heat,—when the Jews gathered round him, and began the conversation which our passage records.

That part of the scene which alone I ask you to notice, is his keeping outside the holy place and the most holy, as though he might not enter there, but remain, like one of the multitude, in the outer court, which even "publicans and sinners" might enter. For this there were several reasons.

1. *Personal.*—He belonged to the tribe of Judah,

not to that of Levi. It could not be personal
uncleanness that kept him without the veil ; but
only Levi's family had access to the holy place, and
only Aaron's family could enter the holiest of all.
He could not, then, enter the chamber which was
the emblem of God's immediate presence without a
breach of law ; and he "came not to destroy, but
to fulfil the law." It "became him to fulfil all righteousness."

2. *Ceremonial.*—The holy of holies could only be
entered with blood ; and he had none to present.
The lamb, the goat, the bullock, all belonged to
others. The time had not yet come for his having
to do with blood. Things that differ must not be
confounded ; the shadow must not be mixed up
with the substance ; the sacrifice must still be left
in Levitical hands, and the altar must not be served
by a son of Judah.

3. *Typical.*—He was himself the true sacrifice,
the bearer of sin. As such he lived and died. In
all that he did, and in all that he refrained from
doing ; in the places that he visited, and in the
places that he abstained from visiting, he kept this
in view. He was loaded with *our* sin, *our* curse,
our condemnation, *our* leprosy ; and, as such, he
must keep at a distance from the holy and the
clean. Not merely was he the rejected of men,—
thrust outside their dwellings, their cities, their
synagogues, having no place to lay his head, treated
as a madman, a Samaritan, a devil ; but he was the
outcast, the condemned One ; with the law's brand

upon him; "made sin for us;" made "a curse for us." As such, his true place was outside the city of God; outside the dwelling of the Holy One. If permitted to resort to Jerusalem, he can only do so as a stranger or wayfaring man, who comes in with the crowd during the day, but retires at night. If allowed to frequent the temple, he can only come as far as the outer court, on the common footing of a sinner,—just as the publican might do. He might stand and see the daily sacrifice offered; he might watch the shedding of the blood and the consuming of the victim; but only as one of the crowd. He might stand, on the day of atonement, and see the two goats chosen by the high priest; he might listen to the confession of sin over the head of the one, and mark the pouring out of the other's blood; he might see the high priest take the basin, and carry the blood into the holiest, Himself standing on the outside, and, though the Blessed One, waiting amid the crowd to receive the priestly blessing of another. More than this he might not do. Were he to go beyond the circle thus marking off the limits within which he was to walk, he would not have been acting as the Sin-bearer, nor submitting to be dealt with as an outcast and a curse for us.

Sin had banished us from God, casting us out of his paradise, and hindering us from appearing in his presence. The Son of God came to take our place of banishment, that, by so doing, he might effect our restoration. He became, in all respects, a *banished* man. His birth in the stable of Bethlehem shewed us this. His flight into Egypt shewed it still more; as if, when he did come to earth, he was not to have a safe abode anywhere, save in a land of strangers. His abode at Nazareth, that ungodly city, shewed it again. His having to resort to the far mountain for prayer, instead of to his Father's house, which was the house of prayer, shewed this also. His never entering the holy parts of the temple, but always remaining outside, shewed this again. And, lastly, his death, "without the gate," finished the manifestation of his humbled, outcast condition here. He is so completely identified with the sinner, the outcast, the banished one, that he is not only deemed unworthy to *live* within Jerusalem, but even to *die* within its walls. As the great sin-offering, he goes without the camp, there to complete his sin-bearing work, and to sum up the testimony which his whole life had given, viz., that he was standing in the sinner's place, enduring the banishment of the banished one, bearing the curse of the cursed one, submitting to the condemnation of the condemned one; and never for one moment contradicting or modifying the testimony, intended to be given by his life, to his sin-bearing character and work; never in anything, great or small, stepping beyond the limits that marked out his mysterious path on earth as "the Lamb of God that taketh away the sin of the world."

Christ's exclusion from the holy of holies would not have been a thing so noticeable, were it not that he had, of all others, a right to enter it,—nay, and to abide there. That inner shrine was his lawful and patrimonial dwelling, his true and proper home. No one, not even Aaron himself, could claim the right of entrance as he could. Not, indeed, as David's Son, but as David's Lord; not as the Son of Judah, but as the Son of God; not as possessed of ritual or legal warrant; but as the Holy One and the Just."

For that solemn chamber, where were the ark, and the mercy-seat, and the cherubim, and the glory, was the special emblem of Jehovah's highest habitation; the type of the presence-chamber in the very heaven of heavens; nay, may we not say, the symbol of that very "bosom of the Father" out of which the only-begotten Son came forth? That holy habitation above had been his abode from eternity; and what, then, more natural than that when he came to earth he should take up his dwelling in that lower sanctuary, which was the shadow and representation of his glorious palace above? Here we should have expected him to have been born and lived while here. And, just as worldly, carnal men would have supposed that the Son of the Highest, when coming to earth, would chose a noble metropolis and a splendid palace for his abode, so spiritual men would have assigned to him the holiest of all, in Jehovah's temple, as his birthplace and his habitation here.

It would have been most suitable; and surely he had a right to it. The temple itself was his Father's house, and the best room in that house would be at his service. Others might be shut out; he would not. The veil that was drawn against others would open to admit him. Who could resist his claim, if he had asked admission? His right was indisputable, as the very Son of God. Judea was his, for it was Immanuel's land. Jerusalem was his, for it was the city of the great King. The temple was his, for it was his Father's house. The holy of holies was his, for it was the express representative on earth of that very heaven which he had left, when coming to do the Father's will.

Yet He entered not that inner sanctuary, nor ever went beyond the altar and the laver without,—the court in which the publican stood and cried, "God be merciful to me, a sinner." He saw daily the priests entering the second court, the holy place, yet went he not in. He saw the high priest, once a year, take the blood of the goat, and enter into the holiest of all, yet went he not in. Though conscious of an innate and inalienable right to enter, He yet remained without, as one who, from some mysterious cause, was excluded from his lawful and patrimonial abode.

SERMON VIII.

THE BANISHED ONE BEARING OUR BANISHMENT.

"*Jesus walked in the temple, in Solomon's porch.*"—JOHN x. 23.

THE one hindrance to His exercise of this his divine right of entrance into the holiest of all, was our iniquity, which was lying on him. That kept him out. Until that was fully borne, he could not enter either the sanctuary below or the presence-chamber above. In taking our sin upon him, as he did from the moment of his incarnation, he had consented to forego for a time his right of entrance into the Father's presence, and into that place where the glorious symbol of that presence dwelt. He had consented to be an outcast, to stand only in the place where sin is borne, not in the place where iniquity is remembered no more. It was as *the banished One* that he passed through earth, having no place to lay his head. It was as the outcast that he never went beyond the outer court of the temple. It was as such that we find him walking in Solomon's porch, thus proclaiming to all who truly understood his character and work, that he was acting as the sinner's substitute,—taking the sinner's place of exile, not merely outside the blessed heaven, where he had dwelt from everlasting, but outside even his Father's house below.

Some speak much of his not having been born in a palace, and dwell on the humiliation of his being without any vestige of human royalty. But these were, after all, but common, and, we may say, carnal things. It was a light thing to be kept out of David's house or Herod's palace; but it was no light thing to be excluded from his Father's house, his own proper home. More than ever David did, would he desire the tabernacles of Jehovah; his flesh and heart would cry out for God; and how peculiar must have been his feelings, in being thus made to stand outside the sanctuary, the very place to which he had so undoubted a right, and in which it would have been his delight to dwell! Instead of communing with his Father in his own holy dwelling-place, he had to resort to the Mount of Olives, and such unsheltered solitudes, as if he had not only no place to lay his head, but no sanctuary to betake himself to, no closet into which he might enter. So strangely shut out was he from all places to which, either as Son of Man, or as Son of God, he would desire to visit or to dwell in!

When he died on the cross, the veil was rent in twain, and he might then have entered. The reasons for his exclusion were at an end; and his banished life was over. Judaic ritualism was exhausted and cancelled. Blood had been shed, to enable *any one* to enter in, priest or no priest, whether belonging to Judah or to Levi; whether on the day of atonement or not. And, in testimony of all this, he might have entered the holiest of all, at his resurrection. But this would have been a small thing, and one which might have raised misconceptions as to the meaning and importance of the very rites that were now to be done away. Instead, then, of entering the earthly sanctuary, he passed upward into the heavenly; instead of claiming his right to enter the typical holy of holies, he did that which was of far deeper signification and higher moment, he entered in and took possession of the true holy of holies above, in token of his having fulfilled his time of banishment, finished his work, and removed every hindrance which stood in the way of those, for whom he was the substitute below, and of whom he was to be the representative above.

See him, then, in these two different conditions,—(1.) walking in Solomon's porch; (2.) seated at the right hand of God.

1. *Walking in Solomon's porch.*—He walks there as the Substitute; our Substitute as truly, as when he groaned in Gethsemane or died on Golgotha. As one consenting for a season to be shut out from the presence of God, that we might enter and dwell in that presence for ever, he stands, or sits, or walks outside the sanctuary. Thus it is that he bears our banishment: he takes upon him not merely the penalty of suffering and death, but that of exclusion from the house and home of God. That penalty he has endured: that exile he has under-

gone: that distance he has experienced: and all this as the Substitute, bearing what we should have borne, in order that we might inherit all to which he could lay claim. Through means of this substitution of the Son of God in the room of the exiled sinner, that sinner finds free access to the innermost shrine of heaven, the very presence of the Father. And the Father's message to each banished one is, enter in! Stand no longer afar off; despair no more, as if the gate were closed. Behold, it is open, wide open! Go in at once, and end your banishment. Go in, and find peace, love, friendship, acceptance, through him, to whose finished work of glorious substitution the Father is bearing such blessed testimony! Why should we depart from the living God, seeing the Son of God has removed all reason for our departure? Why remain in alienation, seeing here is that which has taken away all the hindrances in the way of friendship? Why remain afar off, seeing God asks you to come nigh? Why stand outside, seeing God says, COME IN?

Nor is it bare *liberty* of entrance that has been secured; as if the door had been reluctantly thrown open, and the way grudgingly cleared for us. Such is the efficacy of our Substitute's life and death, that "we have BOLDNESS to enter into the holiest" (Heb. x. 19). We need not hide ourselves in the thicket; we need not run away from God; we need not, in terror and uncertainty, steal slowly and sadly back to our Father's house; we need not wait, nor doubt, nor suspect, nor distrust; we may go at once, and go boldly, to God, on the simple security given to the sinner by the work of the divine Sin-bearer. That work has not simply made it possible for God to receive us, but secured our reception. It has not simply unbarred the gate, but flung it open, as widely open as God himself could fling it. or as any sinner needs that it should be flung. Nay, it has sent out messengers of peace and messages of love, assuring us not only of a welcome when we return, but of God's sincere desire that we should do so. It has not merely removed the restraints on grace which law imposed, and set it free to pour itself out freely; but it has made grace a righteous thing; so that now love is righteousness, and righteousness is love.

It is not possible to imagine greater freeness for the sinner, in his going to God, than has been provided by the vicarious life and death of Him who is "the end of the law, for righteousness to every one that believeth." Nothing can be freer, safer, surer, than "the new and living way." Yet, who goes in; who cares for it; "who hath believed our report?" The tread of returning feet makes no noise in our world; for the home-goers are so few, and so far between each other. But the sound of wandering feet is like the tread of millions. The noise of home-leavers, hastening from their Father's house, they know not whither, fills the wide air of earth; and, while men hear, in that sound, only mirth and joyance, faith hears in it sadness, and unrest, and the cravings of empty hearts, and the self-tolled knell of overhanging judgment, to which, though they will not believe it, they are hastening on.

O men, and friends, and fellow-exiles, we beseech you to turn back on your way of peril and sin. Turn back, lest ye perish! By the death of Him who died the sinner's death, by the life of Him who lived on earth the sinner's life of banishment, we entreat you to bethink yourselves, and turn your footsteps towards your Father's still-open home.

2. *Look at Him within the veil, at the Father's right hand.*—He remained on the outside while here; he has entered in at last, and that, not into the earthly sanctuary, the mere figure of the true, but into heaven itself, there to appear in the presence of God for us. When outside here on earth, he was our substitute; now when within, in heaven, he is our representative. He has gone up and gone in for us. He carries us in along with him, and gives those, who accept his substitution and representation, the same privilege of nearness and fellowship as he has himself. As our High Priest, he communicates between us and God. As Intercessor, he pleads our case. As Representative, he has so identified himself with our persons, that we are lost sight of under his shadow. The Father sees him in us, and us in him. All our imperfection is lost in his glorious perfection; and we, in being presented to the Father, are presented as part of his glorious self; all our uncomeliness for ever

merged in the infinite comeliness of the beloved Son.

From the moment that faith linked us to his cross, and identified us with his person, we became inseparable. In no aspect could God view us, save as part of his Son,—nay, wholly one with him. And this connection, though now one of faith, is ere long to be one of sight. "When he who is our life shall appear, we shall appear with him in glory." His second coming will be the visible completion of the wondrous identification, which faith at first accomplished. Resurrection will bring out, more fully than either life or death, the mysterious oneness between the body and the Head. One cross, one death, one grave, was ours; for his cross was ours, his death ours, his grave ours. So, one glory, one crown, one kingdom, one city, one inheritance, shall be ours hereafter; for all that he has is ours. He, one with us, took our place of exile outside the veil, and bore our shame, our suffering, our death. We, one with him, get his place of nearness to the Father, within the veil, and entrance to the many mansions of the eternal house; receiving the life, the love, the blessing, the eternal gladness, which he has purchased for us, and which he so freely, so lovingly, presents to each one who is now afar off, each banished child of Adam, each prodigal of earth, wandering in the far country, without a home or a Father, without a sanctuary, and without a God.

It is to this *innermost* place in the heaven of

heavens, this *innermost* glory above, that the Lord invites the *outermost* of the sons of men, the *farthest off* of all earth's far-off wanderers. In love he took the lowest place, that he might invite us to the highest. In love he went to the farthest circle of banishment that this earth knows, in order that, by bearing that banishment, he might bring us into the very centre of divine fellowship, and nearness, and heavenly gladness,—to the very bosom of the Father, out of which he himself had come, seeking the lost, and devising means whereby his banished should be restored. Ah, surely there is not anything in our banishment that should lead us, for one moment, to prefer it to our Father's presence, nor anything in the distant land of exile, to make us refuse for it the paradise of God!

SERMON IX.

THE SERVANT OF SINNERS.

"I am among you as he that serveth."—LUKE xxii. 27.

WE find in these words a double reference; first to the *character*, and secondly to the *office*, of the Son of man; to his character as the *lowly* one, to his office as the *servant*. For the purpose of bringing both these things before his disciples, he makes use of those marvellous words, "I am among you AS THE SERVING ONE.

The dispute among the disciples respecting pre-eminence must have grieved and wounded him; more especially because of the *time* when this jealous strife arose. Scarcely had they finished the first solemn supper, the newly-instituted memorial of the body and blood of the Lord; scarcely had the Master ceased warning them of the traitor, and the treachery that was among them; scarcely had their own searching inquiry ended, "Is it I?" when there arose "a strife among them, which of them should be accounted the greatest." How strange and sad, how almost incredible, the scene! Rising from the table of love to contend for the mastery, the one over the other; to wound the ear and heart of the Master with their angry words and selfish arguments; to turn the holy quiet of that upper chamber into a stir of strife, and ambition, and jealous wrangling, in the very presence of the Lord,—how unbecoming, how unkind, how inconceivably selfish and hateful!

To calm this tumult, to allay this strife, to stop the mouths of the disputants, the Lord interposes; and he does so in a way so pointed, yet so mild and loving, as must have overwhelmed the contenders, and covered their faces with shame.

The burden of his rebuke is just this,—" Look at me; am I striving for pre-eminence? Am I coveting honour, or power, or greatness? Am I even exercising superiority over you? Am I not foregoing even my rightful claim of service, and acting as your servant? Instead of demanding service at your hands, I am among you as he that serveth." He admits that this is not man's principle of acting, or estimate of service. He shews that this is not the scale on which earthly distinctions are graduated. Among the nations of the earth each one strives to be uppermost, and covets the titles which rank confers. But with his disciples this order was to be wholly reversed. Man's idea of greatness was that of pre-eminence over his fellow-man, in virtue of which all should be his servants; God's idea of greatness was that of lowly love, in virtue of which a man should be willing to be the servant of all.

To this life of lowly love, this posture of willing service, this place of subjection, and self-denial, and dependence, it was, that he, the Son of God, had stooped from the highest heaven; and was it possible for a man, a sinner, to cherish ambitious thoughts of supremacy or earthly honour? The Son of man had come, not to be ministered unto, but to minister; and, in the fulfilment of that ministry (that *service*), to give his life a ransom for many. And did not this shew the true law of the kingdom, the principle on which God was acting, and on which he was calling us to act; did it not tell us that our aim should be, not to soar, but to stoop; that greatness lies, not in ascending above others, but in descending beneath them; and that the highest seat of honour is, in truth, the lowest place of service,—service that counts no office mean, no labour great, no sacrifice costly,—service that is willing to go down even to the tomb itself in the performance of its offices of love?

Shall we not then covet this honour; this peculiar honour, so unlike all that is human, so truly divine; the honour of lowly service; the honour of resembling Him who took upon him the form of a servant, who girded himself with the towel, that he might wash his disciples' feet, and who has left us this precept for our daily practice, "If I then, your Lord and Master, have washed your feet, ye also ought to wash one another's feet; for I have given you an example, that ye should do as I have done unto you?" When we hear him saying, I am among you as he that serveth, shall we not be ashamed of our pride, and ambition, and love of ease, and fastidiousness, and self-pleasing? When we see him serving, shall we not also serve? When we see him stretching out his hands to all, however unworthy and unloveable, shall we ever turn away, in weariness or in disgust, from any soul on earth, even the unworthiest and most unloveable of all?

But our object at present is not to dwell upon Christ's lowliness and obedience; nor to set forth these as our example; nor to shew the law of the kingdom, that *service* is the true *nobility*. We wish to exhibit the *service* itself of which He speaks; to bring before you Christ the *servant*; not merely Christ the *Father's* servant, doing the Father's will, but Christ a servant to *us* and for *us*; Christ fulfilling this lowly office, in order to meet the case of the neediest.

Let us consider these three things in reference to this service,—*first*, its history; *secondly*, its nature; and *thirdly*, the ends and objects which it is intended to meet.

I. *Its history.*—It is not with His birth in Bethlehem that Christ's service begins. His visit to our first father in Paradise was its true commencement. After that we find him, age after age, visiting the children of men, and always in the character of one ministering to their wants. His intercourse with Abraham, and Isaac, and Jacob, was that of one *offering*, not *asking*, service. In his dealings with Israel, we find the same unwearied, ever-watchful ministry; for the pillar-cloud that led them, that sheltered them, that guarded them by night and day, was the dwelling of the Son of God, the visible exhibition of his presence and service. It was he who ministered to them in the desert. He fought their battles. He selected their encampments. He shaded them from the scorching sun. He drew water for them out of the rock, and brought food out of the storehouses of heaven. In Canaan, too, he ministered to them, generation after generation; and the long record of Israel is the history of his manifold service.

At his birth, his life of service *visibly* began. It was to *serve* that he descended to Bethlehem. And his life at Nazareth for thirty years was a life of service. In the three years and a half of his *public* ministry, he shewed how skilful he was in serving, how willing to undertake it in all its parts. At the well of Jacob we find him serving a needy sinner; in the house of Simon the Pharisee we find him doing the same. In the house of Lazarus we find him ministering to saints. Wherever he goes, we find him still exercising the same lowly vocation; ministering alike to soul and body, to Pharisee and publican, to child or to man, to Jew, or to Samaritan, or to Gentile. The upper chamber, Gethsemane, Pilate's hall, the cross, the grave,—these were all places of service. After his resurrection, on the way to Emmaus, on the shore of the lake, we find him still the same.

At his ascension He only entered on a new department of service; and as the Advocate with the Father, the Intercessor, the Forerunner, we see him still serving. As the priests under the law were, in all things relating to the tabernacle, the people's servants, ever standing ready to do the required work to any Israelite, so is our Intercessor. He stands ready to take up any case that may be put into his hands. He wearies not: he is not provoked; he turns not away; as willing and prompt to serve, even the most unworthy, as in the days of his flesh. For the glory that surrounds him above has not altered his love or his meekness of spirit, nor made him ashamed of the lowly office which he exercised here, as the servant of the needy and the evil.

Nor, when he comes again in strength and majesty, as King of kings and Lord of lords, does he lose sight of his character as the ministering one. Hence in that passage in which he refers to this day of glory (Luke xii. 37), he makes reference to this same gracious office as not even then laid aside, —"Blessed are those servants," says He, "whom the Lord, when he cometh, shall find watching: verily I say unto you, that he shall gird himself, and make them to sit down to meat, and *will come forth and serve them;*" as if, even in that day of triumph and happy festival, there would be something omitted, something incomplete, something incongruous, something not like himself, if he did not then find scope for his old office of condescending love, and appear, even at his own marriage supper, as the servant of his ransomed ones.

SERMON X.

THE SERVANT OF SINNERS.

"I am among you, as he that serveth."—LUKE xxii. 27.

II. *Let us consider the nature of this service.*—It is in all respects like Himself,—like Him who, though he was rich, for our sakes became poor.

(1.) *It is willing service.* There is no constraint, no reluctance, no mere official performance of an appointed duty. In the anticipation of coming to earth as the Father's servant he says, "I delight to do thy will;" and we know that it is as the Father's servant that he is also ours. He is the willing messenger of the Father's grace, the willing executor of the Father's purpose, the willing almoner of the Father's blessing, the willing endurer of the Father's wrath, the willing sacrifice for sin, the willing bearer of our sorrows and burdens. All is willingness with him; most unreserved and perfect willingness. His varied rounds of service are no heavy task. He is the willing servant of the needy.

(2.) *It is a loving service.* Out of no fountain save that of love could such amazing, such endless acts of service flow. The loving and the serving are inseparable. The kind of service which he has undergone, and which he still undergoes, admits of no construction save that of love. Of man's acts of service towards his fellow-man, however great or many, you have still the suspicion that they may be the mere fulfilment of duty, or the payment of a price. But Christ's acts of service cannot be thus misinterpreted. They can mean but one thing; they can spring from but one source; they are the utterance but of one feeling,—love.

(3.) *It is self-denying service.* It is written, "Even Christ pleased not himself;" and how often in the Psalms does he breathe out the heaviness of his spirit when making mention of his unrequited labours! They "gave me hatred for my love;" "they rewarded me evil for good, to the spoiling of my soul." To continue ministering, day after day, in the midst of reproach, and opposition, and rejection, was self-denial and devotedness such as man can hardly either credit or conceive. In encountering the uncongenialities and hostilities of such a world as this, when stooping to serve and bless; in meeting with such unbelief, such ignorance, such frowardness as he had to deal with among his disciples themselves,—his *self-denial* was drawn out to the uttermost; and though his service was truly willing and loving, yet it was *self-denying*, to an extent of which we can have no idea. The Holy One coming into daily contact with sin; the Blessed One meeting with the curse on every side, yet still labouring on, still carrying out unshrinkingly his work of service for the sons of men,—ah! this is *self-denial*, such as could have come forth from no bosom save his own.

(4.) *It is patient, unwearied service.* He has compassion on the ignorant, and on them that are out of the way. He breaks not the bruised reed; he quenches not the smoking flax. He is ever ready with his helping hand. He grudges no toil, no cost. By day or by night we find him ever girt for service. Tender, gentle, and patient, he sends none empty away; he does not upbraid them with requiring his services so often, or with needing the same help again and again, by reason of their own forgetfulness or perversity. He pities, and therefore he serves. He is patient, and therefore he serves. He is tender and gracious, and therefore he serves. Instead of being wearied out with the multitude of applicants, his only complaint is, that so few avail themselves of his help:—"Ye will not come to me." Instead of grudging the labour of supplying so many ever-recurring wants, he speaks as one to whom a favour is done, in allowing him to be the servant of the neediest.

(5.) *It is free service.* It cannot be bought; for what gold could purchase it? Neither does it *need* to be bought, for it is freely rendered. It is without money and without price. Service, without wages asked or given, is an unknown thing among men. Man cannot command the service of his fellow-men without money. But it is not so with God. All is of grace. The love is free, the gift is free, the life is free; so the service afforded to us, by him who came to serve, is altogether free! It is freely presented to us, nay, pressed upon us by One whose delight is in serving, whose honour is in serving, and whose one regret is that there are so few among the needy ones of earth who will allow him to serve! Oh, that you would but accept the service of the Son of God! Oh, that you would allow him to gird himself with the towel, that he may wash you! Oh, that you would give him the joy, the honour, that his heart is set upon, of ministering to you, of attending on you, of guiding your steps through the gloom, and the storm, and the weariness, and the warfare of the desert, till he land you in the promised kingdom, and set you down at his marriage-supper,—there and then to know what the service of love can do, even for the weakest and unworthiest of those whom the blood has washed.

III. *Its ends and objects.*—It is to sinners that this service is rendered; and there is much in this to exhibit the ends which it has in view. They to whom Christ presents himself as the willing, loving, self-denying, patient servant, are not some nobler race of creatures, worthy of such condescension. They are the ungodly, who have no claim upon this gracious One, nothing to recommend them to his regards, save their poverty, their misery, their helplessness, and the impossibility of their delivering themselves, or finding their way out of this region of darkness into the kingdom of light.

No question is made as to the character of the persons to be saved; no objection is raised as to their unfitness or undeservingness; no hesitation is intimated as to the difficulty of the case, or the greatness of the guilt, or the strength, and toil, and care needed in undertaking it. No one of these things is mentioned, nor any such barrier for a moment supposed to exist. This gracious servant of the needy is willing to be employed by any one, no matter who, let him be the poorest, and the sickliest, and the feeblest of all who ever sought a helper, a protector, or a guide, on their way to the kingdom.

We need forgiveness. He ministers this in all its fulness; not once, nor seven times, but seventy times seven; bringing forth to us each hour, for our new sins, the new forgiveness out of the treasury of God; making us feel how exceeding abundant must be the grace of our God, that can afford such endless pardons to be thus so freely ministered.

We need cleansing. He serves us also in this; girding himself with his towel, and washing us till we are clean every whit; aye, washing us hourly; marking with the eye of faithful, patient service every spot that soils us, and purging it off with the clean water of the heavenly laver; attending our steps as we pass along this world's polluted highways, and ready every moment to cleanse our feet from each newly contracted defilement.

We need healing. He ministers healing to us. He healeth all our diseases. With unwearied care and heavenly skill, he watches every turn they take, and applies at once the suited remedy. Our languor he revives, our insensibility he quickens, our callousness he softens, our parchedness he refreshes, our wounds he binds up, our sickliness he turns into health. Thus he serves us in patient love.

We need strength. He serves us in this also, with untiring patience, placing all his strength at our service, nay, perfecting his strength in our weakness. He is ever helping our infirmities, giving us his arm to lean upon, nay, carrying us, as a shepherd his sheep, when too feeble to go, sustaining us in our weariness, reviving us in our faintness, watching our steps that we may not stumble, teaching our hands to war and our fingers to fight,—nay, giving us the victory. No sense of feebleness or helplessness should ever lead us to despond. No hosts of enemies, whether of hell or earth, no terrors of battle set in array against us, should cause us to turn back. To them that have no might he increaseth strength. In all our varied weaknesses he is at hand to serve.

We need wisdom and guidance. He ministers these to us, according to our need. He is made unto us wisdom. He guides us with his eye. He pities our ignorance and perplexity, and takes his willing place at our side, to instruct and to lead. His infinite resources he places at our disposal, and invites us to accept of his service, in the communication of all wisdom, and knowledge, and prudence, and true enlightenment of soul. If we are foolish, or dark, or misled, or stumbling, it is because we will not have him to serve us! O folly without a parallel, to decline or to slight such an offer as this!

We need faith and love. He increases our faith; he prays for us, that our faith fail not; he marks it when feeble and ready to give way, and strengthens it anew. So with our love. He kindles it, and cherishes it, preventing it from being cooled or quenched in this unkindly clime. Oh, what should we do for faith or love, were it not for this ministering One! Is your faith feeble, and unbelief obtaining the mastery? Or, is your love becoming chill and heartless? Accept the proffered service of the gracious Son of Man; allow him to do that in which he delights, to minister to you in these things; so shall your faith wax strong, and your love become fervent like his own.

We need protection. He is our shield and buckler. In the battle he covers our head, and thrusts danger from us. Ever ready, at our right hand and at our left, before and behind, he wards off the stroke, or anticipates and prevents the evil. Unweariedly serving us as our protector, and wielding for us the weapons of battle, he enables us to say, with tranquil confidence, The Lord is on my side; I will not fear though thousands set themselves against me.

But I cannot number our wants. They are numerous as the moments that run on. Each day brings forth its new ones, and repeats the old. How blessed, how comforting, in such a case, to have one to minister to them all, and that one none other than the Son of God himself! The Lord is our Shepherd, we shall not want. Jesus himself is he who waits to serve, to supply, and to satisfy. What can make us fear or despond? What can make our hands hang down, or our knees wax feeble? Our strength may be small; he will increase it. Our faith may be feeble; he will give it might. Perplexities may beset us; he will guide us through. Sorrow may press us down; he will minister consolation. Sin may struggle hard for the mastery; he will subdue it. In every scene, and place, and duty, and struggle, and trial, he will be at our side, as the servant, to minister to us in everything, so that in nothing we may be found lacking.

"I am among you as he that serveth." Thus he speaks to us now; coming into the midst of us, and proffering his gracious services. I am come, not to receive, but to give; not to be filled, but to fill; not to be healed, but to heal; not to be gladdened, but to gladden; not to be ministered unto, but to minister! Oh, who is there that can listen coldly to such an announcement, or refuse such a proffer of service? Shall condescending love like this be trifled with or set at nought?

Is there some one here, like Peter, ready to say, Surely this is too much! "Lord, thou shalt never wash my feet! I cannot bear the thought that thou shouldst perform an act so menial for such as I am." Then hear the answer,—" If I wash thee not, thou hast no part in me." If thou wilt not allow me thus to minister, then thou canst not be mine! Strange, yet blessed thought! We cannot be saved, we cannot have any part in him, unless we allow him thus to perform for us his service of lowly love! It is as the servant that he is the Saviour! In saving, he serves; and in serving, he saves!

Do we not often lose sight of this? And, in losing sight of it, how much do we miss! We should be holier, as well as more blessed men, if we did but allow the Master to serve us as he desires. We should be wiser, stronger, more full of faith, and love, and zeal, would we but consent to let him minister to us in all the varied service which we need so much, and which he is so willing to perform. The Father's servant for our profit, and our servant for the glory of the Father, he presents himself this day to us, seeking to be employed by us in his lowly office, and grieving only at this, that there are so few who will employ him; and that even those who do, either through false humility or self-reliance, do not give him, even to the ten thousandth part, the extent of the employment that he desires.

SERMON XI.

CHRIST THE HEALER.

"If I may but touch his garment, I shall be whole."—MATT. ix. 21.

HERE, we may say, we have the record of one who had learned to do justice to the love of God,—to the grace of the Lord Jesus Christ. Not of many can this be said, in a world of unbelief like ours; but here is one. We do not know her name; no other part of her history is told us; she is brought before us simply as one who trusted in the Son of God, who had tasted that the Lord was gracious. Like a sudden star, she shines out and then disappears. But her simple faith remains as our example.

It is not the great multitude "thronging" Christ that here draws our eye. It is the woman and the Lord; the sick one and her Healer; the sinner and the Saviour. From every one else our eye is turned, and fixed on these. In this brief narrative concerning them, we find such things as the following:—

I. *The way in which these two are thrown together.*—The Lord has just received the ruler's message concerning his little daughter, and he is hastening to Capernaum. His direct errand is about her.

But, on his way, the Father finds much for him to do; and, by chance, as men say, this sick woman crosses his path and detains him a moment; for it is only sickness, or sorrow, or death, that either detain him or hasten him on. In his blessed path as the healer, he is ever willing to be arrested by the sons of men; counting this no detention, no trouble, no hindrance, but the true fulfilment of his heavenly mission. Opportunities such as these were welcome to him; nor was he at any time too busy, too much in haste, to take up the case of the needy, however suddenly brought before him. To him no interruption was unwelcome which appealed to his love or power. These *by-errands* of the Son of Man were often his most blessed ones, as at Nain, and Jacob's well, and the sycamore of Jericho. I know not whether we prize our own *by-errands* sufficiently, our "accidental" opportunities of working or speaking for God. We like to plan, and to carry out our plans to the end; and we do not quite like interruptions or detentions. Yet these may be, after all, our real work. Little can we guess, when forming our plans for the day, on what errands God may send us; and as little can we foresee, when setting out even on the shortest journey, what opportunity may cross our path, of serving the Master, and blessing our fellow-men. Whitefield, on his way to Glasgow, is drawn aside unexpectedly to tarry a night in the house of strangers. To that family he brings salvation. A minister of Christ misses the train which was to convey him to his destination. He frets a little, but sets out to walk the ten miles as best he may. He is picked up by a kind stranger in a carriage, a man of the world, who has not been in the house of God for years. He speaks a word, gives a book, thanks the stranger in the Master's name for his kindness, and joys to learn some years after that he missed the train in order to be the messenger of eternal life to a heedless sinner.

II. *The occasion of their being brought together.*—It is the *incurability* of the woman's ailment by earthly skill that throws her upon the heavenly physician. Man has done his utmost for twelve years, but has failed. She gets worse, not better. But man's failure brings her to one who cannot fail. Man's helplessness shuts her up to help that is almighty; and sends her to one who can do exceeding abundantly above all she asks or thinks. How slow are *we* to turn from man to God! Not twelve years, but many times twelve years do we continue in our trouble, trying successive remedies, —going to one and another and another physician, crying, Heal me, heal me. We hew out cistern after cistern; and still, as each one breaks, we try another. We go the round of vanity, and pleasure, and sin, endeavouring to fill our empty souls; and turning away at last with the despairing cry, "Oh, who will shew us any good?" But, like the prodigal, we begin to bethink ourselves. "There is bread enough in our Father's house," we say;—Shall we not arise and seek it? We have tried man, shall we not try God? We have gone to earthly wells, shall we not try the heavenly? Thus earthly disappointment is the introduction to heavenly blessedness. The uselessness of human medicines sends us to the balm of Gilead, and to the physician that is there. Nor does he reject us because we have tried him last, and because we would fain have done without him if we could. He welcomes us as if we had come to him first; nor does he upbraid us with our delay. Blessed failures, happy disappointments, that thus throw men, with their poor aching hearts, upon the loving-kindness of the Lord!

III. *The point of connection between them.*—It is the woman's malady. Incurability is the *occasion* of the connection; but the point or link of connection is the *disease* itself. Had it not been for this, she would not have sought the Lord. It is not that which is *whole* about her, but that which is *diseased*, that draws the healer to the sick one, and the sick one to the healer. So, it is *sin* that is our point of connection. Not our good, but our want of good, nay, our evil, our total evil. Our death and his life; our weakness and his strength; our poverty and his riches;—these are the things that meet and clasp each other. All connection with the Son of God must begin with our *sin;* for he came not to call the righteous, but *sinners*, to repentance; he receives *sinners;* he saves the *lost*. This is the point in dispute between the Saviour and the self-righteous sinner. This is the truth that we are so slow to learn; yet it is the essence of the gospel. Did we but fully know and act upon this, how differently should we treat the Lord! Distrust and distance would be ended, for the *cause* of these would be taken out of the way. We stand aloof from him because we do not see in him *the receiver of sinners;* nor thoroughly recognise either his absolute goodness or our absolute evil. A good thought, a fervent feeling, an earnest prayer, a sorrowful tear;—these are great things in our eyes; because we think they will recommend us to Him, and form so many points, at which he and we may come into contact with each other. Alas for our folly and unbelief; and alas for the misery and the darkness which they produce! We will not trust him for his own grace and goodness; we must bribe him to bless us! We would hide the evil in us, and we would display the good, in order to induce him to take us into favour. But it is not thus that he receives. It is with sin he deals, and we must bring him that. It is with disease that he deals, and we must bring him that. If we refuse, there can be no meeting between Him and us, till we meet before the throne.

IV. *The woman's need of Christ.*—Hers had been a sore and long sickness; a great and a long need. Yet it was her need that made her welcome. Blessed need that makes us welcome to the Lord!

As with the woman, so with us. We need Christ! And what an amount of need is implied in this! A man that needs an hundred pounds is needy; but the man who needs ten thousand is far more so. That we need *Christ*,—nothing less than Christ, yet nothing more,—is the most appalling, yet also the most comforting announcement of a sinner's state that could be made. Nothing could be said more fitted to awaken, to alarm, to humble, than this,—you need *Christ*. Such is the nature and the extent of your need, that less than the Incarnate Son and his fulness cannot avail you. We need *Christ!* This is the reason for our coming to him, and for his receiving us. We go to him, we deal with him, we make our case known to him,—*because we need him*. It may be our sense of sin or our want of a sense of sin; it may be our ignorance, our stupidity, our insensibility, our conscious absence of all goodness;—it matters not. Only let these bring us at once and directly to himself. The emptiness is ours; but the fulness is his; infinite fulness dispensed by infinite love.

V. *Christ's need of the Woman.*—Does it sound strange to say that Christ needed the woman? It is true; and as blessed as it is true. The speaker needs his audience as truly as the audience needs the speaker. The physician needs the sick man as truly as the sick man the physician. The sun needs the earth as truly as the earth needs the sun. You may say, what would the earth be without the sun ? Yes; but what would the sun be without an earth to shine upon ? What would become of its radiance ? All wasted. It would shine in vain. So Christ needed objects for the exercise of his skill, and love, and power. His fulness needed emptiness like ours to draw it out: otherwise it would have been pent up and unemployed. He is glorified, not simply in the possession of fulness, but in the *using* of it. If it remain within himself, he is unglorified, and the Father is unglorified. He needed opportunities for drawing out his treasures. He needed the publican as truly (though not in the same sense and way) as the publican needed him. He needed Mary Magdalene and the woman of Sychar, and Simon the leper, and Lazarus of Bethany, as truly as they needed him. How cheering ! The Lord hath need of us ! He needs guilty ones to pardon ; he needs empty ones to fill ; he needs poor ones to enrich ! How precious and how ample is the gospel contained in this blessed truth !

VI. *The woman's thoughts of Christ.* — Her thoughts of herself are poor. She is modest and diffident; unwilling to obtrude herself on the Master. She is in earnest about her cure ; but she takes the quietest way of obtaining it. Her desire to touch his garment is not error or ignorance, as if supposing that some virtue lay in its hem. Nor is her wish for secresy, unbelief, but simply humility ; —humility, accompanied with such faith in him, that she feels assured that a touch of his raiment will suffice. She is unwilling to detain or trouble him; and she has such high thoughts of him as to convince her that a direct appeal is not needed. A touch will do; one touch of his garment! Thus she thinks within herself, in the simplicity of her happy faith. She knows his fulness is infinite, and that simple contact with him in any form will draw it out. The healing virtue in him is irrepressible. Like the sun, he cannot but shine. Like the garden, he cannot but give out his fragrance. Only let her come within touch of his raiment, and all is well.

She touched, and as she believed, so was it to her. All was well.

Let such be our thoughts of this heavenly healer. He is the same in heaven as on earth. There still goes virtue out of him to heal the sons of men. Let us do justice to his love and skill,—thinking no evil of Him, but only good. The simplest form of connection with him will accomplish the cure. Listening to his voice,—that will do it. A look at his countenance,—that will do it. A clasp of his hand,—that will do it. A touch of his garment, even of its hem,—that will do it. For "as many as touch him are made perfectly whole."

SERMON XII.

CHRIST THE CLEANSER.

" He that is washed needeth not, save to wash his feet, but is clean every whit."—JOHN xiii. 10.

This washing of the disciples' feet was one of the last of our Lord's acts on earth, as the servant of his disciples, the servant of sinners. How fully did that towel, and that basin, shew that he had "taken upon him the form of a servant," (Phil. ii. 7), and that he had come "not to be ministered unto, but to minister!" This last act of lowly love, is the filling up of his matchless condescension; it is so simple, so kindly, so expressive; and all the more so, because not referring to positive want, such as hunger, or thirst, or pain, but merely to bodily comfort. Oh, if he is so interested in our commonest comforts, such as the washing of our feet, what must he be in our spiritual joys and blessings! How desirous that we should have peace of soul; and how willing to impart it!

This scene of condescending love is no mere show. It is a reality. And it is a reality for us to copy. Love to the saints; love shewing itself in simple acts of quiet, lowly service; service pertaining to common comforts; this is the lesson for us, which the divine example gives. If *He* did this, what should *we* do? "If I your Lord and Master have washed your feet, ye also ought to wash one another's feet."

But, in the midst of this scene and its lesson, there suddenly rises up a spiritual truth, called forth by Peter's remonstrance. The whole transaction is transferred into a *type*, or *symbol*, by the Lord himself. The earthly all at once rises into the heavenly, as he utters these words, "If I wash thee not, thou hast no part in me." It is as if he had lighted up a new star in the blue, or rather withdrawn the cloud that hid a star already kindled, but hindered, in its shining, by an earthly veil.

Accepting, then, this spiritual truth as a vital part of the transaction, let us study its full meaning, as thus unveiled to us. The words of this tenth verse might be thus translated, or at least paraphrased:—"He that has bathed (or come out of the bath) needs only, after that, to wash his feet; the rest of his person is clean." Here, then, we have first the bathing; and, secondly, the washing.

I. *The Bathing.*—The reference here may be to "the fountain opened for sin and for uncleanness;" in which we are "washed from our sins in his own blood" by "Him who loved us" (Rev. i. 5). The bath is the blood, and the bathing is our believing. From the moment we bathe, that is, believe, we are personally and legally clean in God's sight; our "bodies are washed with pure water" (Heb. x. 20). We may accept the reference here, as being either to the *temple*, or to the *bath*. He who bathes, say in the morning, is clean for the whole day. Our believing is our taking our morning bath. *That* cleanses our persons; and during all the rest of our earthly day we walk about, as men forgiven and clean; who know that there is no condemnation for them, and that God has removed their sins from them, as far as east is from the west. Connecting the washing here referred to, with the temple service, the meaning would be this:—We go to the altar and get the blood, the symbol of death, sprinkled upon us, implying that we have died the death, and paid the penalty, in him who died for us. From the altar we go to the laver, and get the blood washed off from our persons, proclaiming that we are *risen* from the dead, and therefore in all respects most thoroughly clean,—"clean every whit,"—all over clean in our persons before God.

This is the *bathing;* and thus it is that we are cleansed, realising David's prayer, "Purge me with hyssop, and I shall be clean; wash me, and I shall be whiter than the snow." When I believe in Christ as the fountain, as the altar and the laver, that is, when I receive God's testimony concerning his precious blood, I am washed. I become *clean;* as Christ said to his disciples, "Now are ye clean *through the word* that I have spoken unto you." When I believe in Christ as the righteousness, that is, when I receive God's testimony concerning his divine righteousness, I am straightway righteous. When I receive him as the life, I have life. When I receive him as Redeemer, I am redeemed. When I receive him as the sinner's surety, I am pardoned; there is no condemnation for me. When I receive him as the dead and risen Christ, I die and rise again.

Such are the results of this divine bathing. They are present and immediate results. They spring straight from that oneness with him in all things into which my believing brings me. As a believing man, I enter upon his fulness; I become partaker of his riches; and so identified with himself, that his cleanness is accounted my cleanness, his excellence my excellence, his perfection my perfection. As he was the Lamb without blemish, and without spot, so I am "clean every whit;" and to me, as part of the cleansed Bride, the Lamb's wife, it is said, "Thou art all fair, my love; there is no spot in thee."

II. *The Washing.*—This is something different from the bathing, and yet there is a likeness between the two things. Both refer to forgiveness; or rather, we should say, that the first refers to personal acceptance, the latter to the daily forgiveness of the accepted one. The washing is not that of the person, but of the person's feet,—those parts which come constantly into contact with the soil and dust of the earth. Considered personally, and as a whole, he is far above the earth, and beyond its pollutions; for he is with Christ in heavenly places; but, considered in parts, his *feet* may be said to be still upon the earth. In one sense he is "clean every whit," seated with Christ in heaven; in another, he is still a sinner, walking the earth, and getting his feet constantly soiled with its dust, or "thick clay." Our Lord here speaks of the *washing* in reference to this latter condition; and contrasts the *continual washing* with the *one bathing;* the daily pardons, upon confession, with the one acceptance, in believing; an acceptance with which nothing can interfere. With the *sense* of acceptance, we may say that many things can and do interfere; but with the acceptance itself, nothing can, either within or without, either in heaven or on earth.

The person who is bathed, is exposed after coming from the bath to constant soiling of his feet; but that is all. His person remains clean. The priest who has washed at the laver, is constantly getting his feet soiled with the dust of the temple pavement, or with the clotted blood which adheres to it. But this does not affect his person. That remains clean. So is it with the believing man. Personally accepted, and delivered from condemnation, he is every moment contracting some new stain, some defilement which needs washing. But this defilement does not affect his personal forgiveness, and ought not to lead him into doubt as to his acceptance. He himself is clean, through his reception of the word spoken to him by his Lord and Master; and he goes about the removal of his ever-recurring sins, as one who knows this. He betakes himself to Christ for the hourly removal of his sins, as one who has tasted that the Lord is gracious; he comes for the washing of his feet to him who has already bathed his person.

It is this distinction between the "bathing" and the "washing" that meets the difficulty felt by some, as to a believer constantly seeking pardon. He that has bathed needeth not save to wash his feet; but still he does need to have these washed. He that has been accepted in the beloved, has not daily to go and plead for acceptance, nor to do or say anything which implies that the condemnation, from which he has been delivered, has returned; but he has to mourn over, to confess, to seek forgiveness for daily sins. The two states are quite distinct, yet quite consistent with each other. The complete acceptance of the believing man does not prevent his sinning, nor do away with the constant need of new pardons for his sins; and the recurrence of sin does not cancel his acceptance, nor is the obtaining of new pardons at variance with his standing as a forgiven man.

It is this distinction which answers a question often raised, "Are all our sins, *future* as well as past, forgiven the moment we believe?" In one sense they are; for from the time of our believing, we are treated by God as forgiven men, and nothing can interfere with this. But in another they are not; for, strictly speaking, no sin can be actually forgiven *till it exists*, just as no one can be raised up till he actually fall, and as we cannot wash *off* the soil from our feet until it is *on* them. That God should treat his saints as *forgiven* ones, and yet that he should be constantly *forgiving*, are two things quite compatible,—and the "bathing and washing" of our text, furnish an excellent illustration of their consistency. All such questions have two sides, a divine and a human one. The mixing up of these two, or the ascribing to the one what belongs to the other, confuses and perplexes. The keeping of them separate makes all clear. With the *divine* side God has to do, with the *human* we have to do. Eternal forgiveness is God's purpose: daily forgiveness is our enjoyment and privilege.

We are apt to get into confusion here, and to feel as if our daily sins did interfere with our acceptance, and ought, for the time, to destroy our consciousness, or assurance of acceptance. Our Lord's words here clear up this difficulty, and rectify this mistake. "He that hath bathed needeth not, save to wash his feet." Our state of "no condemnation," is one which our daily sins cannot touch. These sins need constant washing; but that does not affect the great truth of our personal cleanness in the sight of God, our having found grace in the eyes of the Lord. To suppose that it could do so, would be to misunderstand our Lord's distinction between the bathing and the washing.

Let us learn, then, how to deal with our daily sins, in consistency with this distinction. Suppose I sin,—suppose I get angry; shall I conclude that I have never been accepted, or that this sin has thrown me out of acceptance? No; but holding fast my acceptance, go and confess my anger to the Master. Suppose I allow the world to come in, and perhaps for days I become cold, and prayerless; shall I say, Ah, I have never been a forgiven man? or, This has broken up the reconciliation? No; but, undisturbed in my consciousness of pardon and reconciliation, I simply take my worldliness, my coldness, my prayerlessness to God; I go and wash my feet as often as they need it, and that is every moment; but, in doing so, I never lose sight of the blessed fact, that I have bathed, and that as nothing can alter this fact, so nothing can invalidate its effects. It abides unchanged. Once bathed, then bathed for ever!

Shall we sin, then, because grace abounds? Shall we soil our feet because our cleansing has been so perfect, and because the washing is so easy? No. How shall we who are dead to sin, live any longer therein? So far from being now in a more favourable position for committing sin, we are placed in one which, of all others, is the most effectual for delivering us from it. The conscious completeness of the pardon is God's preservative from sin; and it is the best, the most effectual. There is none like it. It is the source of our power *against* sin, and *for* holiness. Without this, progress in goodness, freedom in service, and success in labour are all impossible.

The bathing and the washing are, both of them, God's protests against sin; and, if understood aright, would be our most effectual safeguards. They come to us like Christ's words to the woman, "Neither do I condemn thee; GO AND SIN NO MORE." And what more likely to deepen our hatred of sin, than this necessary intercourse with our holy Master, in the reception of constant forgivenesses from his priestly hands. The more that we have to do with Him, the more are we sure to become like him; nor is anything more fitted to make us ashamed of our *sins*, than our being compelled to bring them constantly, and to bring them all, small and great, for pardon to HIMSELF.

It is thus that the Highest stoops to the lowest, and discharges toward them the offices of happy affection and considerate sympathy in the most menial things of life. Shall we not imitate his love, and by our daily acts of kindly service to our fellow-saints, knit together the members of the blessed household? However great in rank, or riches, or learning, shall we not stoop? "High in high places, gentle in our own." Shall we not thus win love? Not so much to ourselves, as to the beloved One; shewing his meekness in ours, his gentleness in ours, his lowliness in ours, his patience in ours; thus melting hearts that would not otherwise be melted, and winning affections that would not otherwise be won. "For as He is, so are we in this world."

SERMON XIII.

THE SURETY'S BAPTISM.

"I have a baptism to be baptized with; and how am I straitened till it be accomplished!"—LUKE xii. 50.

MESSIAH was announced, by the prophets, as King of Peace and King of Righteousness. He was to be Solomon and Melchisedec in one; the great antitype of both. He was to conquer and cast out him who had brought in all the discord; to restore unity and order to a broken and dismembered world. He was to reconcile the various parts of creation, so that not only were God and man, heaven and earth, to be at one, but even the lower races of creation were to have their variances removed, and the lion and the ox, the wolf and the lamb, the leopard and the kid, were to dwell together in peace. Everything connected with his person, his work, his word, his reign, was *peace*. His was to be the "covenant of *peace;*" his name was to be the "Prince of *Peace;*" and in his days there was to be "the abundance of *peace.*"

At verse 51 there is an apparent denial of this: "Suppose ye that I am come to give *peace* on earth? I tell you, Nay; but rather division." This, however, clearly means that the *first* results of his coming were not the expected ones of peace. He was indeed coming on an errand of peace; but there was something before that,—something introductory to it, yet altogether unlike it. Before the light there must come the darkness; before the still small voice there must come the earthquake, the whirlwind, and the lightning. So, before the peace of Messiah's reign there must come fire, and war, and division, and persecution, and the sword. Before Israel is planted in their land, to enjoy the abundance of Messiah's peace, there must come the "tribulation such as never was nor shall be."

The fire spoken of in the 49th verse is not the fire of Pentecost, nor the symbol of the Holy Ghost, nor the figure of purification. It is manifestly the fire of vengeance, so frequently referred to by the prophets as the precursor of Messiah's coming and reign. Ps. l. 3, "Our God shall come, and shall not keep silence; a *fire* shall devour before him." Ps. xcvii. 3, "*A fire* goeth before him, and burneth up his enemies round about." Isa. ix. 5, "This (the last battle) shall be with *burning and fuel of fire*." Isa. x. 17, "And the light of Israel shall be for *a fire*, and his holy one for *a flame*." Isa. lxvi. 15, "Behold, the Lord will come with *fire*, to render his anger with fury, and his rebuke with flames of fire; for *by fire*, and by his sword (his "flaming sword," Gen. iii. 24), will the Lord plead with all flesh." So John the Baptist announced Christ as the Avenger who was to "burn up the chaff with *unquenchable fire*" (Matt. iii. 12).

So Paul proclaims him as to come "with *flaming fire*, taking vengeance on them that know not God." So do Peter and Jude, and John in the Revelation. It is *fire* that is so specially and so awfully associated with Messiah and his day.

Of this fire the Lord here speaks, adding, "What will I if it be already kindled?"—meaning, "Would that that day were come,—that day which is to bring glory to me and my people,—to purge the earth from sin, and make all things new. It is not for its own sake, or for the destruction which it brings, that he longs for the fire, but for the glorious results that are to follow.

He then announces himself as the bringer of fire, the kindler of that terrible flame in which creation is to be wrapped, when the wicked are consumed, and when the alloy of the ancient curse is to be burned out of it for ever. "I am come to send fire on the earth." He tells also with equal distinctness his desire for the arrival of that awful day. Not that he loves the night; but it is the herald of the morn. Not that he desires the day of wrath; but it is the introduction of the day of everlasting peace.

Having thus adverted to his second coming and the woes then awaiting the world, he turns to his first coming, and the woes about to come upon himself. The world's baptism of fire was certainly to come, but his own baptism of fire must come first. "I have a baptism to be baptized with." The fire that is to burn up his enemies and purge creation must first descend on him, for he is the great demonstration to the universe that "our God is a consuming fire." The sword that is to go through the world must first awake against the Man that is Jehovah's fellow. The cup of trembling that is to go round the nations must first be given into His hands. In the sorrow, and the wrath, and the death, that are to visit this evil world, He must first have his bitter share. O dreadful baptism of the Son of God! a baptism which the sons of Zebedee vainly thought they could partake of along with him; a baptism which neither man nor angel could endure; a baptism whose shower of infinite wrath was too fiery, too resistless, too overwhelming, to be borne by any, save one who was superhuman, superangelic,—truly divine; for who but God can bear the wrath of God, and not be totally consumed?

The baptism of the Son of God, here spoken of by himself, was the baptism of wrath; for he who was made sin for us must be baptized with this baptism. Because of this he cried out in his anguish, "Thy wrath lieth hard upon me; thou hast afflicted me with all thy waves;" "Thy fierce wrath (or 'burnings,' Ps. lxxxviii. 16, Heb. xii. 29) goeth over me." It was thus that the shower, which should have expended itself on us, exhausted itself on him. It was thus that righteousness made way for grace, and, satisfying itself upon the Surety instead of the sinner, proclaimed righteous pardon to the condemned, and righteous liberty to the captive. For the Son of God there was the baptism of fire, in order that for us there might be the baptism of grace and peace.

It is the knowledge of this fiery baptism of our divine Surety that gives to us the reconciliation and the peace which, as sinners, we need. The more thoroughly that we know that baptism, and enter into its gracious meaning, the more do we realise the reconciliation of the covenant, and feel assured that there is no condemnation for us. The knowledge of his condemnation becomes thus the assurance of our own forgiveness, and the discernment of the wrath that has come down on him, conveys to us abiding and unchanging peace ; because it is wrath which has wholly and for ever passed away from us.

It was of this fiery baptism that He himself spoke when he said, "Now is my soul troubled." Of this he spoke more fully in Gethsemane, when his sweat was as it were great drops of blood falling down to the ground. Of this he spoke upon the cross, when he cried out, "My God, my God, why hast thou forsaken me ?" Of this he spoke in the Supper, when he said, "This is my body broken for you. . . . . This cup is the New Testament in my blood, shed for many, for the remission of sins." It is of this fiery baptism of wrath, under which he died, that our own baptism is the memorial ; for it is called " baptism into death," and we are said to be "baptized into his death," as if we in baptism were so identifying ourselves with him, as to be baptized with the baptism wherewith he was baptized, and to be brought under the same descending flood of divine wrath as came down on him.

This baptism the Son of God must undergo; and he knew this. It was appointed him of the Father, and arranged in the eternal covenant. "I *have* a baptism to be baptized with." He knew it; he knew the reason of it; he knew the result of it; and he knew that it could not pass away from him. He had come to fulfil all righteousness; he had come to be made a curse for us. As the fulfiller of the Father's will he must undergo the appointed baptism. As the Redeemer of the captive, the Substitute for the sinner, the Man who "pleased not himself," he must undergo it. It was his lot, his divinely ordained lot. He knew it, and he went on to meet it. "I have a baptism to be baptized with." He saw Gethsemane in his path, but he turned not aside. He saw Golgotha before him, but on he went, straight to the agony of its cross and death. To do the will of Him who sent him, and to finish his work, at whatever cost,—this was his desire.

But still he felt, in regard to that awful baptism, the human sensitiveness and shrinking which made him in Gethsemane cry, "If it be possible, let this cup pass from me." "How am I straitened," he says, "till it be accomplished!"

SERMON XIV.

THE SURETY'S BAPTISM.

"I have a baptism to be baptized with; and how am I straitened till it be accomplished!"—LUKE xii. 50

IN this awful utterance of our Substitute, as he looked forward to the cross, we have,—

1. *A longing for the baptism.* He desired its accomplishment. He knew the results depending on it, and these were so divinely glorious, so eternally blessed, that he could not but long for it,—he could not but be straitened till it was accomplished. The cup was inexpressibly bitter, but the recompence for drinking it was so vast, that he could not but long for the hour when it should be put into his hands. Just as he said at another time, "With desire have I desired to eat this passover with you before I suffer;" so here he says, "I have a baptism to be baptized with, and how am I straitened till it be accomplished!"

2. *The consciousness of fear and bitter anguish in contemplating it.* He was truly man, both in body and soul. As man he shrunk from pain, he was weighed down with burdens, he was subject to sorrow; he looked on death as his enemy, and he made supplication with strong crying and tears

unto him that was able to save him from death. His utterances in the Psalms are the fullest intimation of his feelings in these respects. Thus he cries, "Rescue my soul from their destructions, my darling from the lions;" "O Lord, rebuke me not in thy wrath, neither chasten me in thy hot displeasure; for thine arrows stick fast in me, and thy hand presseth me sore. I am feeble and sore broken: I have roared by reason of the disquietness of my heart." . . "My heart is sore pained within me, and the terrors of death are fallen upon me: fearfulness and trembling are come upon me, and terror hath overwhelmed me." . . "Save me, O God, for the waters are come in unto my soul; I sink in deep mire, where there is no standing; I am come into deep waters, where the floods overflow me. I am weary of my crying; my throat is dried: mine eyes fail while I wait for my God." Such are the utterances of his human soul under the pressure of its infinite sorrows. He did not shake off the burden, yet the weight was intolerable. He did not refuse the cup, yet its gall and wormwood were such as to wring from him many an awful cry. He did not turn back from the anguish, or the darkness, or the death, yet he speaks as one overwhelmed with the very thought of them.

If, then, his humanity was thus proved to be true and real, altogether like our own, in everything save sin, how true and real must have been those sorrows which thus agonized that holy yet true humanity! His burdens were all real; his pangs were all real; his terrors were all real, as were his hunger and his thirst,—real as was his death upon the Roman cross, or his burial in Joseph's tomb. His divine nature did not relieve him of one grief, or make his sufferings mere shadows. It fitted him for being filled with more sorrow than any man could be. It conferred on him an awful, we may say a *divine*, capacity of endurance, and so made him the subject of sharper pain and profounder grief than otherwise he could have been. So far from his suffering less truly, or to a less degree, because he was the Son of God, he was, in that very way, made capable of an amount of bodily and mental agony of which, as a mere man, he could not have been susceptible.

And as the sorrow was thus all real,—increased, not lessened by his Godhead,—so was his substitution for us as real. "Surely he hath borne *our* griefs, and carried *our* sorrows; he was wounded for *our* transgressions, he was bruised for *our* iniquities." His endurance of our penalty was as true as was his partaking of our sorrow. It was "the chastisement of *our* peace that was on him." The more that we contemplate this his suffering, his baptism, the more will the whole reality of his sin-bearing work appear. He, "his own self, bare our sins, in his own body, on the tree."

3. *The straitening in regard to its accomplishment.* Like Paul, he was in a strait between things which pressed in opposite ways, and which must continue to press till the work was done.

(1.) *He was straitened between the anticipated pain, and the thought of the result of that pain.* How fully was this feeling brought out in that remarkable passage recorded by the Evangelist John (xii. 27), "Now is my soul troubled; and what shall I say? Father, save me from this hour: but for this cause came I unto this hour. Father, glorify thy name." Here was the straitening expressed in our text; the same straitening that we find again in the scene of the garden agony.

(2.) *He was straitened between grace and righteousness.* Till the great sacrifice was offered, there might be said to be conflict between these two things. The reconciliation was not actually accomplished between them. Mercy and truth had not yet met together; righteousness and peace had not yet kissed each other. Between his love to the sinner and his love to the Father there was conflict; between his desire to save the former and his zeal to glorify the latter there was something wanting to produce harmony. He knew that this something was at hand, that his baptism of suffering was to be the reconciliation; and he pressed forward to the cross, as one that could not rest till the discordance were removed,—as one straitened in spirit till the great reconciliation should be effected. "I have a baptism to be baptized with, and how am I straitened till it be accomplished!"

Such was the baptism of the Son of God, and such the straitening of spirit, till it was accomplished. It was infinite suffering to which He looked forward; suffering from which his soul would naturally shrink; yet he could not rest, till the life-time's endurance had been completed, and the great work done. He pressed forward in the path of suffering, nor did he stay, till he had reached its end. The spirit was willing, though the flesh was weak.

And now, as the result of this accomplished baptism, we have forgiveness and salvation proclaimed to us. He has finished transgression, made an end of sin, brought in everlasting righteousness, made reconciliation for iniquity. No second baptism like his is needed now. The one baptism has done the work. No second cross requires to be erected on some new Golgotha. His one cross has completed the great propitiation, and brought redemption to the captive. No second death can be demanded now, by law or righteousness. The one death of the Prince of Life has secured for us the everlasting life, which no other death could have done. The knowledge of this one baptism, this one cross, this one death, is all we need to put us in possession of forgiveness and life, of righteousness and glory.

What, then, remains for us but that we enter into his rest, reaping what he has sown, and gathering fruit from the vine which he has planted? So complete is the Father's testimony to the accomplished baptism of his Son, the finished work of the Substitute, that, in receiving that testimony, we receive the full measure of blessing purchased for us by that baptism and death.

Nor are the results of this bloody baptism of the Son of God limited or temporary. The whole earth is yet to share them. The eternal ages are yet to know them. There come, no doubt, first the sword, the discord, the persecution, and the fire. All these have been doing their work on earth, and shall do so, yet for a little season. But ere long the sword shall go through earth for the last time ; division shall disturb its peace for the last time ; persecution shall seize its victims for the last time ; the fire shall be kindled for the last time. And then shall come the peace, and the love, and the holiness. Then shall come the deliverance of creation, the reign of peace, the kingdom of glory, the new heavens and new earth, wherein dwelleth righteousness. Then shall He see of the travail of his soul, and shall be satisfied. Then shall He reap the fruit of his awful baptism. That baptism will not then seem too bitter or too terrible, when its issue shall be seen to be so glorious and eternal. Nor will the time then seem to have been too long, even though the kingdom should be deferred for many a day ; seeing there is to be so infinite a compensation for the sickness of hope deferred, and so blessed a termination of the long, long ages of delay.

SERMON XV.

THE SURETY'S SORROW.

"Now is my soul troubled."—John xii. 27

This twenty-seventh verse connects itself, not so much with the three previous verses, as with the twenty-third. The first announcement is, "The hour is come, that the Son of Man should be glorified;" the second is, "Now is my soul troubled."

The connection between these two statements does not seem at first sight very plain. The second is not the statement we should have expected to follow the first. Rather, we would say, it should have been "Now is my soul *glad*," not "*troubled;*" for the prospect of the glorifying ought naturally to call up joy, not sorrow. We feel at a loss to know why he should be so troubled, when arriving within sight of the glory.

Was earth so desirable an abode, that the thought of leaving it should sadden him? Did he wish to remain among sinners and enemies? Did he prefer the land of death, and curse, and woe, and shame, to the glorious heaven above, to the society of angels, to the honour of the throne of the majesty in the heavens? That, we know, could not be. He, far more than David ever did, longed for the wings of the dove that he might fly away and be at rest.

Why, then, did the near prospect of the glory thus overwhelm him with sadness? If there was nothing in the glory to produce this, what occasioned it? It was evidently no common sorrow; it was something new and terrible, even to him whose life was one weighty sorrow, and whose acquaintanceship with grief was of thirty-three years' standing. "Now is my soul troubled."

In bringing out the import of our Lord's words here, let us take up these four questions:—

I. *What was the trouble of his soul?*—As it could not be the glory itself, it must have been something either on this or on the other side of it; something which lay on his way to it, or was to be encountered immediately after it. It could not be the latter, as the entrance into the glory was the absolute ending of every thing like sorrow. It must, then, have been something which lay on this side of it,—something which he had to pass through in order to reach it.

There were three things which occasioned trouble to Christ when here; (1.) The sorrows and sins which he saw on earth; (2.) Sin imputed to him; (3.) The wrath of God on account of this imputed sin. The first of these was a constant source of sorrow to the compassionate Saviour; but there was nothing in the present scene to make it peculiarly so. The burden of sin, and the wrath of God, due to him as the Sin-bearer, were also continual sources of sorrow; and increasingly so, as the great crisis drew nigh, when the whole load of that sin and wrath was to press upon him in all its terribleness. The sin laid upon him was that which he infinitely abhorred; need we wonder, then, that, as it pressed more and more upon him, his soul should be troubled, nay, become "exceedingly sorrowful, even unto death?" The wrath and curse, due to this sin which was laid upon him, was that which he infinitely shrunk from: for, as the Son of the Blessed, he could not but be troubled at being made "a curse;" and as the object of the Father's divine complacency and love, he could not but feel troubled at the outpouring of the Father's wrath.

Such was the trouble of his soul. All along these things had been felt, and they had made him the man of sorrows. But as the great hour drew on when the Lamb was to be slain, the weight of the burden increased,—till, as he came within sight of the cross, it oppressed him so fearfully, that it seemed as if he would sink under it, ere he reached his destination. Intense was this trouble of his soul. So intense must have been his hatred of sin, and his shrinking from the Father's wrath. So intense also must have been his love to the sinner, and his zeal for the glory of the Father.

And if sin, though but imputed, was so hateful to him, what ought that sin, which lives in us, and pervades our whole being, to be to us? If divine wrath, though brief and for another's sin, and with all heaven's glory beyond, was so intolerable, what will that wrath be to the lost sinner, which is for his own guilt, and which will therefore burn into his innermost conscience. not for a day or a lifetime, but for a whole eternity, with no prospect of cessation or diminution, or glory beyond it all ?

II. *Why was he thus troubled now, and not before.* —In a certain measure he was always troubled, for he was, from his birth, the Sin bearer; but as he drew nearer the crisis, the sorrow increased, and the burden grew heavier. He realized more of that awful hour when the whole wrath should be poured out upon him; and the nearness of the glory reminded him of the greater nearness of the sorrow that lay on this side of it, and through which he must pass, in order to reach the blessedness beyond. The very vision of the glory, too, would serve to enhance and augment the trouble, as the dark peaks of Sinai look darker and more terrible, when the sun is seen going down behind them, and by his radiance bringing out each fierce and rugged cliff in full relief against the glowing sky.

Christ's soul was thoroughly human, in everything but sin; and hence objects, whether of joy or sorrow, affected him in proportion to their nearness or their distance. He always knew that the Father's will would infallibly be accomplished; yet it was not till the Seventy returned to him with joy, saying, "Lord, even the devils are subject to us through thy name" (Luke x. 21), that he "rejoiced in spirit." He knew that Lazarus was dead before he came to Bethany; yet it was not till he stood by his tomb and addressed the weeping all around, that he "wept." The *nearness* of either, or joy, or grief, affected him as it affects us. Our natures do not admit of our feeling them as much when they are far off as when they are near. So was it with Him. He knew the sorrow that lay before him, and doubtless it had thrown its shadow over him long ere this; but as he neared it, that shadow grew darker and darker, till, as he actually came within sight of the cross, his soul was troubled.

He must go to the cross with the full knowledge of what he is to suffer there. That suffering is not to overtake him unawares. He is to know, before he drinks it, the bitterness of the cup which the Father hath given him to drink, the anguish of that baptism with which he is to be baptized. He must see the sword that is to smite; and try the sharpness of its edge before it awakes against him. He must have a foretaste of the wrath and the curse, of death and of the grave, that he may calmly measure them, and give to them the entire acquiescence of his understanding and will. It was only thus that he could offer himself up as a *free-will offering*, fully cognisant of, and acquiescent in, all that was to be inflicted on him by the Father's justice. It was needful that he should suffer *willingly;* and in order to do so, he must suffer *knowingly;* the blow must not take him by surprise; he must give his own full consent to all that he was to endure; not to shut his eyes, and be led, as it were, blindfold to the cross, but to see it all, know it all, consent to it all; and then, after having thus seen and known and consented, go forward to the place of sacrifice, saying, Not my will, but thine be done.

Twice at least before he went to the cross, the Father brought the cup which he was to drink of, and placed it by his side, that he might look into it, and measure it and taste it; once at the time before us, and again in Gethsemane, when his "soul was exceeding sorrowful even unto death," and his "sweat, as it were, great drops of blood falling down to the ground." In both of these cases, there seems to be the same meaning and the same result. In both of them the Father was bringing the cup of wrath, and setting it down by his side, that he might fully know what he was about to drink; that having examined the contents, and tasted some of the infinitely terrible mixture, he might express his calm determination to drink it all, in that day when it should be put into his hands for this end; nay, might say, before heaven, and earth, and hell, holding the cup which he had examined up to view, "I delight to do thy will, O God;" "the cup which my Father hath given me to drink, shall I not drink it?"

The best commentary on these words of our text are those Psalms in which Christ speaks as the Sin-bearer, as the 38th or 40th, or 69th or 88th. In them we find Christ examining the bitter cup, and trying its contents, and tasting them day by day; and though, on such occasions as the present, or in Gethsemane, his soul was specially troubled, yet often, at other times also, was he made to feel the sorrow to which he had subjected himself for us. Each time that he used them he would enter into the trouble of soul which they express; but as the consummation drew nearer, he would enter more deeply into that trouble; and at each successive time they would acquire a more profound and solemn meaning. With us, familiarity with sorrow, and continual repetition of its bitterness, would harden and produce indifference. With Christ it was otherwise; for, though all was human, yet all was perfection in him; and each time these Psalms were read by him, they would convey a deeper and deeper experience of the awful realities which they expressed. For, though uttered in the feeble language of man, which could not fully enunciate the great things of God, yet, as understood and interpreted by the Son of God according to his perfect wisdom, what a reality would these cries of anguish convey to his soul; what a depth of meaning would each word possess!

How fully did the Son of God understand the conflict into which he entered for us; measure the weight of the burden which he bore for us; realise the sin which was laid upon him; take the dimensions of the wrath which was to be poured out on him for us, and examine the contents of the cup which he was to drink for us!

III. *Why did not his divine nature ward off the trouble?*—This question may be answered by another, Why did not his divine nature prevent sin from being imputed to him at all? If his Godhead did not do the one, why should it do the other? We know that the Godhead, so far from hindering the imputation of sin, was that which made it possible for sin to be imputed to him. Had he not been divine, there could have been no imputation. If, then, his Godhead did not hinder, but help the imputation of sin, it surely would not hinder the *consequences* of that imputation. If the imputation was real, the sufferings must be real. His Godhead availed not to diminish or neutralise the sorrow, but to give to that sorrow its infinite value and sin-bearing character. The union of the divine nature with the human was, not to interfere with the actings of the human, but to make them efficacious; not to ward off suffering, but to impart to it its vicarious potency; not to make the cup less bitter, but to make its contents healing and saving; not to save the victim from the cross, but to make crucifixion atonement; not to ward off death, but to impart to that death the character of an infinitely precious ransom; not to bar the grave against the entrance of the mighty victim, but to make that grave the womb of immortality and incorruption, the cradle of the church, the well-spring of resurrection-life and everlasting glory.

Besides, think what is meant by the divine nature warding off the suffering? If it mean anything at all, it must mean the turning of that suffering into a mere form or pretext. This, we are sure, was not the case. Instead of making the sufferings less real, it made them more real. The union of the divine with the human nature enabled the latter to bear more suffering than it otherwise could have done; and to have called in the Godhead in order to ward off the suffering, would have been to have called it in to hinder one of the very results contemplated by the union. The payment of the penalty was the suffering and the death of the Christ; and to have interfered with that suffering, or with that death, would have been to have hindered the payment of the ransom. Nay, and even when the human nature of the Lord was sinking under the pressure of the sorrow, it was not the Godhead that was sent to mitigate that anguish, or to sustain him under it; it was an angel,— "there appeared an angel from heaven strengthening him." For the Godhead to have interposed to shield Him either from the suffering or the death, would have been to maim his work, to destroy his substitution, and to turn the payment of the awful penalty from being one of the greatest of all realities into a mere pretence.

IV. *Why did not the joy in prospect of the glory outweigh and neutralize the sorrow?*—Here, again, we must remember that Christ's humanity was perfect; that the divine was not mixed up with the human, nor the human mixed up with the divine.

Each acted according to its nature. The glory therefore, however great, could not prevent Christ's human soul being acted on by the sorrow, according to its greatness, and according to its nearness. The cause of the sorrow was infinitely great, and the sorrow itself was at hand, therefore it was impossible for human nature not to feel profoundly that which was so great and so near. Had the sorrow been like our sorrow, then the difference between it and the glory would have been so great as to have made him call it a "light affliction," not worthy to be compared with the glory to be revealed. But his sorrow was not like ours. It was not indeed lasting; but it was unutterably vast; its vastness could only be measured by the greatness of our sins, and the greatness of him who was bearing them. There is no proportion between our suffering and our glory, any more than there is between time and eternity; but there is some proportion between Christ's sufferings and Christ's glory; it was, if one may so speak, the proportion between two eternities, two infinities. No wonder, then, that with such an infinity of suffering, the glory should have been for a season shut out, the human nature of Christ should have been bowed down under the awful load, and his soul made exceeding sorrowful even unto death. No vision of the coming glory could make his present suffering less, or alter the necessity for his bearing it, however much it might tend to sustain him under it. The sin laid on him was still the sin, the wrath was still the wrath, the curse was still the curse; and all these were infinitely terrible, to one who so thoroughly understood them; nor could the glory, however bright, lessen that terribleness, or mitigate the suffering which it was producing in the soul of the Son of God.

Oh, if his trouble of soul were so great, what must the sin be which produced it? Yet what must be the completeness of that deliverance from trouble, which is the portion of the believing soul, in consequence of his bearing it all? Not a pang remains for us; not a drop of bitterness is left behind. All is peace.

But, on the other hand, what must be the wrath of God against the transgressor? What must be the torment of the eternal curse which the lost sinner is to bear? And what must be that hell, that unending and unchanging hell of woe and torment, in reserve for those who, having rejected the sin-bearing of the divine Substitute, shall be compelled to bear the penalty of their guilt, without help, without alleviation, and without sympathy, suffering the vengeance of eternal fire!

SERMON XVI.

THE SURETY'S THIRST.

"Jesus saith, I thirst."—John xix. 28.

THREE things need our notice here : the thirst, the cry, the answer. They are not trifles, nor accidents, either in themselves or in connection with the great event of which they form a part. They have much to tell us of the Sufferer, and the nature of his sufferings ; and they help us to get at the meaning of the mysterious transaction of that hour, —an hour of the deepest darkness that ever rested over earth, yet an hour which proved the forerunner of the brightest and most blessed day-spring that ever shone from heaven.

1. *The thirst.*—It was a *true* thirst, and as deep and sore as it was true. It was a thirst corresponding with the character of him who felt it. He was human, and He was divine. It was, of course, humanity that thirsted ; but it was humanity in union with divinity, and therefore made more susceptible of suffering, more capable of enduring what alone it would not have been capable of undergoing. Christ's humanity was perfect ; but that only made it more sensitive,

more acutely alive to suffering, so that his hunger, his thirst, his weariness, instead of being mitigated or made unreal, became more real and intense, more unmodified and harder to bear, than they are or can be in our imperfect humanity. The perfection of humanity implies the perfection of suffering, whenever that perfect humanity comes into contact with suffering at all. Pre-eminence in sorrow, and pre-eminence in joy, must be the portion and prerogative of such exalted perfection. It is only perfection such as this that can sound the depths of creature-sadness, or reach the heights of human joy. Had there been one taint of imperfection, about either the body or the soul of Jesus, he could not have tasted the whole bitterness of our anguish; he could not have drained our cup; he could not have paid our penalty; he could not have felt that extremity of thirst, regarding which he uttered the bitter outcry in the hour of his conflict with death, and with the powers of darkness, upon the cross.

Christ was filled with the Spirit, "without measure," in a way and to an extent such as no other man ever was or could be; yet this did not exempt him from pain, or make his thirst unreal, or alleviate one pang which fell to his lot as the Sin-bearer. With that Spirit He was filled; by that Spirit he was sustained and strengthened; by that "eternal Spirit" he offered himself without spot to God;" but in no way and at no time did this Spirit come between him and suffering, either to blunt the edge of the weapon or ward off the stroke. The indwelling of the Spirit in him added to his perfection, and every addition to his perfection was an increase of his susceptibility to suffering; so that he felt pain more than we can do; he felt weariness, hunger, thirst, more than we can do. The Spirit that dwelt within him could not, indeed, feel the pain or the thirst; but the human nature thus inhabited by the Spirit was made capable of containing or receiving more pain, and thirst, and sorrow than it could have done otherwise, even as perfect humanity.

Christ was God-man; very God as truly as very man. But this did neither prevent nor nullify his sufferings. No abatement could be made from his sorrows, either in respect of number or intensity, because of his Godhead. That Godhead seemed only to present him as a broader mark for the arrows of his enemies; to make him a more capacious vessel for containing the fulness of the divine wrath due to him as the sinner's substitute. The Godhead could not, indeed, suffer, nor hunger, nor thirst, nor weep; but, by its union with the manhood, it could make all these endurances more true and more intense to that humanity with which it was united; not only attaching to these sufferings a value which they could not otherwise have had, but imparting to them a profound reality, which, in other circumstances, could not have belonged to them. We need to be cautious in using language respecting Christ not expressly employed in Scripture ; but, seeing the love of Christ is called the love of God, and the blood of Christ is called the blood of God, may we not term the thirst of the Son of God upon the cross, " the thirst of God ?"

How true was the humanity of Christ! That thirst proclaims him truly a man ; in body and in soul a man ; in sorrow and in joy a man. His Godhead did not neutralize his manhood, nor make any of its actings less truly human. That which was divine in his person made that which was human more thoroughly human than it could have been in any other circumstances. As his humanity shewed forth his Godhead more illustriously, so his Godhead brought out his humanity into fuller, wider, truer, and more perfect action, exhibiting it in an extremity of weakness and suffering, to which it could not otherwise have been reduced without wholly giving way. No mere man could have passed through Gethsemane and Golgotha, could have endured the agony of the one, and the thirst of the other, without being annihilated.

And what does this thirst mean ? Is it a mere vain exhibition of what humanity can bear ; of what the Creator can enable the creature to endure ? No. He thirsts as the sinner's substitute; and his strength is dried up like a potsherd, because the heat of divine wrath was withering up his moisture. That thirst is *expiatory;* for he suffers the Just for the unjust. He thirsts, that we might not thirst. He is parched, that we might not be parched. He is consumed with wrath, that we might not be consumed. That thirst is the bearing of your sin and your hell, O believer. That thirst is the unsealing of the eternal fountain, that its waters might flow forth to the parched and weary sons of earth. How much we owe to that awful thirst! How much we owe to the love of Him who thirsted upon that cross for us!

II. *The cry.*—"I thirst," or, "I am thirsty." These are common words among us; and the cry, in itself, does not strike us as remarkable. "I am thirsty," says the child to its mother. "I am thirsty," says the traveller on the highway. "I am thirsty," says the sick man on his hot bed of fever. We are familiar with the cry; it is that of a fellow-mortal; and we know that it will be met with a quick response, for it is a cry for something which can be easily and cheaply supplied.

But when such words come from the lips of the Son of God, the case is wholly different. It is no remarkable thing to hear a beggar asking alms on the highway or at our door; but when the great Roman general, the conqueror of kings, is reduced to poverty, and begs his bread, we are amazed; an interest is immediately excited, and we ask, How is this? So, when the cry comes from him who is God over all, the Creator of heaven and earth, the framer of all earth's fountains and streams, the fashioner of man's soul and body, we are startled.

How can this be? Whence does it arise? What can it mean? Is the cry a real and natural one? Is it the true expression of deep-felt pain in the divine utterer? or is it the mere indication by him of what, in such circumstances, a crucified malefactor would feel, but which he himself, in virtue of his exalted nature, could not possibly have been supposed to suffer?

One thing strikes us much here. His is the only cry heard at this time. There are two men on crosses beside him; but they utter no cry. One spends his breath in reviling, the other in praying; but they do not say, "I thirst." This is a peculiarity which we cannot fail to notice. Of the three sufferers, the Son of God alone utters the cry of thirst. How great must that thirst have been! how bitter the cry thus wrung from his expiring lips!

Specially does this appear when we call to mind the meek and uncomplaining character of the holy sufferer. Only once or twice, in a life of unutterable sorrow, did he allow any expression of his grief to escape him, as when he said, "Now is my soul troubled;" and when in Gethsemane he said, "My soul is exceeding sorrowful, even unto death;" and now on the cross, when he exclaimed, "My God, my God, why hast thou forsaken me?" and again, in the words of our text, "I thirst." Intense and overpowering must have been his thirst ere it could have extorted from him such an utterance at such a time.

SERMON XVII.

THE SURETY'S THIRST.

"Jesus said, I thirst."—JOHN xix. 28.

THE present is the only reference which the Lord makes to pain of body; the others are to the griefs of his troubled soul. No doubt, in the Psalms he alludes once or twice to his bodily sufferings, as when he speaks of his bones being out of joint, his heart melted like wax, his strength dried up like a potsherd. But these intimations of corporeal pain are few; it is of the sorrows of his soul, in connection with the wrath of God, that he speaks so fully. In the Gospels, this cry of thirst is the only expression of bodily anguish that is recorded; and from the way in which it is introduced we are plainly given to understand that even this cry would not have been uttered had it not been for the fulfilling of Scripture. However terrible the thirst, the cry would have been repressed, had it not been for what was written in the Psalms concerning this,—"In my thirst they gave me vinegar to drink" (Ps. lxix. 21). For thus the Evangelist writes: "After this, Jesus, knowing that all things were now accomplished, that the scripture might be fulfilled, saith, I thirst."

Not that the cry was unreal, and merely uttered, as one might say, to serve a purpose. The cry was the embodiment of the most real anguish ever felt on earth. But this anguish was, as we see in the Psalms, only poured out into the Father's ears; for these Psalms which I refer to are the secret and confidential utterances of Christ in his intercourse with the Father. The outpourings of his human griefs, the outcries of his anguished spirit, were not for man's ears; only on the present occasion he allows himself to be overheard by man, in order that thereby he might put honour upon the Father's word, and shew himself in all things the obedient Son, the doer of the Father's work, the fulfiller of the Father's will.

Terrible was that cry, "I thirst;" for it was the cry of God. It is a fearful thing, they say, to see strong men weep, or hear strong men cry; but here was One stronger than the strongest, higher than the highest, the Son of God himself, constrained to give vent to his suffering in this piercing cry, "I thirst!" To what an extremity of weakness is he here reduced, and under what a burden of agony is he weighed down, when he utters it! He would rather not utter it; he has repressed it long; he has put forth his strength in repressing and in bearing up under the pain, uncomplaining; but now he can refrain no longer; he must cry out, that he may give vent to the long pent-up agony.

Terrible was that cry; for it was the cry of One

sinking into death under the condemnation of man's sin, under the weight of infinite guilt. It was the cry of One subjected to the wrath of him who is a consuming fire ; of One who felt himself about to be overcome of his great enemy, in deadly conflict ; of One who knew that no help was nigh; that he was to be left unsuccoured by God and man.

Such was the cry of the Substitute,—a piercing, bitter, agonising cry ! No parched and weary Ishmaelite, throwing himself down in despair beside a dried-up well, ever uttered such a cry as this. But it is the very bitterness of the cry that tells us its efficacy. It is a cry wholly relating to the sufferer himself, not to us ; it is the cry, not of intercession, but of agony ; yet, it is not on that account the less sufficient and satisfying for us. It tells of propitiation fully made, of redemption gloriously accomplished, of the debt paid to the last farthing. It tells us, too, of love ; love immeasurable and unutterable ; love triumphing over shame and anguish, over hunger and thirst ; love which many waters could not quench, nor the floods drown ; love to the Father, love to the sinner ; the love of the Shepherd to his flock ; the love of the Head to the members ; the love of the elder Brother to his brethren ; the love of the Redeemer to his Church ; the love of the Bridegroom to his bride-elect ; the love that passeth knowledge, and whose breadth and length, whose height and depth, are beyond all measure and comprehension; the love of the Just to the unjust; the holy to the unholy; the heavenly to the the earthly; the Creator to the creature; the love of the Only-begotten of the Father, like himself, infinite and divine.

That awful cry, as it was the expression of the bodily anguish which was filling him, as the Substitute, so was it the indication of that bodily torment from which his people have been delivered by his endurance of it in their stead. He drank it that they might never taste it; for "they shall hunger no more, neither thirst any more, neither shall the sun light on them, nor any heat;" "God shall wipe away all tears from their eyes, and there shall be no more death, neither sorrow nor crying, for the former things have passed away" (Rev. xxi. 4).

That awful cry, as it was the expression of the bodily endurance through which the Surety passed, so is it the announcement of the bodily torment of the lost for ever. Oh, what must hell be! What must be the unquenchable fire! What must be the everlasting thirst! What must be the weeping, and wailing, and gnashing of teeth! "Have mercy upon me," cries the rich man in hell, "and send Lazarus, that he may dip the tip of his finger in water, and cool my tongue, for I am tormented in this flame" (Luke xvi. 24). Such is the eternal thirst, and such its awful utterance. A day's thirst, under a scorching sun, is terrible; what must be an eternity of thirst in the heat of the devouring fire! O lost soul, you must thirst for ever! Because thou hast, while here, forsaken the fountain of living water, and hewn out for thyself cisterns, broken cisterns, that can hold no water, therefore, instead of the living water, clear as crystal, thou shalt drink of the WINE of the fierceness of his wrath; "the wine of the wrath of God, which is poured out without mixture into the cup of his indignation, and shalt be tormented with fire and brimstone, in the presence of the holy angels, and in the presence of the Lamb" (Rev. xiv. 10).

III. *The Answer.*—From above there came no answer. God was silent. From around there came derision. Man answered with laughter and with vinegar.

It is not God's wont to be silent in such a case. He feeds the young ravens when they cry. He regards the prayer of the needy. His ear is ever open to the cry of the destitute and the sorrowful. But here he answers not a word. No wonder that Christ should say, "My God, why hast thou forsaken me?" He thirsts, but the Father seems not to regard his thirst; he cries, but the Father gives no heed to his cries. When Hagar cried out for thirst in the desert of Beersheba, God sent his angel and led her to the unseen well. When Israel cried at Marah, God sweetened the bitter waters for them; and when they cried in Horeb, he smote the rock, and the waters gushed forth. When Samson cried out for thirst at Ramath-Lehi, God opened a spring for him in the very jaw-bone which he had used as a weapon.

But now God answers not. It is not Hagar, nor Israel, nor Samson, that cries, but One far greater and more beloved than these. Yet God answers not. This is the crisis of the abandonment; God must have forsaken him, when a cup of cold water is denied. An angel came to the Sufferer in Gethsemane to strengthen him; but no angel comes with a cup of water to quench his thirst. All heaven seems to stand aloof.

Ah! this is the hour and the power of darkness. He has taken the sinner's place, and he must bear the sinner's anguish, both in soul and body. He must suffer the sinner's thirst, as well as die the sinner's death. Every drop of the cup given him he must drink; and neither he himself nor his Father will interfere to put aside the draught, or to abstract a single drop. The Father's love to the Son is still the same; but righteousness stays his hand, and restrains the forth-putting of his delivering power. His readiness to hear the prayers of the beloved Son remains unaltered; but love to sinners, love to the Church, constrain him to shut his ear against this last cry of anguish. Ah! that "no answer" from heaven, that silence of the Father, is the proof that the great surety-work for us is going on successfully, and approaching its consummation. In the infliction of judicial wrath, and the withholding of fatherly deliverance in the hour of need, we see the inflexible carrying out of those principles of law and justice on which alone substitution can proceed, forgiveness be founded, and salvation secured. It is not of diluted wine, nor of a half-filled cup, that the sin-bearing Son of God must drink. The wine must be unmixed, and the cup full; otherwise the sin is not wholly borne, nor the great work perfected, of the just for the unjust. Love would have said, Oh, hear that cry, and quench that thirst; but law said, Not so, else the sacrifice is blemished, and the suretyship rendered invalid.

Thus the Father kept silence; he, who alone could have relieved that anguish, stood aloof. Justice took its course, and law was satisfied. The sacrifice was completed and the penalty exhausted; for, immediately after this, Jesus said, "It is finished," and, bowing the head, he gave up the ghost.

SERMON XVIII.

THE SURETY'S THIRST.

"Jesus said, I thirst."—John xix. 28.

Oh, well for us that thus the work was so completely done! What glad tidings of great joy to us come forth, not only from that thirst and that cry of the Son of God, but from the silence of the Father! It is finished, said the Son on earth. It is finished, said the Father from heaven. And it is when we learn the meaning of that thirst and that cry; when we so learn their meaning as to add our Amen to the "It is finished" of the Father and the Son, that the great reconciliation begins between us and God ; and in proportion to our increasing perception of the completeness of the wondrous sacrifice, our peace deepens, our joy overflows, our hope kindles into new brightness ; the shadows of the cross bringing out, in full relief, the vision of the approaching glory.

But it is not only from heaven that there is no response ; from earth there comes no answer, or, at least, no sympathy. Man does not understand the thirst, and heeds not the cry of the Sufferer. If ever there was an appeal of anguish that could reach man's heart, and call forth any latent spark of love or pity, it was this cry from the cross. This seemed to be God's last appeal to man,—his last test, applied, to see if there was any goodness, any right feeling remaining in him, any sympathy with the Son of God. For when was the cry for water refused, or the thirst of the dying mocked? But man heeds not the anguish of the Crucified. God's last appeal to him is in vain. He meets the cry of the Son of God with mockery.

It would seem that Jesus was offered vinegar more than once, and possibly among some of those who presented it there might be a feeling of pity; for the simple fact of its being vinegar is no proof of its being meant as insult, seeing that vinegar was the only thing at hand; being the usual drink of the Roman soldiers. If this were the case, it only shews how utterly unable man was, even if willing, to relieve the anguish of the Sufferer. Help from man was vain. All that he could offer was but like the feather wetting the lips of the dying. But it is clear, both from the passage itself and from the Psalms, that the offering of the vinegar was meant as mockery. The Jew said, in taunt, and with pretended misunderstanding of his words, "This man calls for Elias;" and the Gentile presented his vinegar; thus between them completing the mockery. This is the last venting of man's enmity against the Son, the last drop of the old serpent's venom poured upon the seed of the woman.

It was not, indeed, in man's power fully to

relieve this awful thirst; yet he could have done something; and even had he failed, he could have shewn his pity. But pity is not in his bosom where God is concerned. "This is the heir; come, let us kill him," is his feeling. He has got God into his power; he has got the Son of God hanging helplessly on a tree; and his enmity to God now gets vent to itself. He can mock God safely now. Samson has lost his strength, and his enemies may work their fill of malignity against him. Thus man's hatred of God comes out in all its bitterness; and it does so, just at the very point where God's love was coming out in its fulness. Never did love and hatred, kindness and enmity, so meet together. Never was love so requited, and kindness so mocked, as here. God has come down to prove man: he dwelt on man's earth; he lived a life of service for man; he emptied himself; he reduced himself to the extremity of weakness and suffering; he put himself into man's power, and appealed, not to his highest and noblest feelings, but to the commonest sympathies of mere humanity. But all in vain. In such circumstances even the worst malefactor would be pitied and relieved. The fact, however, of the sufferer being a holy man shuts out their sympathy; and the fact of his being the Son of God rouses their hatred. That very thing, which ought to have overawed them, and drawn out their profoundest sympathies, is that which calls forth insult, which extinguishes pity, which steels them against the Sufferer's cry, which rouses all hell in their bosoms! Towards men they would have acted and felt as men; towards God they are as devils!

Now is their time for taunt, and insult, and cruelty. So long as he is going about, doing miracles, they are afraid to touch him. They know not how he may avenge himself. But now, when he is dying on a cross, they may hate and mock him as they please. Now, when the lion of the tribe of Judah is in chains, and expiring of his wounds, they may trample on him at will. O man, such is thy heart! Such is the extent of thy enmity to the God in whom thou livest, and movest, and hast thy being!

But though, *at the time*, there was no response from heaven, and nought but mockery on earth, this state of things was only for an hour. The silence cannot last; the cry of the only-begotten Son must be heard, though at another time and in another way. Him the Father heareth always; and this appeal of the Son of God for something to quench his thirst is not unheeded. The answer is denied at the moment, but only that it may be given in all its largeness thereafter. The denial of the request finished the mighty work, through means of which, a glorious answer was to be vouchsafed, in which he was not merely to have his thirst quenched, but to see of the travail of his soul, and to be satisfied. His death, which immediately followed this silence, was the smiting of the rock, from which the waters were to gush forth which were to quench the thirst both of soul and body ; and not his own thirst alone, but that of millions,—the whole vast multitude of the redeemed from among men.

Yes ; God's answer to the cry of his Son is his raising him from the dead, crowning him with glory and honour, exalting him to be a Prince and a Saviour, to give repentance and forgiveness ; depositing in him those gifts for the rebellious, which he was to bestow on men ; making him King and Head over all things, and investing him with a kingdom which shall have no end. He humbled himself to the death of the cross, and therefore God hath highly exalted him. Thus, in the end, the Father's love to the Son is manifested, and his righteousness vindicated. He hath done all things well.

And then, how has God avenged himself on man for his refusal to heed the cry of his Son ? Here, too, evil has been overcome of good ; and where sin abounded, there grace has much more abounded. Man mocks the thirst of God, but God pities and relieves the thirst of man. He makes man's wrath to praise him, and to be, besides, the means of blessing to himself. This crucified Christ, whom man only insults, is the appointed Saviour ; and man, though he knew it not, has been carrying out God's redeeming work. Man, though he meant it not, has been slaying the sacrifice by which reconciliation is accomplished. He has been helping to smite the rock, from which the living water was to gush forth to satisfy the thirst of sinners.

Herein is love; not man loving God, but God loving man; so loving man as to persist in his great work of grace, notwithstanding man's utmost hatred and rejection. Here is the fountain which love has opened, and which flows in the waste places of earth like a river. Here is God's provision, not only for man's pardon, but for his fullest joy. The Surety thirsted that we might not thirst; he drank of the vinegar that we might not drink it; he drained the cup of wrath that we might never taste it; he was wounded that we might be healed. And, standing by that very cross, where the Son of God was mocked in his thirst, and refused a cup of cold water to moisten his parched lips, the messenger of God's free-love lifts up his voice, and says, "Let him that is *athirst* come; and whosoever will, let him take of the water of life freely."

SERMON XIX.

THE SURETY'S CROSS.

"The cross of our Lord Jesus Christ."—GAL. vi. 14.

THE death of the cross has always been, above every other, reckoned the death of shame. The fire, the sword, the axe, the stone, the hemlock, have in their turns been used by law, as its executioners; but these have, in so many cases, been associated with honour, that death by means of them has not been reckoned either cursed or shameful. Not so the cross. Its victim, nailed in agony to the rough wood, suspended naked and torn to the gaze of multitudes, has always been reckoned a specimen of disgraced and degraded humanity; rather to be mocked than pitied. With Jew and Gentile alike, evil and not good, the curse and not the blessing, have been connected with the cross. In men's thoughts and symbols it has been treated as synonymous with ignominy, and weakness, and crime. God had allowed this idea to root itself universally, in order that there might be provided a place of shame, lower than all others, for the great Substitute who, in the fulness of time was to take the sinner's place, and be himself the great outcast from man and God, despised and rejected, deemed unworthy even *to die* within the gates of the holy city.

Not till more than four thousand years had gone by, did it begin to be rumoured that the cross was not what men thought it, the place of the curse and shame, but of strength and honour and life and blessing. Then it was that there burst upon the astonished world the bold announcement, "God forbid that I should glory, save in the cross of our Lord Jesus Christ." Greek and Roman, Jew and Gentile, prince, priest, philosopher, Rabbi, Stoic, Epicurean, Pharisee, barbarian, Scythian, bond and free, North, South, East and West, looked to one another with contemptuous impatience, indignant at the audacity of a few Jews, thus affronting and defying the "public opinion" of nations and ages ; assailing the faiths and unbeliefs of earth with this as their only sword; striking down the idols with this as their only hammer ; and with this, as their one lever, proposing to turn the world upside down.

From that day the cross became "a power" in the earth ; a power which went forth, like the light, noiselessly yet irresistibly, smiting down all religions alike, all shrines alike, all altars alike ; sparing no superstition nor philosophy ; neither flattering priesthood, nor succumbing to statesmanship ; tolerating no error, yet refusing to draw the sword for truth ; a power superhuman, yet wielded by human, not angelic hands ; "the power of GOD unto salvation."

This power remains;—in its mystery, its silence, its influence;—it remains. The cross has not become obsolete; the preaching of the cross has not ceased to be effectual. There are men among us who would persuade us that, in this late age, the cross is out of date and out of fashion, time-worn, not time-honoured; that Golgotha witnessed only a common martyr scene; that the great sepulchre is but a Hebrew tomb; that the Christ of the future and the Christ of the past are widely different. But this shakes us not. It only leads us to clasp the cross more fervently, and to study it more profoundly, as embodying in itself that gospel which is at once the wisdom and the power of God.

The secret of its power lies in the amount of divine *truth* which it embodies. It is the abridgment of the Bible; the epitome of Revelation. It is pre-eminently the voice of God; and, as such, conveying his power as well as uttering his wisdom. "The voice of the Lord is powerful; the voice of the Lord is full of majesty."

Yet is the cross not without its mysteries, or, as men would say, its puzzles, its contradictions. It illuminates, yet it darkens; it interprets, yet it confounds. It raises questions, but refuses to answer all that it has raised. It solves difficulties, but it creates them too. It locks as well as unlocks. It openeth, and no man shutteth; it shutteth, and no man openeth. It is life, yet it is death. It is honour, yet it is shame. It is wisdom, but also foolishness. It is both gain and loss; both pardon and condemnation; both strength and weakness; both joy and sorrow; both love and hatred; both medicine and poison; both hope and despair. It is grace, yet it is righteousness; it is law, yet it is deliverance from law; it is Christ's humiliation, yet it is Christ's exaltation; it is Satan's victory, yet it is Satan's defeat; it is the gate of heaven and the gate of hell.

Let us look at the cross as the divine proclamation and interpretation of the things of God; the key to his character, his word, his ways, his purposes; the clue to the intricacies of the world's and the Church's history.

I. *It is the interpreter of man.*—By means of it God has brought out to view, what is in man. In the cross man has spoken out. He has exhibited himself, and made unconscious confession of his feelings, especially in reference to God,—to his Being, his authority, his character, his law, his love. Though "the determinate counsel and foreknowledge of God" (Acts ii. 23) were at work in the awful transaction, yet it was man who erected the cross, and nailed the Son of God to it. Permitted by God to give vent to the feelings of his heart, and placed in circumstances the least likely to call forth anything but love, he thus expressed them, in hatred of God and of his incarnate Son. Reckoning the death of the cross the worst of all, he deems it the fittest for the "Son of the Blessed." Thus, the enmity of the natural heart speaks out, and man not only confesses publicly that he is a hater of God, but he takes pains to shew the intensity of his hatred. Nay, he glories in his shame, crying aloud, "Crucify him, crucify him;" "This is the heir, come let us kill him;" "Not this man, but Barabbas." The cross thus interpreted man; drew the mask of pretended religion from his face; and exhibited a soul overflowing with the malignity of hell.

You say, "I don't hate God; I may be indifferent to him; he may not be in all my thoughts; but I don't hate him." Then, what does that cross mean?—Love, hatred, indifference;—which? Does love demand the death of the loved One? Does indifference crucify its objects? Look at your hands! Are they not red with blood? Whose blood is that? The blood of God's own Son! No: neither love nor indifference shed that blood. It was hatred that did it; enmity; the enmity of the carnal mind. You say that I have no right to judge you. I am not judging you. It is yon cross that judges you, and I am asking you to judge yourselves by it. It is yon cross that interprets your purposes, and reveals the thoughts and intents of your heart. Oh, what a revelation! Man hating God; and hating most, when God is loving most! Man acting as a devil; and taking the devil's side against God! You say, "What have I to do with that cross, and what right have you to identify me with the crucifiers?" I say, "*Thou* art the man." Do not say, "Pilate did it, Caiaphas did it, the Jew did it, the Roman did it; I did it not." Nay, but you did, you did. You did it in your representatives,—the civilised Roman and the religious Jew; and until you come out from the crucifying crowd, disown your representatives, and protest against the deed, you are verily guilty of that blood. But how am I to sever myself from these crucifiers, and protest against their crime? By believing in the name of the crucified One. For all unbelief is approval of the deed and identification with the murderers. Faith is man's protest against the deed; and the identification of himself, not only with the friends and disciples of the crucified One, but with the crucified One himself.

The cross, then, was the public declaration of man's hatred of God, man's rejection of his Son, and man's avowal of his belief that he needs no Saviour. If any one, then, denies the ungodliness of humanity, and pleads for the native goodness of the race, I ask, what means yon cross? Of what is it the revealer and interpreter? Of hatred or of love? Of good or of evil? Besides, in this *rejection* of the Son of God, we have also man's *estimate* of him. He had been for thirty years despised and rejected; he had been valued and sold for thirty pieces of silver; a robber had been preferred to him; but at the cross, this estimate comes out more awfully; and there we see how man undervalued his person, his life, his blood, his word, his whole errand from the Father. "What think ye of Christ?" was God's question. Man's answer was, THE CROSS! Was not that as explicit as it was appalling?"

As the cross reveals man's depravity, so does it exhibit his foolishness. His condemnation of him, in whom God delighted, shews this. His erection of the cross shews it still more. As if he could set at nought Jehovah, and clear the earth of him who had come down as the Doer of his will! His attempt to cast shame upon the Lord of glory is like a child's effort to blot out or discolour the sun. And as his erection of the cross was the revelation of his folly, so has been his subsequent estimate of it, and of the gospel which has issued from it. He sees in it no wisdom, but only foolishness; and this ascription of foolishness to the cross is but the more decided proof of his own foolishness. He stumbles at this stumbling-stone. The cross is an offence to him, and the preaching of it folly.

My friend, what is that cross to *you?* Is it folly or wisdom? Do you see, in the way of salvation which it reveals, the excellency of wisdom, as well as the excellency of power and love? Has the cross, interpreted to you by the Holy Ghost, revealed your own heart as a hell of darkness and evil? Have you accepted its exposition of your character, and welcomed it also as salvation for the lost,—reconciliation between you and God?

II. *It is the interpreter of God.*—That "the Word was made flesh" is a blessed fact, fraught with grace to us. But incarnation is not the whole of the Bible; no, not half of it. It is not at Bethlehem, but at Golgotha, that we get the full interpretation of

God's character. "Unto us a child is born" is the dawn; "It is finished" is the noon. The cross carries out and completes what the cradle began.

It is as the God of grace that the cross reveals him. It is love, free-love, that shines out in its fulness there. "Hereby perceive we the love of God, because he laid down his life for us" (1 John iii. 16). It is as "the Lord, the Lord God, merciful and gracious," that he shews himself. Nor could any demonstration of the *sincerity* of the divine love equal this. It is love stronger than shame, and suffering, and death; love immeasurable; love unquenchable. Truly, "God is love." In his treatment of the Son of God, man was putting that love to the test. In the cross he was putting it to the extremest test to which love could be put. But it stands them all. Man's most terrible tests but draw it forth the more copiously, and give it new opportunities of displaying its riches. What more extreme test can man ask, or God give, than this?

But *righteousness* as well as grace is here. The God who spared not his own Son is "the righteous Lord who loveth righteousness," and who "will by no means clear the guilty." We learn God's righteous character in many ways. We learn it from its dealings with righteousness, as in the case of all unfallen ones; we learn it still more fully from its dealings with sin, as in our fallen world; but we learn it, most of all, from its dealings with both of these at once, and in the same person, on the cross of

Christ. For here is the righteous Son of God bearing the unrighteousness of men. How shall God both reward and punish at once; reward the righteous one, yet punish the substitute of the unrighteous? Surely righteousness will deal mildly with sin, when found laid on one so righteous, and so beloved for his righteousness? It will mitigate the penalty, and spare the beloved one? No; it does not. It will not admit of the principle that sin is less sin, or less punishable, in such circumstances. Even when found lying on the most righteous and the most beloved of all, upon the very highest person in the universe, it must be dealt with as sin, and punished as truly as when found upon the common sinner. There must be no exemption, and no mitigation. How terrible is the righteousness of God, as interpreted by the cross of Christ! How infinitely holy, how gloriously perfect, how inexorably just, is the God who gave his Son! His love is no weakness, no good nature, no easy indifference to wrong and right. It is righteous love; and, as such, the cross proclaims it with loud and most unambiguous utterance. All the divine perfections are seen here in harmonious glory, mercy and truth, grace and justice; the perfection of holiness combined with the perfection of love. A righteous Judge and a righteous pardon! Righteousness forgiving, saving, justifying, glorifying; taking the side of law in condemning sin, yet taking the side of love in delivering the sinner himself.

O wondrous, glorious cross! Blessed interpreter

of God to us! Scene of the great self-manifestation, the great revelation of the mind and heart of God! O cross of Christ, tell us more and more of this grace of God! Preach reconciliation to the alien, pardon to the guilty, assurance of God's free yet holy love to the dark and suspicious soul! Speak to our hearts; speak to our consciences; pour in light; break our bonds; heal our wounds;—all by means of thy interpretation of the divine character, thy revelation of the righteous love of God!

SERMON XX.

THE SURETY'S CROSS.

"The cross of our Lord Jesus Christ."—GAL. vi. 14.

III. *It is the interpreter of law.*—It tells us that the law is holy, and just, and good; that not one jot or tittle of it can pass away. The *perfection* of the law is the message from Calvary, even more awfully than from Sinai. The *power* of law, the *vengeance* of law, the *inexorable tenacity* of law, the *grandeur* of law, the unchangeable and infrangible *sternness* of law,—these are the announcements of the cross. Never was there so terrible a proclamation of law, and so vivid a commentary upon it, as from the cross of Christ. In the crosses of the two thieves there was the declaration of law, but not half so explicit as in the cross of the righteous Son of God. He who has most honoured the law is the one whom the law refuses to let go; nay, whom it compels to suffer most. All his life-time's honour of the law seems to go for nothing. It stands him in no stead, now that he has undertaken to answer for the sinner. There is no relaxation of law in his behalf. Law,—unpitying, relentless, remorseless law,—demands from him the double debt; first, the fulfilment of all its precepts, and then, the endurance of its penalties as if he had fulfilled not one of its statutes, but had broken them all.

Thus by the cross does God interpret the law to us; shewing us, with divine expressiveness, what it is, and what it can do. It was law that condemned the Son of God. It was law that erected the cross, and nailed the Sin-bearer to it. It was law that afflicted him and put him to grief. It was law that shed his innocent blood. Surely, of all the many illustrations and interpretations which law has received in the world's history, there is none like this.

By the cross does God protest against all attempts to destroy or dilute, to mutilate or modify the law. Man thinks it too strict, too broad; nay, affirms that Christ came to mitigate it, and to give us a salvation founded on a modified law, and obtained by our obedience to such a law. God, in the cross of Christ, says, I do not think so. See yon cross, and my Son upon it, bearing the law's penalty. Would I have made him to do so, had it been too strict? Did he obey too much? Did he suffer too heavily? Thus in the cross God upholds the law as well as expounds it; protesting against the idea that the gospel is just the law lowered and relaxed, so as to suit our fallen state of being; and proclaiming to us a gospel founded upon a fulfilled, an unmodified, an unchangeable law.

O man, read the divine comment on the law as given on the cross, and learn what sin is, and what righteousness is. Man, in erecting that cross, was no doubt making a mock both at law and at sin; he was refusing the love of God as well as the law of God; he was, like Cain, rejecting the sin-offering, and saying, "I need it not." But God was exhibiting to us the reality and the darkness of sin. In the cross God was condemning sin, and shewing how different his estimate of it was from that of man. And there is nothing so fitted to convince, to overawe, to overwhelm the sinner as the sight of that cross. "They shall look on me whom they have pierced, and mourn." It is the sight of the *cross* that brings a man down to the dust; that produces genuine repentance,—godly sorrow, such as law alone could not accomplish. Look, then, and be smitten to the heart by the spectacle of the Lamb of God on the tree, wounded for our transgressions, bruised for our iniquities; "made under the law;" enduring the curse of the law, that from that curse we might be redeemed.

IV. *It interprets sin.*—As the interpreter of law, it is necessarily the interpreter of sin; for as "by the law is the knowledge of sin," so that which expounds the law must also discover sin. The cross took up the ten commandments, and on each of their "Thou shalts" and "Thou shalt nots," flung such a new and divine light, that sin, in all its hideousness of nature, and minuteness of detail, stood out to view, as it never did before, "the abominable thing" which Jehovah hates. Sin was on the earth before Sinai's thunder awoke the desert and shook the camp of Israel. But it was hidden, or but dimly seen. As the war-rocket sent up at midnight shews the whole ground and camp, so did the blaze of Sinai light up the law and discover sin. There was sin upon the earth before the Christ of God died. But it was, with all the illumination of Sinai, but imperfectly known. As the lightning of heaven, more potent and penetrating than the most brilliant war-rocket, bursting down at midnight on some plain or valley, lights up the landscape, far and near, so did the heavenly glory of the cross unfold, in awful vividness and infinite detail, "the exceeding sinfulness of sin."

It shewed that sin was no *trifle* which God would overlook; that the curse was no mere threat which God could depart from, when it suited him. It shewed that the standard of sin was no sliding scale, to be raised or lowered at pleasure; that the punishment of sin was no arbitrary infliction; and that its pardon was not the expression of divine indifference to its evil. It shewed that sin was no variable or uncertain thing; but fixed and precise; a thing to which God was pointing his finger and saying, I hate *that*, and *that*, and *that*. It shewed that the wages of sin is death; that the soul that sinneth must die; that sin and its fruits and penalties are *certainties*, absolute certainties, before which heaven and earth must pass away. It shewed that sin is no mere misfortune, or disease; but *guilt*, which must go before the Judge, and receive judicial doom at his hand. It shewed all these, when it shewed us our divine Substitute, dying the Just for the unjust; God lowering none of his demands, nor abating aught of his wrath, even in the case of his beloved Son.

The cross shewed us, moreover, that the essence of sin is hatred of God; and that man is, by nature, just what the apostle calls him, a "hater of God" (Rom. i. 30). The law had told us but the one half of this. In saying, Thou shalt love the Lord thy God, it pointed to sin as the want of love. But that was all. The cross goes farther than this, and shews us sin as enmity to God, and man as a murderer of the Lord of glory. Is not this a discovery of the malignity of sin, such as had never been imagined before? O what must man be, when he can hate, condemn, mock, scourge, spit upon, crucify, the Christ of God, when coming to him clothed in love, and with the garments of salvation? And what must *sin* be, when, in order to expiate it, the Lord of glory must die upon the tree, an outcast, a criminal, a curse, before God and man, before earth and heaven!

V. *It interprets the gospel.*—That good news were on their way to us, was evident from the moment that Mary brought forth her first-born, and, by divine premonition, called his name "Jesus." Good will to men was then proclaimed. But the Substitute had then only *commenced* his mission of grace. Step by step the good news unfolded themselves, as he passed over our earth, doing the deeds and speaking the words of love. But not till the cross is erected, and the blood is shed, and the life is taken, do we fully learn *how* it is that his work is so precious, and that the tidings concerning it furnish so glorious a gospel. The gospel is good news concerning a divine Sin-bearer; concerning that death which is everlasting life to us; concerning that blood which purges the conscience from dead works, cleansing sin, and reconciling us to God. The cross is reconciliation between us and God, and that is good news. The cross is the bruising of the heel of the woman's seed, and the bruising of the serpent's head; and that is good news. The cross is the adjustment of every question raised by law and righteousness, by God or by conscience;—the righteous and honourable settlement of every claim that can be made against the sinner. And that is good news. The cross is the appointed meeting-place between the sinner and God, where the ambassadors of peace take their stand, beseeching the wanderer to turn and live, the rebel to be reconciled to God ! There the covenant of reconciliation was sealed; there peace was made; there the debt was paid; there the ransom was given. And are not these glad tidings of great joy?

VI. *It interprets service.*—We are redeemed that we may *obey*. We are set free that we may *serve*,—even as God spoke to Pharaoh, "Let my people go, that they may serve me." But the cross defines the service, and shews us its nature. It is the service of love and liberty; yet it is also the service of reproach, and shame, and tribulation. We are crucified with Christ! And this brings out our position as saints. We are crucified followers of a crucified Lord. We are crucified to the world, and the world to us, by the cross of Christ. But besides this, we have to take up our cross, and bear it. It is not *his* cross we bear. None but he could bear it. It is a cross of our own; calling us to self-denial, flesh-denial, and world-denial; pointing out to us a path of humiliation, trial, toil, weakness, reproach, such as our Master trod. Yes; it is a cross *of our own* that we are to bear; not, indeed, of our own making or seeking,—for self-made, self-sought crosses are evil, not good,—but still a cross of our own. There is a personal cross for each, which we are to take up and bear; a cross which is the true badge of discipleship, the genuine mark of authentic service. What he bore for us is done; it cannot be borne over again; the cross of Christ is not for any but himself to carry. But as he had a cross to bear for us, so have we a cross to bear for him, and "for his body's sake, which is the Church."

"Follow me," he says; and we cannot but yield to the almighty voice. He draws us out of the world, and we follow him. He leads us in at the strait gate, and we follow him. He guides us along the narrow way, and we follow him, our cross upon our shoulder and the crown before our eye. Smoothness, and brightness, and greenness, are not the features of the narrow way; but rather thorns and briars, darkness and dust, and ruggedness, all along; fightings without, and fears within. The road to the Kingdom is not so pleasant, and comfortable, and easy, and flowery, as many dream. It is not a bright sunny avenue of palms. It is not paved with triumph, though it is to end in victory. The termination is glory, honour, and immortality; but on the way there is the thorn in the flesh, the sackcloth, and the cross. Recompence yonder; but labour here! Rest yonder; but weariness here! Joy and security yonder; but here endurance and watchfulness,—the race, the battle, the burden, the stumbling-block, and ofttimes the heavy heart.

In entering Christ's service, let us, then, count the cost. In following him, let us not shrink from the cross. It was his badge of service for us; let us accept it as ours for him.

To the world the cross is an offence and a stumbling-block. It is so in two ways. It makes those, who have taken it up, objects of dislike to others; and it is itself an object of dislike to these others. Thus while it unites the saints, it divides them from the world. It is the banner round which the former rally and gather; it is the mark against which the arrows of the latter are turned.

For there are "enemies of the cross of Christ," and enemies of Christ himself. Of them the apostle says, "their end is destruction." Thus the cross is both life and death, salvation and destruction. It is the golden sceptre; it is the iron rod. It is the

Shepherd's staff of love; it is the Avenger's sword of fire. It is the tree of life and cup of blessing, it is the cup of the wine of the wrath of God.

O enemy of the cross of Christ, know your awful doom. Do not take refuge in fancied neutrality; reasoning with yourself that because you are not a scoffer, nor a profligate, you are not an enemy. Remember that it is written, "He that is not for me is against me;" and that, "The friendship of the world is enmity with God." That cross shall be a witness against you, in the day when the crucified One returns as Judge and King. The early Christians had a tradition among themselves, that the cross was to be the sign of his coming; appearing in the heavens, as the herald of his advent. Whether this is to be the case or not, the cross in that day will be the object of terror to its enemies. They would not be saved by it, and they shall perish by it. They would not take its pardon; they must bear its condemnation. The love, which it so long proclaimed, shall then be turned into wrath. The glorious light beaming forth from it, to light them to the kingdom of light, shall then become darkness; their sun shall set, no more to rise; their night shall begin,—the long, eternal night that has no dawn in prospect, and no star to break its gloom.

SERMON XXI.

THE CROSS THE EXPRESSION OF MAN'S UNBELIEF.

"They cried, saying, Crucify him! crucify him!"—LUKE xxiii. 21.

CRUCIFIXION was the death of the outcast only, the *Gentile* outcast. *Stoning* was the Jewish death, *crucifying* the Gentile death, or rather the Roman death; the death devised and inflicted by the fourth great beast of Daniel, when exercising his power in trampling down the nation of God with his iron feet. "Crucify him," then, meant, Let him die the worst of deaths, the Gentile death, the death that is so specially connected with the curse; the death that proclaims Him to be not merely an outcast from Israel, an outcast from Jerusalem, but an outcast from the Gentile, an outcast from the race.

He to whom this cry is directed, is a Gentile ruler; and it is striking to observe the Jew handing over his fellow-Jew to the abhorred Gentile, the conqueror of his city and nation. With what a hatred must these crucifiers have hated their victim, when they give him over to the Gentile to have their utmost malice executed upon him!

He, against whom they thus furiously shout forth their bitterness, is the Son of God; not merely a holy man, but one in whom the fulness of the Godhead dwells; one who has been sent of the Father to carry out his purpose of love. It is against "the Word made flesh," the "only-begotten of the Father, full of grace and truth," that the cry is raised, "Crucify him! crucify him! let him die the worst of deaths; not this man, but Barabbas." It was not his human holiness merely that excited the hatred and the outcry; it was his divine perfection. It was not merely man hating man because better than himself; it was man hating God; man seeking to rid himself, and rid his world of God altogether; man seizing the opportunity he had now got, in having God in a human form within his power, of making away with Jehovah, as the Being to whose absolute dominion he would not submit, and whose presence on the earth, in human form, was altogether intolerable.

Who were they who raised the cry and made this awful demand, in the name of justice and religion, upon a Gentile ruler, for the death of the Son of God?

They were the Jews, the Jews of Jerusalem; not the more ignorant and irreligious Jews of Samaria or Galilee, but the Jews of Jerusalem. Nay, and chief among these haters of Messiah were the men who professed most to be looking for his advent; the best educated, most learned, and, according to their ideas, most devout and religious of the nation. They were not Egyptians or Persians, or Greeks or Romans, worshippers of false gods; but children of

Abraham, men who studied Moses and the prophets, men well-read in the Scriptures, and worshippers of the one Jehovah. They were the choice men of a nation which had been trained up, for well-nigh two thousand years, in the knowledge of God; with whom God had taken infinite pains,—to teach, to guide, to elevate, to keep from surrounding falsehoods, and superstitions, and sins. They were a people that knew more of truth, heavenly truth, than any other on the face of the earth. They were, beyond comparison, the best educated, most enlightened nation on the earth. No blessing had been grudged, no miracle withheld, no privilege refused, no cost spared, to make them the nation of nations, religiously, morally, and intellectually, nay, and physically as well. They were, then, the best specimens of the race,—the representatives of humanity in its best estate,—the exhibition of the natural man, improved to the uttermost, by knowledge, and law, and government, and religion.

It was to this people that Messiah was proposed, for reception or rejection. If *they* rejected him, who could be expected to receive him? If they hated him, who could be expected to love him? If they treated him with dishonour, who could be expected to honour him? If the best portion of the race, who had been expressly separated from the rest, and divinely trained, in order to be ready for his advent, refused him, what could be expected of the worst; what could be expected of the race as a whole? As God gave Adam, and to our race in him, all advantages for standing, so did he give to Israel, and to our race in them, all advantages for receiving his Son. Yet, with all these advantages and privileges, they rejected him! "He came unto his own, and his own received him not." Their cry was not, "Crown him," but "Crucify him;" not, Let the King live for ever, but, Let him die the worst of deaths.

It was thus that man rejected Christ,—civilised man, educated man, religious man! It was thus that the natural heart spoke out, and shewed the depths of its enmity and atheism,—the extent of its desperate *unbelief*. Yes, it was the *unbelief* of the human heart that here told itself out, and cried, "Crucify, crucify!"

All unbelief, then, is rejection of the Son of God. Whatever be its evasions, and subterfuges, and excuses, and fair pretences, this is its essence,—rejection of the Christ of God. In thousands of cases it does not reach the length of the rejection in Pilate's hall; but not the less true is it that such is its true and ultimate form of expression; that to such a height all unbelief is tending, and would assuredly rise, did circumstances call it forth; and that the great reason why, in so many cases, it does not ripen into this awfulness of aspect, is, that man is not so directly confronted with the Son of God, face to face, and the natural heart is not so explicitly shut up to the choice between Christ and Barabbas, nor so immediately and peremptorily called to decide upon the reception or rejection of the Son of God. Were the natural heart, even in its best estate, called upon to speak out, by the demand being made upon it for immediate and unreserved affection and allegiance to Messiah, it would rise up into the same awful attitude of enmity, and manifest its unbelief, in the same terrific outcry for the crucifixion of the Son of God.

And why this desperate rejection; this feeling of man towards the Christ? For many reasons; but chiefly for this, that God's religion, of which Christ is the beginning and the ending, is so thoroughly opposed to man's religion, or man's ideas of religion, that to accept Jesus of Nazareth would be a total surrender of self, a confession of the utter absence of all goodness, an overturning of every religious idea or principle, which the flesh had cherished and rested on. In such a case, and with such an alternative, it does not seem so incredible that man should resist to the uttermost the claims of Christ upon his faith and his heart. His alternative is,—the denial of self, or the denial of Christ; the rejection of his own claims to be his own saviour, or the rejection of the claims of Christ; the crucifixion of the flesh, or the crucifixion of Christ. With such an alternative, what will the natural unbelief of the human heart not resort to; and what but the almightiness of the Divine Spirit can effectually oppose the claims of self, and prevent the most daring rejection of Christ, or turn that rejection into a cordial and trustful reception? Nothing else will overcome the unbelief, or turn it into faith and love. Allow it to take its own way, and run its course, and it will end in the crucifixion of the Lord of glory. It will prefer self, the flesh, the devil,—the worst of criminals to Christ. "Not this man, but Barabbas!"

It is supposed by many that such a thing as the rejection of Christ could only have occurred among uneducated, uncivilized, lawless, irreligious men. But no.

Education will not hinder rejection of Christ. They who crucified Him were educated men; not ignorant and brutal.

Civilisation will not hinder rejection of Christ. It was the civilised Roman, and the more civilised Jew, that crucified him. Civilization is a poor rampart against the assault of man's natural unbelief.

Law will not hinder rejection of Christ. The Roman is the representative of man's law, and the Jew of God's; yet both combine to reject Christ's claims, and to crucify himself.

Religion will not hinder rejection of Christ. Christ was crucified by men who had more of what man calls *religion* than any other on the earth. They prayed, they fasted, they gave alms, they multiplied sacrifices; yet they crucified Christ! It was the Scribes and Pharisees, the religious and respectable men of Israel, that were the foremost in rejecting Messiah. God's way of dealing with them, as announced by Christ, was so opposed to their ideas of the way in which they ought to be dealt with, that rejection of the claims of Jesus, and hatred of his person, were necessary elements in, or at least indispensable deductions from, their religion. How often among ourselves, does a man's religion, or religiousness, or ritualism, form the great hindrance to his reception of the gospel! It is not Christ that is his religion; it is his religion that is his Christ! This being the case, the Christ of God cannot be prized, or loved, or trusted in; he can only be rejected, hated, crucified.

This rejection of Christ shewed itself in various aspects, in the different characters and events described by the evangelists, in this last scene in Jerusalem. In all of them, however, it is *unbelief* that is shewing itself,—the same unbelief that still induces opposition to Christ, the same unbelief that keeps an anxious sinner oftentimes so long in darkness and distrust. And, as we judge of the real nature of a thing best, when fully developed and carried out, so we learn the true nature of all unbelief, from the modes in which it expressed itself at this great scene of rejection, enacting at Jerusalem, from the hour that Judas sold his Master, up to the moment when the thief railed on him from the cross.

Look at Judas then,—there is unbelief. The traitor is neither more nor less than an unbelieving man carrying out his unbelief in betrayal of his Lord. His is the unbelief that treats Christ as a piece of merchandise, bought and sold between man and man! O unbelieving man, thou art Judas, thou art the traitor; for all unbelief is betrayal of the Lord.

Look at the disciples; "they all forsook him, and fled." Professing to love him, they treated him as one unworthy to be suffered for. That act of forsaking was the unbelief even of the converted man, coming out and shewing itself again. Especially in Peter do we see it. In him there is open denial, and in that denial we see the old heart of unbelief again speaking out. O backslider! remember this, all unbelief is a forsaking of the Lord, a denial of the Master. Say what you will, this is your crime. You think you are not so bad as Peter. The difference is only in degree, hardly even that.

Look at Herod; he mocks him, and sets him at nought. Here is another phase of unbelief. O unbelieving man, thou art Herod; thou and thy companions are Herod with his men of war; for all unbelief is mockery of the Lord. You say you never mocked him; yet that unbelief, if unfolded, would make you a Herod.

Look at the Soldiers; they scourge and buffet him. There again is the natural heart *acting* itself out. These indignities and wounds are but another utterance of man's enmity. O unbelieving man, thou art the executioner; for all unbelief is a buffeting and scourging of the Son of God.

Look at the Scribes and Pharisees, the Jewish crowds that demand his execution, and shout,

"Crucify him! crucify him!" There is the evil heart of unbelief giving vent to itself. These crowds are fair specimens of the race; they are no worse than you are, O unbelieving man. In like circumstances, you would have said and done the same; for all unbelief is a crucifixion of the Son of God. Thou art the Scribe, thou art the Pharisee, thou art the vociferating Jew; it is the voice of *thy* unbelief that cries, "Crucify him! let him die the death, let him die the worst of deaths!"

Look at the thief that is nailed beside him; he rails at him there. Ah, surely unbelief might have been silent in such circumstances! Yet no; even upon the cross it reviles. O unbelieving man, thou art the reviler of the Son of God.

Look at the crowd around the cross; they wag their head, and taunt, and jest. It is still but man's natural unbelief that is speaking out. O unbelieving man, thou art the taunter, thou art the jester, thou art the mocker, of Jesus of Nazareth.

Look at the soldier that pierces his side, after he has breathed his last. He is determined to make sure of his death. Unbelief will not bear the thought that there should be the very chance of life left. O unbelieving man, thou art the soldier: it is thy spear that is drawing out the blood and water; it is thy unbelief that not only says, Let him die the death; but, let us make sure of his death; let there be no mistake as to this.

Learn, then, the true nature of all *unbelief;* its deceitfulness and desperate malignity; its rooted hostility to Christ and to his claims upon man; its determination to be satisfied with nothing but his death; its resolute rejection of his person, and work, and grace; its natural and unchangeable watchword, "Not this man, but Barabbas;" "Crucify him! crucify him!"

Nor has this unbelief anything to say for itself. It cannot be accounted for by anything in the object presented. "They hated me without a cause" (John xv. 25). "For my love they give me hatred" (Ps. cix. 5). This is the plain statement of the fact. The object was most loveable, most trustworthy, most glorious; but man would have none of it. Here was the Being who, of all others, was most fitted to call up love and trust; for here was the only-begotten of the Father, full of grace and truth; here was the embodiment of divine love and loveableness. But God's love is met with man's hatred; the most unambiguous revelation of divine love calls forth the most fearful utterance of human hatred and unbelief!

O man! can that heart of yours be anything but evil, which thus deals with God and his love? Can that unbelief of yours be a trifle? Can it be anything but the most resolute and guilty enmity; enmity which, though it may often slumber for a season, yet which, the moment it awakes and recovers strength, breaks forth in mockery against the Son of God, and demands his instant condemnation and crucifixion,—"Crucify him! crucify him!" Be ashamed of it; abhor it; cast it utterly away.

When Christ comes again in his glory, how will unbelief appear? It will be seen to be *rejection* of the Son of God,—rejection the same as Israel's. You will be of those that "pierced him." All that distrust, these misgivings, that standing aloof, will be seen in their proper character. Your unbelief brings you amongst those who "have not obeyed the gospel," and that brings you under the rod of him who comes to take vengeance upon such. Christ *may* come soon; but, whether or not, let the thought of the great day shut you up to *immediate faith*, immediate reception of Him whom Israel crucified.

SERMON XXII.

LIFE AND FRUITFULNESS THROUGH DEATH.

"Verily, verily, I say unto you, Except a corn of wheat fall into the ground and die, it abideth alone: but if it die, it bringeth forth much fruit."—JOHN xii. 24.

It is strange that, in a world made by the God only wise and good, there should be such a thing as *death*. It is more wonderful that this death should come out of a thing so glorious as life. But, beyond these, there is a wonder greater still,—that life should grow out of death, and corruption be the seed and parent of incorruption.

Yet this last is the process which God has been carrying on in our earth, since the threatening took effect against Adam: "In the day that thou eatest thereof, thou shalt surely die."

It needs no great power to bring death out of life. Man can effect that without an effort. But to bring life out of death needs other power than man's. Man can kill, but God only can make alive. It is the *Creator* alone that can *quicken;* and hence the apostle sets these two things together when he says, "God who *quickeneth* all things, and *calleth those things which be not* as though they were" (Rom. iv. 17). The power to destroy life has been given to the creature; but the power to impart it is a prerogative of Godhead and a function of Omnipotence. Thus all of death that is in us we owe to ourselves, and all of life that is in us we trace solely to God, to him whose name is "Jehovah," who not merely is King "eternal and immortal," but "who *only* hath *immortality*" (1 Tim. vi. 16).

We can, however, go a step farther than this; and it is to this higher point that the apostle leads us when he says, "Thou fool, that which thou sowest is not quickened except it die" (1 Cor. xv. 36). These words are peculiar, and the thought embodied in them is not one which man has ever owned, far less originated. The apostle is speaking, no doubt, especially of the resurrection of the body, yet in so doing he enunciates a wider, more universal, and more subtile truth,—a truth unacknowledged by philosophy, but largely recognised in Scripture, and taught by many natural processes,—that death is the way to life, that the dissolution of the lower life is necessary in order to the development of the higher. Yes; this is the sum of the divine testimony concerning life and death; that the latter, instead of being the destruction or extinction of the former, is the preparation for and introduction to it; that the ascent from a lower kind and narrower region of life to a loftier and wider is through DEATH. This is the narrow isthmus, or rather the subterraneous passage, through which God is conducting us, from the bleak coasts of this poor moorland lake to the shores of that fair ocean, whose waters spread themselves out under calmer skies, and break upon a sunnier shore.

"That which thou sowest is not *quickened* except it *die*." Strange words, and most marvellous truth! Yet the apostle speaks as if this were one of the plainest and commonest of nature's laws; so that a man must be a fool, if he has not read that law in the every-day processes of sowing and springing. And as it is with the seed, so is it with man himself. It is by means of darkness that we reach the light. It is by falling that we rise; by going down into the depths of the valley that we find our way up to the mountains of immortality beyond. It is through winter that we pass into spring. It is by dying that we are made to live,—live for ever; for the life that is not reached by death seems but half secure. The life that lasts,—the life that is truly immortal and eternal, is only obtained by dying. It is *resurrection-life* that is the truest as well as the highest form of life, the surest as well as the most glorious immortality. It admits of no reversal and no decay. These souls of ours are quickened to an endless life, by having first passed through a death of trespasses and sins; and these bodies must go down into the grave, and there be dissolved, that every particle of mortality may be shaken out of them, ere they can be made partakers of the glory in reserve for them. They are sown in weakness, that they may be raised in power; they are sown in corruption, that they may be raised in incorruption. It is the grave, the abode of putrid loathsomeness, that is the womb of the undecaying and the undefiled. John Howe, in commenting on the expression, "armour of light," exclaims, "Strange armour that a man can see through!" so may we say here, "Strange life that is the offspring of death; how unlike the child and the parent to each other!"

Yet we shrink from death and abhor the grave! What! "are we afraid of becoming immortal?" Are we reluctant to part with weakness, and disease, and corruption? Do we refuse to enter the porch and gate of life's temple? Are we dismayed at the prospect of going into the robing chamber, where the vestments of this vile flesh are put off, and the raiment of a glorious immortality put on? Fools that we are! Do we not remember that "that which is sown is not quickened except it die?"

But our Lord's words add another truth to those already noticed on this point. It is not merely *life*, but *fruitfulness*, that is to be reached through death; so that death is the parent of fruitfulness, and to retain life is to be *unproductive*. "Verily, verily, I say unto you, except a corn" (or grain) "of wheat fall into the ground and die, it abideth alone: but if it die, it bringeth forth much fruit." It is as if he said, Look at that grain of wheat; it contains in it both life and fruitfulness; but these are locked up, imprisoned in it; nor can they be disengaged or set loose, so as to unfold and multiply themselves, save by death. The fruitfulness that is in it must remain all folded up and lost, unless death come in to break up its prison : it is life that is keeping it from living, and multiplying, and replenishing the earth; the outer life is imprisoning the inner, and not till that outer life has perished can the inner life flow out upon the world; the germs of a higher excellence are so closed up in its secret cells, so bound together, that they cannot expand or shew themselves, till the dissolution of that which we call life has bidden these secret treasures come forth. The various elements of higher being and powers of propagation are so wrapt round with this covering, this coating of life, that ere they can come forth death must do its work, breaking the bars of the prison-house, and making the deep cells of happy life to give up their wondrous inmates.

Thus, that which seems to us the destruction of all fruitfulness, is its true paternity. That which appears to dissolve all excellence, to wither up all beauty, to scatter all sweetness, and to mar all power of reproduction, is the very thing by which these are led forth from inactivity and inertness to do their work upon the earth, and to fulfil the end of their being. Death, which is in itself an evil and a penalty, is yet God's instrument for opening prisons, and unloosing chains, and disengaging the higher vitalities and perfections of being. And we cannot but notice that our Lord, having thus vindicated the connection between productiveness and death, adds, by way of application, " He that loveth his life shall lose it; but he that hateth his life in this world shall keep it unto life eternal."

Take that brown rough bulb, and preserve it with all care from damp and frost, and the foot of the destroyer; what is the result? Nothing. "It abideth alone." Whatever may be its treasures, they lie hidden. But cast it into the ground and bury it, and immediately a change comes over it. Corruption seizes it. Part after part falls off and dies. This, however, does not affect its inner vitalities, save to call them out, and send up to man the hidden beauty. It shoots up in its greenness to the sun; leaf after leaf unfolds itself; blossom after blossom comes forth from the mysterious recesses in the mouldering root; till the lily itself waves before us in its comeliness, and we feel "that Solomon in all his glory was not arrayed like one of these."

Such is the law of creation, of the new as well as of the old creation: through darkness to light; through death to life; through corruption to fruitfulness and glory.

But our Lord's words primarily and especially concern himself. He was the grain of wheat (sower and seed in one); and, as such, he must fall into the ground and die; for, without his dying, his coming would profit nothing, his incarnation would be barren. It was death that was to draw out his treasures, and unlock the storehouse of his unsearchable riches.

That he was the true seed, in which were deposited all life and fruitfulness, a few passages will shew. "It pleased the Father that in him should all fulness dwell." "In him dwelleth all the fulness of the Godhead bodily." "In him are hid all the treasures of wisdom and knowledge."

The Christ, the Incarnate Word, is the one divine depository of all the riches of Godhead, whether the riches of grace or of glory, of wisdom or of power. And as he is the one depository, so is he the one channel of conveyance, to the creature, of all this fulness of the everlasting God. He is to the Creator what the eye, the ear, the tongue, the whole bodily frame, are to the creature. He is the one fountain-head of divine blessing, the one outlet of heavenly love, the one medium of intercourse between the finite and the infinite, the human and the divine. The invisible becomes visible in Him, and he that hath seen him hath seen the Father. That which man calls *development* is a reality only as connected with him; and *progress* is but a name or a falsehood, save as rooted in him. Man has many Christs, but the true Christ is one.

SERMON XXIII.

LIFE AND FRUITFULNESS THROUGH DEATH.

"Verily, verily, I say unto you, Except a corn of wheat fall into the ground and die, it abideth alone: but if it die, it bringeth forth much fruit."—JOHN xii. 24.

THE seed, then, is divine; and, as such, it contains an infinite store of treasure. But this is not enough. How are its riches to be made available for us? Let the following statements be considered:—

I. *Incarnation is not enough.*—No doubt, in the incarnation is wrapt up the love of God,—the love of Father, Son, and Holy Ghost; and the simple announcement, "the Word was made flesh," "unto us a Child is born," is glad tidings of great joy. Still there is something awanting. It is the beginning, but it is not the end. Is love to meet with no obstructions? And if sin opposes, and righteousness opposes, and law opposes, what is love to do, or how is it to reach the sinner? The Son of God might take flesh and dwell among us; but this did not secure life for the dead, or pardon for the condemned, or salvation for the lost, or victory over man's great enemy, or honour to God's broken law

The fountain must be unsealed, else its waters are useless; the box of spikenard must be broken, else its fragrance will not flow out to cheer man's fainting heart, or heal this world's polluted air.

II. *Power is not enough.*—Love, though armed with almighty power, finds mighty barriers. It is hedged in by righteousness, and righteousness is stronger than power, as much stronger as the moral is higher and greater than the physical. And just as God *cannot* lie, so omnipotence cannot conquer law, or set its provisions aside. Mere strength cannot come to the judgment, or prevail with the Judge. In the eye of law, power is unknown; in the decisions of the judgment-seat, it is not recognised as an element at all. Power, however great, cannot reach the criminal, though it may walk round the walls of his dungeon, and try its energies against the massive gratings. Infinite power dwelt in the man Christ Jesus; and this was, no doubt, good news." But, till something has been done to cause this power to flow out, and do glorious things *in righteousness*, it is unavailable for the sinner, whatever it may be for the righteous. The vessel may be full, but there is a wall of iron between it and us."

III. *Suffering is not enough.*—The Son of God did truly suffer; more truly and more greatly suffer than any other being has done or can do. His burden of grief was the heaviest ever borne by man; and from the cradle to the cross he was the Man of sorrows, the suffering One both in body and in soul. Yet these tears and groans were not enough; they could not unlock the heavenly treasure deposited in him, nor draw forth the provision for a needy world contained in his unsearchable riches. If any amount or intensity of suffering could have done this, it would have been that of the man Christ Jesus; but even *his* suffering was not enough. It was part of the process, but it was not the whole. Something deeper and more penal, something that had in it more of condemnation and wrath, was needed. Only such suffering as ended in *death*, could draw out the life and fruitfulness wrapt up in the divine seed.

IV. *Holiness is not enough.*—At his conception he was "the holy Thing;" and during his life he was "the holy One;" and in his walk on earth there was seen an *obedience*, which, of all other obediences, was the most perfect; both for admiration and example. Yet this did not touch the law's inexorable penalty, nor help to bear the legal curse. He that would save us must be a substitute, as well as an example, and must undergo the law's *last* sentence, ere he is in a legal condition to bless, or to pour out the divine love on us, in pardon, and healing, and joy.

V. *Death alone can do the work.*—The love that stops short of this effects nothing; and, however large it seems, or near it comes, it but mocks the sinner. If the fulness treasured up for us in the "Word made flesh" is to come forth, then he must die. There must be the pouring out of the soul unto death. Even *he* is not at liberty to communicate his love and joy to us, save through his own death; his death as the payment of the righteous penalty, and the fulfilment of the unchangeable sentence, "The soul that sinneth it shall die." He, though the true wheat, must "abide alone," except he die.

He has died, the Just for the unjust; dying the sinner's death, and bearing the sinner's curse. Thus he "brings forth much fruit." All that made this fruitful One barren has been taken away. *Death* has done what *life*, in all its divine vigour, could not do. In the sinner's grave, to which the Surety went down, the dissolution of legal bonds has been effected, whereby the fulness, hitherto pent up and imprisoned, comes forth to a dead world, like spring sending up its warm breath and covering earth with verdure.

This truth is not here spoken for the first time. It is the truth wrapt up in the first promise respecting the woman's seed, the man with the bruised heel. It is the truth to which Abel's sacrifice pointed so explicitly. It is the truth coming out in all the Levitical sacrifices and rites. It is the truth uttered by prophets: "When thou shalt make his soul an offering for sin, he shall see his seed, he shall prolong his days." It is the truth announced by apostles: "Without shedding of blood is no remission." It is the truth to which such prominence is given in the Apocalypse, when the Son of God is seen as the Lamb slain, and when the saints sing, "Thou hast redeemed us to God by thy blood." It is this which the apostle Paul had specially in view when he interprets the tabernacle veil as meaning "the flesh" of Christ (Heb. x. 20). That which shut out the worshipper from the mercy-seat was the symbol of the body of the Son of God! The veil, which was hung before the holiest, said to the Israelite, "Godhead is within; the mercy-seat is within; the glory is within; but there is a hindrance which makes them at present unapproachable. Ere you can draw near, that veil must be 'RENT,' and then all is open; but till that is done there is no access to God, even to that God who has come down to make his dwelling in the midst of you." The flesh, or body, of Christ said to every one, "Godhead is within; Jehovah has come down; he is at your side; but ere this can profit you that body must be broken, that flesh must have its life poured out."

These, then, are the glad tidings which we bring. This veil has been rent in twain from the top to the bottom; the way is open for the sinner; go in at once into the holiest; go in now, go in as you are, and stand boldly before the mercy-seat. It is now the throne of grace for you! Yes; the good news to the sons of men are not merely that the Word was made flesh, but that that flesh was wounded, that body broken for us. The good news are, that the corn of wheat has fallen into the ground and died. Having died, it has not merely been again "quickened," but has itself become the quickener of the dead. It is death that has imparted to it this productiveness, this life-giving energy. It will not now abide alone; it will bring forth much fruit, and that fruit will remain.

The extent of this fruit-bearing we do not yet see. It is only one here, and another there, whom we see quickened from the death of sin by the all-vivifying power of him who, as the last Adam, is made a quickening spirit (1 Cor. xv. 45). But, in the day of his glorious re-appearing; when he comes with the ten thousand of his saints, those who have slept in him, and those who shall be alive at his return; when he comes to smite Antichrist, to bind Satan, to deliver creation from its groans, to bless Israel, to be a light to the Gentiles, to set up his righteous kingdom, and to make all things new; it shall be seen what he has done by dying. In that day, when he presents to himself the Church of the first-born, the redeemed from among men, without spot or wrinkle, a great multitude that no man can number, we shall learn the extent and excellency of that fruitfulness which he acquired by dying. Heaven and earth, men and angels, shall then see why it was that this corn of wheat fell into the ground and died.

That which is true of the Head is true also of the members, though in different manner and degree. The better life, both of soul and body, is only reached by death. And as the "quickening" comes by death, so does the fruitfulness. It is not merely the "eternal weight of glory" that is to be wrought for them by their present affliction, but their fitness for future service as God's kings and priests; their power of eternal ministry in the kingdom hereafter; their completeness, both of character and qualification, for the unending work; the kind and amount of their everlasting success; in other words, their "fruitfulness" depends on their assimilation to their Lord here, in weakness, in humiliation, in suffering, and in death.

Hence we sorrow not as those who have no hope, as to their life, or their glory, or their fruitfulness. Their life is hid with Christ in God; and when he who is their life shall appear, they also shall appear with him in glory.

The heathen sorrowed without hope. To the philosophic Athenian, even the bold Roman, death was gloom, and nothing else. There was no hope about it. Their Elysian fields were poor, and the prospect of reaching them a sorrowful uncertainty. To them death connected itself with no hope, no brightness, no triumph. It was not *sunset* to them; for that bids us be on the outlook for another Sun, as bright as that which set. It was not *autumn*, nor *winter*; for these speak of returning spring and summer. It was not the *seed* cast into the rough soil; for that predicts the future tree or flower, more beautiful than the seed. It was pure and simple darkness; all cloud, shadow, desolation. The death of childhood and youth was especially bitter and terrible; nor can anything be more touching, nor more expressive of the "sorrow without hope," than the emblems, which we still find carved upon Grecian or Etrurian tombs. A shattered pillar; a ship gone to pieces; a race lost; a harp lying on the ground, with snapped strings, and all its music lost; a flower-bud crushed, with all its fragrance in it;—these were the sad utterances of their hopeless grief. The thought that death was the gate of life, came not in, to cheer the parting or brighten the sepulchre. The truth, that the grave was the soil, and the body the seed sown by God's hand, to call out all the latent life; that the race was not lost, but only a little earlier won; that the column was not destroyed, but transferred to another building and another city, to be "a pillar in the temple of God;" that the bud was not crushed, but transplanted, for fuller expansion, and with all its odour unexhaled and unimpaired, to a kindlier soil and air; that the harp was not broken, nor its music spilt and lost, but handed up to a truer minstrel, who, with a finer touch and heavenlier skill, will bring out all the rich compass of its hidden music, which man would not have appreciated, and which earth would but have spoiled;—these were things which had no place in their theology, hardly in their dreams. They sorrowed as those who had no hope.

But the death even of the ripe and aged, was to

them a thing of darkness and fear. It was less strange and sad than that of childhood and prime; but it was still a perplexity, an unsolved mystery.

And do *we* not sometimes forget that this mystery has been cleared away? Not that we doubt the personal safety or blessedness of the departed heir of the kingdom; but we speak of his usefulness being ended, or at least only prolonged here on earth, in the good deeds, or good words, or good report which he has left behind, and by which he, being dead, still speaketh, and still is useful. Now, no doubt, that which the text calls "fruitfulness" is thus carried out; so that a saint's death becomes a thing of life to thousands, and a saint's memory becomes as fruitful as his living person was. But there is another productiveness, which spreads itself out over eternity, and which death, so far from destroying, only develops. It is for this that he is educating here,—for this that he is undergoing his training below, and serving his earthly apprenticeship. The fitness for service,—whether of priesthood or of kingship, for we are kings and priests unto God, the power of working truly and successfully for God, acquired here by hard experience, during years of doing and suffering,—these, so far from being lost, or superseded, or thrown by, are but matured and unfolded hereafter; transferred from a narrow corner here to the spacious universe of God; set free from fetters and limits, to spread themselves out over a far wider range of objects, in the exercise of a ministry, at once priestly and kingly ; a ministry as perfect and successful as it is boundless and everlasting.

No man's usefulness ever ends. The true becomes truer ; the powerful becomes more powerful ; the noble becomes nobler ; the fruitful becomes more fruitful ; the successful multiplies successes ; and without fear of reverse, or failure, or discomfiture, or weariness, the liberated saint rejoices in the anticipation of an eternal future of usefulness,—usefulness in all respects illimitable, usefulness far beyond that of his most productive days on earth. The corn of wheat, before it fell into the ground, was comparatively barren; but having fallen into the **ground** and died, it brings forth much fruit.

SERMON XXIV.

THE RISEN CHRIST AND THE THINGS ABOVE.

"If ye then be risen with Christ, seek those things which are above, where Christ sitteth on the right hand of God."—COL. iii. 1.

THE word "if" is not, in this place, expressive of doubt. It does not imply that those "saints at Colosse" were uncertain as to whether they were risen with Christ. Rather, it is the apostle's way of denoting the surest of all certainties. Thus he uses it in Rom. v. 10, "*If* when we were enemies we were reconciled to God;" and in verse 15, "*If* through the offence of one many be dead." So that more truly it might be rendered "since," as assuming the fact, and setting it down as beyond all doubt.

No countenance is here given to uncertainty or non-assurance on the part of a saint, as if he were one not entitled to say more for himself than "*If* I be a saint." The gospel does in no way, and by no word, directly or indirectly spoken, encourage uncertainty, or give us leave to call it humility. The result of a believed gospel is not uncertainty, but certainty; not trouble, but peace; not the continuance, but the expulsion of all anxiety. The gospel presents me with that, in believing which I am entitled to say, " I *am* a child ; forgiven, saved, risen." Such is its nature that, in receiving it, so far from being brought into uncertainty, or kept in uncertainty, I am relieved from all uncertainty ; my soul is set at rest. I am not only warranted, but commanded to claim my sonship. My not claiming it, my standing still in doubt as to reconciliation between me and God, shews that I have not yet fully understood the freeness and meetness of the grace which the gospel makes known. For God here presents to us such a gospel as to shut each hearer of it up to this alternative,—either to doubt the good news, or enter into conscious friendship with himself.

Sad it is that uncertainty such as this should be so common amongst us, as if there were no sin in it, no blame attaching to those in whom it exists ; as if God's sovereignty would account for it entirely, and as if man's rooted self-righteousness, his evil heart of unbelief, were not the true and real cause.

Yet sadder still, that man should be *contented with* this uncertainty; soothing his conscience to sleep with the idea that he may be a Christian though he has no assurance ; nay, that his very doubtings are the best evidences of his faith ; as if unbelief could be the fruit of faith, or distrust the offspring of confidence ! Surely matters have come to a low ebb indeed, when such is the case with us; not in rare examples, but in instances innumerable; when assurance is the exception, and doubting the rule ; when peace with God is strange in the Church, and uncertainty tinges with gloom the religion and the life of so many who name the name of Christ.

May we not ask, What is there about this uncertainty so attractive and loveable, that we should fondle it so tenderly, and cling to it so desperately? Does it bring peace? That it cannot do: for its very nature is to distract and trouble us. Does it console us under the pressure of life's sore calamities? It cannot; for it is itself our heaviest burden. Does it heal our wounds? No; it is daily inflicting wounds, but healing none. Does it sweep off the clouds that overshadow us in our pilgrimage, or brush aside the entangling thorns and briars of the wilderness? No; it is itself the thickest cloud, the sharpest thorn that can wound us. Does it raise us above the world, or make us holier men? That it cannot do. It drags us down, and hinders all holy walking. Does it enable us to serve the Lord more truly or fervently? No; it keeps us in dark bondage; so that thus chained and prisoned, we cannot serve him. Does it conform us to the image of God's Son? Ah, no; in him we see the true filial spirit and the devoted life; and how can these exist in us so long as we know not in what relationship we stand to God; so long as we are uncertain whose we are, and whom we serve.

If, then, uncertainty be such a thoroughly unprofitable thing; if it be such a hindrance, such a sore evil, such an enemy to our souls, why cherish it as many seem to do? Why cling to it, instead of casting it away? Why not abhor it, and ourselves because of it?

The condition, then, of a saint, is one of *certainty*. That certainty is this,—he is risen with Christ. It is not that he ought to be risen, or that he hopes to be risen, but that he *has* risen. This is the blessed fact that forms the commencement of his history as a saint. This event stands at the very threshold of his career; nay, constitutes its outset. His life is the life of a risen one. His story is that of one who has risen. He cannot tell of his change without telling of resurrection. He cannot speak of his new course and conversation, without referring to resurrection. He cannot account for the high level on which he stands, or the privileges which encompass him, or the hopes that rise before him, save by tracing all these back to this one fountain-head,—RESURRECTION.

What, then, is the meaning of this fact or event in the life of a saint, which forms the commencement of his history? It cannot in any way be understood of the resurrection of the body, which is the Church's hope. For that is altogether *future;* and is, besides, connected with the *second* coming of the Lord, whereas this is connected with His *first*. The privilege or blessing, pointed at by the apostle here, is something *past*, something which had commenced when they believed; whereas the resurrection of the body is still a thing for which we wait and long.

Nor does the apostle's statement simply mean

that the resurrection of Christ has secured to us certain blessings, or opened a door for us into the participation of certain privileges, or made sure to us the title or right to certain future glories. All this is true ; but it is much below the whole truth, and only very partially expresses the apostle's great idea regarding the standing and privilege of a saint.

He is telling us in what light God looks upon the soul that has believed on his Son, and therefore in what light we are to look upon ourselves. He is shewing us under what special character God is dealing with us; on what footing he has set us; to what extent he is placing to our credit the work of his Son; in what way he regards him as our complete substitute, and us as doing, suffering, passing through, and deserving, all that he did, suffered, passed through, and deserved.

Hence, pointing to the cross of Christ, he says, that cross was *your* cross—" Ye were crucified with Christ," and on that cross *you* endured the wrath which you had incurred; *you* paid the whole penalty, so that there is not a farthing of it remaining unpaid. Pointing to the death of Christ, he says, that death was *your* death—" Ye died with Christ;" it was *you* who then died, and in dying met the full demand of the inexorable sentence; "The soul that sinneth it shall die." Pointing to the grave of Christ, he says, that grave was *your* grave;—" Ye were buried with Christ;" there you lay, victims to the law's righteous requirements, and the Lawgiver's righteous execution of these in full; there you lay, during the three days in which your Substitute was lying there, just as those who have refused the Substitute shall lie eternally, bearing the penalty which no time can cancel or exhaust. Pointing to the resurrection of Christ, he says: That resurrection was *your* resurrection; "Ye rose with Christ;" having exhausted every claim against you, and paid to the full each farthing of the righteous penalty, so that law has nothing now to insist upon against you. Yes; it was *you* that rose eighteen hundred years ago, when your Substitute arose. In rising, you left behind you in the grave all the guilt that laid you there. It was the prisoner's dungeon in which you were laid; but you have come forth from it, because the reasons why you entered it no longer exist. It was *law* that chained you there, and it is the same law that now unchains you; because it has nothing now to say against you. It was *righteousness* that cast you into that prison, and barred its gates against your return from it; and it is the same righteousness that has brought you forth in triumph, having found far more and stronger reasons for your deliverance than for your imprisonment. You have thus come forth from the cell to which your transgressions had consigned you; and not as one that has evaded justice, but as one who has satisfied it to the full, having given it far more than it sought. You have come forth, not with the felon's brand upon you, not with the shame and stigma of your former life, to darken and disgrace you, but as one risen to a new life altogether; a new life in the eye of righteousness, in the eye of the law, and in the eye of God; as one entirely severed from his former self; between whose present and former self there is such a great gulf fixed that he is entitled to say, I am no longer the same individual, I have acquired a new personality, a new legal identity.

The mighty truth here taught is, in fact, just this: Being identified with our Substitute in death, *we, i. e.*, our former self, perished. That death destroyed our identity; it cut the legal link for ever between our present and our former selves, so that law cannot identify us as the individuals against whom it thought to urge its overwhelming claims. It is baffled; it is brought to a stand; and to every one of its charges we can confidently plead "not guilty," on the score of not being the same individuals against whom the charges are laid. Again; being identified with our Substitute in resurrection, a new personality has been formed; a new individuality has been established in law; and it is on the footing of that new personality, that new individuality, that we stand, and bid defiance to every accusation that the law without, or conscience within, can press against us.

In *believing*, this identification between us and our Surety took place. In *believing*, we became legally one with Him, in death and resurrection; that is, we died and rose again. In *believing*, the mighty legal spell was wrought, the mighty legal miracle was accomplished, whereby our former self passed entirely away, and a new self came up into glorious being.

Nor is this new personality a mere figure, or fiction, or romance. Those who never realised the momentousness of that central doctrine of the Word of God, the substitution of the righteous for the unrighteous, nor tasted the peace which comes from the knowledge of that substitution, may say that this is but a figure. But they who feel that this legal transference of guilt from themselves to their Surety lies at the root of all their peace and hope, will neither be stumbled at the apostle's statement in our text, nor look upon it as the mere boldness of figure. For whatever difficulty there may be in understanding the *nature* of the transaction, or the very manner in which it is accomplished, still the thing itself is sure, and its results, in so far as God and we are concerned, are of the most real and blessed kind.

It is on this new legal personality that God acts in his treatment of us. It is on this ground that he confers his favour, and pours out his blessings. He deals with us, not according to what we *were*, but according to what we *have now become*, in consequence of our oneness with him in whom his soul delighteth. This oneness is our claim for blessing. This is the plea which we present, and which we know God rejoices to accept.

Why, then, should there be such unwillingness to identify ourselves with the Son of God? Is oneness with him a thing so shameful, or so terrible? Is our own identity so precious a thing that we are unwilling to part with it, and to sink it in his? Surely this cannot be. What can be more blessed than to lose ourselves in him; to be so completely identified with him that the law and the Lawgiver should treat us as entirely one! What can give our souls a surer resting-place than the knowledge that this treatment of us is the very thing that magnifies the righteousness of Jehovah, and enhances the glory of his incarnate Son!

SERMON XXV.

THE RISEN CHRIST AND THE THINGS ABOVE.

"If ye then be risen with Christ, seek those things which are above where Christ sitteth at the right hand of God."—COL. iii. 1.

THIS new *identity* or new *self* is not a thing gradually formed; wrought out step by step as we advance in likeness to Christ; it is not a thing dependent upon our graces, a thing which is more or less complete, as we are more or less holy men; it is a thing of *state*, not of *character*; a thing of *law*, not of moral fitness; it is therefore formed at once,— the moment that we believe. Then we become one with a dying and rising Saviour; as truly and thoroughly one with him as we shall ever be during a whole long life of holy doings. In believing, we are crucified with Christ; we die, and are buried with him. Thus our former self is gone. It perishes. Twice over it is declared to be gone; once on the cross, and a second time in the grave of Christ. Then we rise to a new life, and acquire a new self,—a new personality. We come forth out of the grave, where we had been buried with Christ, *new men;* not the same individuals in the eye of the law, but others altogether. We obtain a new life, a risen life, a life corresponding to that of him who *rose* as well as *died*, who was not only delivered for our offences, but raised again for our justification. We are risen *with* Christ. He is the risen Head, and we the risen members. "We are risen with Christ!" It is not merely that we are forgiven, reconciled, justified, but we have entered on a new and more elevated condition of being, a resurrection-life, a life which is truly the earnest and anticipation of the glorious state of being which is finally to be ours in the day when this mortal shall put on immortality, and death be swallowed up in victory. This resurrection-life let us realise as already ours; ours in right and title *now*, soon to be ours in reality, when He who is our life shall appear.

The expression "with Christ," which the apostle uses here, is one which applies to much more than to resurrection. *All* that we receive we receive *with* Christ; in conjunction with him; as sharers with him in what he has received from the Father. We are not simply said to receive blessings from Christ or from the Father for Christ's sake, but to receive them from the Father as joint-possessors, joint-claimants, joint-heirs with the Son. "We are made *partakers* of Christ," that is, made fellow-sharers, fellow-partners with him in all that he is and has. He is ours, and all that he has is ours. The love wherewith the Father loves him, the blessedness with which the Father has blest him, the honour with which the Father has honoured him,—all this he shares with us as being one with him; the members of his body; the bride in whose love he rejoices.

And as it is on this *oneness* between us and Christ that God acts in his treatment of us, so it is upon this that we are to act continually in our intercourse with him, and in our whole life on earth. Our life is to be the life of risen ones. Our whole walk and conversation are to be those of men who feel that they have died and risen, and that in this sense also they have become new creatures in Christ Jesus; old things having passed away, and all things having become new.

It is to this that the apostle refers in the words of our text, when he says, "If ye then be risen with Christ, seek those things that are above, where Christ sitteth at the right hand of God," as if he would remind us that they who have *died with Christ* have died to all things *beneath;* and that they who have *risen with Christ* have, by their new life, been brought into connection with things above. Their death with Christ severed for ever the tie to earthly things; their resurrection with Christ fastened at once and for ever a new tie which links them to what is heavenly; their former connection with what is earthly has ceased, and a new connection has begun with heavenly things; they are to be not so much dwellers upon the earth as inhabitants in heaven, like angels come down to visit earth on some gracious errand, yet still mindful of their own proper home, their true descent, and rank, and character. "Our conversation is in heaven, whence we look for the Saviour, the Lord Jesus Christ." And if our conversation is in heaven, should not everything about us, everything said or done by us, correspond to this dignity?

What have Christ's risen ones to do with the vanities, or pomps, or pleasures of earth? The world has its own followers, and these things are for *them!* But for us who are risen with Christ, there are other things provided. We have other company, other joys, other hopes. Earth has too long detained us; heaven is now the home of our souls.

Seek the things that are above! Do we not need the counsel? Are not our eyes ever turning downwards? Are we not, like Lot's wife, too often looking back, remembering that Sodom out of which we have been taken? And what attraction do we find there, so fascinating, so irresistible, that we experience such difficulty in looking upwards? Is the bleak desert fairer than the blue starry heavens? Is the society of the world better than the companionship of angels and saints, nay, of God and Christ and the eternal Comforter? Strange that we should need a *command* to do what seems so natural, so unavoidable, so blessed! Yet we do require the command; and that not once in a lifetime, when some sore temptation besets us, but each day and hour!

Seek the things that are above! Heaven and the things of heaven; God and Christ, and the angels, and the saints, the kingdom, the city, the glory, the crown;—these are all *above*, and these are our treasures; why then should we still cling to earth and mind the things below?

Love not the world! for if we love this world we cannot love the world to come; if we love the world, we cannot love the Father; if we love the world, we cannot seek the things above. The friendship of the world is enmity with God, and therefore companionship with the things of the world cannot fail to hinder us from setting our affection on the things above. There must be no compromise, no lingering, no half-heartedness. All must be decided; for what can be more expressive of decision and unwavering consistency than the idea of our being actually *risen* men! This sets aside all vain excuses, all idle pleas for mingling with the world. Either you are risen, or you are not risen. If you are not risen, then, of course, there can be no appeal of this kind to the conscience at all. Go on in your worldliness; fling yourselves headlong into the torrent of earth's vanities; but know that the end of these things is death! But if you are risen, then there is an end of all debate. The point is settled. You cannot take part with the world in its follies, and gaieties, and sins! What, risen with Christ and yet a worldling! Impossible. Risen with Christ, yet singing its idle songs, hurrying through its mazy dance, partaking in its mirth and revelry! Impossible. If you be risen with Christ there is no alternative; you *must* seek the things above.

The apostle evidently takes this for granted; that there is no alternative in such a case. The unrisen may seek the things below, but the risen *must* seek the things above. The unrisen may linger amid the vanities of earth, but the risen must set their affection on the things of heaven!

The things that are above, are those on which our eye, our heart, our hopes, are resting; we are seated with Christ in heavenly places, and hence our delight in the things connected with these heavenly places; we are come to mount Sion, to the city of the living God, the heavenly Jerusalem, to an innumerable company of angels, to the general assembly and church of the first-born, which are written in heaven, and to God the Judge of all, and to the spirits of just men made perfect, and to Jesus the Mediator of the New Covenant. And having come to these, we are conversant with these; we live amongst these; we realise these more truly than the things around, which we hear, and see, and handle. These are the scenes, and sights, and sounds, that occupy our souls! We have ceased to be citizens of earth's polluted cities; we are citizens of the New Jerusalem which cometh down out of heaven from God. We have ceased to be inhabitants of earth; we have become the inhabitants of heaven. We have ceased to call anything on earth our own, for we are heirs of God and joint-heirs with Christ, so that *all things* are our heritage; as it is written, "He that overcometh shall inherit all things." We have a home, but not in the palaces or haunts of the world; a house not made with hands, eternal in the heavens.

The things that are above are the *real and the enduring;* therefore we seek them, for all below is shadowy and transient; passing away like the morning cloud. The things that are above are the things congenial to our risen natures, therefore we seek them. All other things are repulsive, not attractive, because unsuitable and uncongenial; they have nothing in common with us, nor we with them. The things that are above are the satisfying and gladdening, and therefore we seek them. Nothing here can *fill* us, nor impart one hour's real enjoyment. But the things above both fill and gladden; we feel, even in the *anticipation* of them, far more of rest and peace diffusing themselves through our souls than in the full *possession* of what the world calls joy. The things that are above are the infinite and eternal. All else are narrow and limited; they have at the most but a life-time's duration; no more. But the things above have no limit either as to space or time. All connected with them is *illimitable;* so that we can look forward to an enjoyment of them which fades not, and changes not, and shall never end! Of this we have the *earnest* already, and the *reality* will not be long behind. It only awaits the coming of Him who is to shake the things that can be shaken, in order that those things which cannot be shaken may remain.

The things that are above are thus those round

which all our hopes and joys are daily gathering. They are our portion, our heritage, our treasure. What have we upon earth to compare with them, or to desire beside them? Day by day they are gathering more of our hopes and joys. One by one the affections of earth are loosening from the things of earth, and fastening themselves to the kingdom that is to come. One by one the objects of endearment here are detached from us and pass upwards, becoming part of the things above. We begin to feel as if heaven contained far more of our heart's affections than earth; and as if the command to seek the things above were becoming easier and more natural, seeing we have so many fewer objects now to love on earth, so many more to love in heaven. And as flower after flower is transplanted from the wilderness below to the paradise above, we feel as if that paradise were assuming more and more truly the aspect of our real and proper home; the home of our kindred, and the home of our hearts; the home into which no foe shall enter, and out of which no friend departeth; the home where the shadow never falls, but where the sunshine ever rests; where the Lamb that is in the midst of the throne shall lead us to living fountains of water, and God shall wipe away all tears from our eyes.

SERMON XXVI.

FAITH IN AN UNSEEN CHRIST.

"Blessed are they that have not seen, and yet have believed."—
JOHN xx. 29.

HERE is another "beatitude" in addition to what Matthew gives; and from the same lips that spoke the others. For Christ was himself the "Blessed One;" and well knew who were "blessed," and what made them so. He knew not only who were to be partakers of the great beatitude, "Come, ye blessed of my Father," but who are partakers of blessing now. The substance of his statement here is just this: "The blessed ones are the believing ones; and of these the most blessed are they whose faith rests most simply on the bare word of God, without either sight or sign."

Man neither understands nor likes this way. He says, Had I seen Christ and his cross, I should certainly have believed. He glories in his proverb, "Seeing's believing," in opposition to God's, "Believing's seeing;" thus denying that "faith is the substance of things hoped for, the evidence of things not seen," and forgetting how the Lord spoke at Bethany,—not, "If thou shouldst *see* thou shouldst *believe*," but, "If thou shouldst *believe*, thou shouldst *see*." There is, no doubt, blessedness in *seeing* (John xx. 20) ; and there is blessedness in *believing* ; and there is blessedness in *believing after seeing ;* but that of which the Lord here speaks is a blessedness different from these, and truer than all of them,—the blessedness of believing without seeing. Others may be blessed ; for any kind of true connection with the Lord must make us blessed; but they are the most blessed who have not seen, and yet have believed. The actual sight of Christ contributed much less to the blessedness of those who saw him, than we generally suppose. Tens of thousands saw him, yet remained unbelieving and unblest ; and in the case of multitudes of others, the sight of him only led to further unbelief, and hatred, and rejection. Even in the case of those who saw and believed, the seeing was not such a special advantage and blessing as we sometimes think. Thomas saw and believed ; yet the Lord will not allow him or us to suppose that this is best. He tells us that, far better than this, is the blessedness which flows from simple faith, in the absence of all visible or sensible helps ; simple faith, that counts God's testimony sufficient, and owns a risen Lord, though, in doing this, it is unassisted by eye, or ear, or hand.

But how and why are these believing ones so specially "blessed?"

1. *They throw themselves upon the bare word of God.*—All that they believe, they believe simply because God has said it ; so that their faith rests

on no divided evidence ; and the foundation they build on is not partly strong and partly weak, partly iron and partly clay, partly rock and partly sand, but wholly rock, wholly iron, wholly strong. They take God's testimony as their sole authority for everything. This makes their faith sure ; far surer than if it had sprung out of what is seen by their own eye. This makes it also far more unwavering and unchanging than if it rested on sight ; for sight may change ; to-day bright, to-morrow dim ; but God's testimony changes not. Not sense, nor feeling, nor touch, nor taste, nor vision, but the naked word of Him that cannot lie; —this is the true foundation of a sinner's faith. That is the surest and truest faith, that thus comes into contact with, and rests directly on, the *bare rock*, with nothing between. Nothing can shake faith, in such a case, but that which shakes the evidence of God's own being and faithfulness. Changes and uncertainties, in themselves or in man, cannot shake them, so long as they know that with God there is no variableness, neither shadow of turning.

2. *They come directly into contact with God himself.*—No cloud, no distance, no medium of any kind, comes between them and God. They deal directly with God ; the soul touches him who is a Spirit, needing no interpreter nor introducer. We speak to God, and he speaks to us, as he did to Moses, face to face. We are of necessity cast upon God himself, God alone ; and this is blessedness.

Joseph no longer speaks to his brethren through an interpreter, but draws near and speaks in their own tongue, nay, falls on Benjamin's neck, and kisses him.

3. *They get more into the heart and reality of the things of God.*—Sight often crusts over spiritual things, or builds a wall, or draws a veil around them. Simple faith goes in at once to the heart and core of things; it goes beyond what is outer, and takes up its dwelling in the region of the invisible and divine. Instead of cruising along the rocky sea-board, it strikes inland, and pitches its tent amid the gardens and by the streams of a richer and more glorious country; it leaves things seen and temporal behind, and holds direct intercourse with things unseen and eternal. It is in itself simpler, purer, and more direct; less drossy and earthly; less mixed or alloyed with elements of frailty, or self, or the flesh; and hence it finds its way into regions into which faith of a grosser kind could never penetrate: it rises up, with a buoyancy all its own, into a higher atmosphere, disentangled and disengaged from the things of earth. Like a being without a body to clog it, it moves more at will, and rejoices in a liberty to which faith of a more material kind is a stranger.

4. *They take fewer false steps, and make fewer mistakes.*—Simple faith sees, as it were, everything with God's eyes, and hears everything with God's ears; it sees nothing with man's eyes, and hears nothing with man's ears; and thus comes to no

false conclusions, and is kept from the continual mistakes into which sense is falling. It sees through the screen, or veil, of the visible into the invisible; it makes the distant seem as the near, and the future as the present. It not only sets the right estimate on the evidence of sense and feeling, but it puts the true interpretation upon all the facts and phenomena coming under the eye or sense. It disputes the point with sense and feeling, with the eye and ear, with consciousness and reason, and triumphs over all. Exercising simple faith on the bare word of him who has given me the sure record respecting his crucified, dead, buried, risen Son, I see myself crucified, dead, buried, risen with him. Though seeing in myself the chief of sinners, I know and believe that there is no condemnation for me. Conscious of foolishness and ignorance, I know and believe that I am wise in Christ. Sensible of hourly defilement all over, I am persuaded that there is no spot in me. I see sin covering the earth, and Satan exercising dominion, but yet I do not believe in the supremacy of sin, and I know that Jehovah reigns. I see no visible Christ, no cross, no throne, no Holy Spirit, anywhere; and yet I believe in a Christ, a cross, a throne, a Holy Spirit, and that these are the most real of all real things. I see the sickness, the death-bed, the coffin, the grave of the saint; and yet I believe not in his sickness, but in his health; not in his death, but in his life; not in corruption, but in incorruption; not in mortality, but in immortality; not in the grave, but in the resurrection. Thus what I see I do *not* believe: nay, I believe in the contrary of what I see. I believe not only *without*, but *against* seeing; and thus I put the right construction upon things seen and temporal, looking at everything with the eyes of God, and tasting the blessedness of anticipating the time when that which is perfect is come, and that which is in part shall be done away. Thus faith judges and sifts everything by the word of God, and is in its turn judged, sifted, purified, by that word, so as to yield the richest fruit, and bring home to our souls the fullest and truest blessing.

5. *They are thus subjected to discipline of the best and most effectual kind.* This life of believing without seeing,—nay, often of believing against seeing, —is excellent training for every part of the new nature. It keeps the body under, while it lifts up the soul; it binds the flesh, while it sets free the spirit; it loosens us from the earthly, and fastens us to the heavenly. It is a divine school, or process of discipline, for every faculty of the renewed being; detaching intellect, imagination, feeling, more and more from the gross and the carnal, and familiarising them with, as well as assimilating them to, the pure and the spiritual. It calms us, too, and keeps us calm in a stormy world. It awakes us and keeps us awake, amid scenes fitted to lull us asleep. It makes us more truly "children of the light and of the day," by transporting us beyond this world of night and darkness, into

the kingdom of the unsetting sun. It greatly increases, too, our longing for the day of sinless vision, when sight shall no longer be a temptation, nor the senses a snare, nor outward glory a hindrance to spiritual feeling, nor the works of God a screen, or wall, between us and God himself. It whets our appetite for the marriage supper of the Lamb, and in thus giving us a time of fasting, prepares us for the day of feasting. How much of true efficacious discipline turns upon our being kept from present vision, and compelled to believe without sight or sign; to live wholly by faith upon an unseen Christ, and in expectation of an unseen kingdom!

For all that we have spoken applies both to past and future. We see neither; the cross and the crown are both invisible; and in regard to both it is true, "Blessed is he that hath not seen, and yet hath believed.' The present want of *vision* is no loss to us now, and shall be no loss to us hereafter. Seeds require darkness to spring in; light injures; so we require the darkness of this world to spring in; light would interfere with our development and growth. We are to flourish in light, but it is our day of darkness here that prepares us for this. Were it not for this day of darkness, this day of the absence of vision, we should be but half prepared for the day of light, and the realm of glorious day.

This is the church's day of *faith*, not of *sight;* for during her Lord's absence, she lives by believing, not seeing. *Others have seen for her;* and she believes what they saw. The disciples saw the death and resurrection for her; the prophets saw the glory and the kingdom for her; and she believes what they saw. She hears the report regarding the cross of Christ from those who saw it; and, believing, she says, "God forbid that I should glory, save in the cross of our Lord Jesus Christ." She hears the report concerning the dying, buried, rising Saviour; and, believing it, she rejoices with joy unspeakable and full of glory. She hears the report of prophets concerning the resurrection from the dead, when the Lord returns to raise and glorify his own; and, believing it, she says, "O death, where is thy sting? O grave, where is thy victory?" She hears the report concerning the future inheritance and kingdom; and, believing it, she exults in the prospect, tasting thereby a peculiar blessedness, which she could not have done in other circumstances, even though God had given her a glimpse of the third heaven itself, or dropped down upon her a gem of the New Jerusalem, as a specimen, or earnest, to sight and touch, of what its glory is to be.

Words like those of our text seem specially written for us in this day of absence, when we must be indebted to faith alone for the knowledge of everything connected either with the sufferings that are past, or the glory that is to follow. We need not ask for a sign; there shall no sign be given but the sign of the prophet Jonas; and, besides, the privilege of the church in this age is to live without any sign or vision, in simple faith upon the word of an unseen God. This is her blessedness and honour. By this she resembles most, and treads most closely in the footsteps of, the Son of God. By this she condemns the world, and crucifies the flesh, and bears witness to the power, the faithfulness, the love of God. For this witness of simple faith, which so honours God, she is honoured of God; and receives from him a recompence of reward, both now and hereafter, corresponding to her testimony.

Let those who have already believed through grace, learn more of their true character; let them remember their testimony, and act according to it, and up to it. Live as believing men; God expects this at your hands. Ask no sign nor vision; ask no evidence of miracle without, or feeling within, to rest your faith upon. God has given you a true report concerning his Son, confirmed with infallible proofs. Let your faith rest simply there, in the absence of sense, or sight, or feeling, or sign, external or internal. Remember how it is written, " If thou shalt *believe*, thou shalt *see*." The vision will come in its due time, and it will be infinitely glorious; meanwhile, walk by faith, till the day break and the shadows flee away. For " blessed are they that have not seen, and yet have believed."

Let those who have not yet believed nor tasted that the Lord is gracious, believe now. Wait not for signs without or movements within. Take the true testimony of God concerning his Son, and rest upon it. It is enough; and it is all true! See how true it is; and what a love it speaks of, what a salvation it announces! Believe, and be saved! But remember, that while "He that believeth shall be saved, he that believeth not shall be damned!"

SERMON XXVII.

CONSECRATION BY BLOOD

"And he brought the other ram, the ram of consecration: and Aaron and his sons laid their hands upon the head of the ram. And he slew it; and Moses took of the blood of it, and put it upon the tip of Aaron's right ear, and upon the thumb of his right hand, and upon the great toe of his right foot."—LEV. viii. 22, 23.

By "the ram of consecration," is meant the ram by which Aaron and his sons were consecrated, or set apart for the service of God. The victim was selected by Moses, who was thus representing God. It was not Aaron and his sons who chose the sacrifice; it was God who made the choice for them, and presented the ram to them that they might put their hands on it, and in so doing, acknowledge it as God's appointed sacrifice, and accept it as their substitute.

Thus, the transaction of sacrifice is here, as elsewhere, shewn to be *twofold*. Moses, as acting for God, exhibits one part, and Aaron, as acting for the people, exhibits the other. Moses chooses; Aaron, in Israel's name, accepts the choice. Moses presents the ram; Aaron, in Israel's name, puts his hand on it, in token of laying sin upon it. Thus, in one sense, God lays our sins upon the sacrifice; but, in another, it is *we who lay our sins*

CONSECRATION BY BLOOD. 213

upon it, when we bring them to it and confess them over its head. It is this latter part of the great transaction that is so fully brought out in the Book of Leviticus, and the other books relating to sacrifice. For though, in one aspect, Aaron represents Christ, in another, he represents, not Christ, but Israel, or the Church. This is especially the case when his sons are associated with him, and when he places his hands on the head of the sacrifice, and confesses sin upon it. He acts and speaks in the name of the people, confessing their sin, and laying it on the Lamb of God. He thus represents, not the Father, but the sinner accepting the sacrifice provided by the Father. He represents, not Christ, but the sinner bringing his sin to Christ, and taking him as his substitute and surety. The Father's act in laying sin on Christ, and our act in laying our individual sins on Christ, are two things not to be confounded, and neither of them to be overlooked.

This personal dealing with the sacrifice, this putting the hand on the head of the ram of consecration, as it was about to be slain, is the first part of the great transaction; and it is that part which represents the *forgiveness* of the individual thus personated by Aaron and his sons. Thus, the beginning of the consecration is forgiveness,—forgiveness through death,—the death of one selected by God to bear his sins. There can be no consecration without forgiveness; and, upon forgiveness, consecration follows forthwith, being, in fact, a continuation of the sacrificial process through which the forgiveness is obtained.

This sacrificial process is very fully given us here. There is, *first*, the selection of the victim. There is, *secondly*, the transfer of the sinner's sin to this selected victim. There is, *thirdly*, the death of the victim. There is, *fourthly*, the transfer of its death to the sinner, by putting the blood upon him. There is, *fifthly*, the sinner's new life after this has been gone through. There is, *lastly*, his entire consecration to God in consequence of his whole man having thus died and risen.

1. *The selection of the victim.*—As, in all cases, the lamb or goat, on these great public occasions, was to be chosen by Moses, so was our great Sacrifice chosen by God. "Behold my servant whom I have chosen," is God's message to us concerning him; and again, he says, "I have exalted one chosen out of the people;" and, in the New Testament, he is called "the Christ, the chosen of God" (Luke xxiii. 35). The great sacrifice, the propitiation for our sins, the lamb for the burnt-offering, is entirely of God's selection. And in this of itself, we have the blessed assurance of its suitableness and perfection.

2. *There is the transfer of the sinner's sin to this selected victim.*—Though, in one sense, this is done by God, through that same eternal purpose by which the victim was selected; yet, in another sense, and as a thing brought about, or becoming a fact, in time, it is the sinner that does this, when

he accepts the sacrifice, and, putting his hand upon it, confesses his sin over it. Then the *actual transfer* takes place; for, up till that moment, the sin had been lying on the sinner. It is upon our acceptance of God's sin-offering that the guilt, which had made us *unclean* in his sight, passes over to the appointed Substitute, and leaves us *clean*. What he asks of us is simply our *sin*, our *guilt;* no more. He is appointed to receive and bear it. He beseeches us to transfer it to him, and to allow him to bear it all. And why should there be unwillingness to allow of such a transfer? Why should the relinquishment of condemnation be so slowly, so reluctantly consented to?

3. *There is the death of the victim.*—According to the process described in our text, *the transfer is made while the victim is alive;* and then, he having been loaded with our transgressions, is led out to be slain. For as death was the due of our sin, so must it be the due of him to whom it is transferred. On whomsoever the guilt is found, on him must the penalty lie; and from him must that penalty be exacted to the uttermost. The soul that sinneth, it must die. *Death*, nothing less than *death*, must be inflicted wherever guilt is found; for law must take its course, and righteousness must have its satisfaction. The only thing that can remove guilt from us for ever, is the *death* of him to whom it is transferred. In no other place can guilt be hidden, so as never to re-appear against us, but the *grave*. Death pays the debt and exhausts the

penalty; nothing short of death. Without that shedding of blood, which is the means of death, and the evidence of its having taken place, is no remission.

4. *There is the transfer of this death to the sinner by putting the blood upon him.*—The sinner's death is first of all transferred to the Surety, who dies as the sinner's substitute. Then the Surety's death is transferred back again to the sinner, and placed to his account as if it had been his own. In *confession*, we transfer our death to the Surety. In *believing*, we transfer his death to ourselves, so that, in the sight of God, it comes to be reckoned truly ours. This transference of the Surety's death to us, is that which is set before us by the putting the *blood* upon us. For blood means death,—or life taken away; and the putting of blood upon us is the intimation the death has passed upon us,—and *that* death, none other than the death of the Surety. The putting the blood upon us is the identifying of us with him,—his death with ours,—so that thus we die with Christ,—and we are buried with Christ; and all in order, as we shall see, that we may rise again with Christ. It is in this way that we become partakers of the baptism wherewith he was baptized; not by being plunged in blood; not by our being brought to the blood, but by the blood being brought to, or applied to us; by having *blood put upon us*, as in the case of Aaron and his sons,—to signify that thus we were dead,—dead with him who died for us,—dead in virtue of the transference

of his death to us by the sprinkling of the blood upon our persons.

It was not Aaron that sprinkled the blood upon himself or his sons. That would have meant that he was putting himself to death with his own hand, as a self-murderer. He neither sprinkled the blood upon himself, nor did he plunge himself in the blood; that would have been the symbol of *suicide*, not of death by the hand of the law. It was Moses, representing God, that sprinkled the blood. Aaron but presented himself in the appointed place, put himself in the appointed position, and forthwith the symbol of death was administered to him. God, by the hand of Moses, sprinkled the blood upon him,—as an intimation that the death of the sacrifice had been transferred to him. It was by this baptism of blood, beside the altar where the sacrifice had died, that symbolised to Israel that which was not fully revealed till after years,—the sinner's death with Christ; and told him that the time was coming when he should be in reality baptized into his death, made partaker of his death, that so he might also be partaker of his burial and his resurrection. It is God that sprinkles the blood of Christ upon the sinner, and so transfers to him Messiah's surety-death upon the cross. And what God asks of every sinner here is, that coming to the great altar of sacrifice, even the cross of his Son, he would allow Him to transfer the Surety's death, with all its everlasting benefits of pardon, and salvation, and life, to him.

O sinner, it is this that thy God this day asks of thee! Not to do anything, but to let him do the whole. Not to put thyself to death, either in symbol or in reality, but to allow him to reckon to thee the sinbearing death of his almighty Son. Wilt thou not consent to this, and, in consenting, receive from his hand the baptism of blood, by which the great death is made over to thee, forgiveness sealed, and cleansing at once received?

Remember that that which God calls cleansing can only be accomplished by *death*. It is guilt that has made thee unclean, and that uncleanness can only be removed by that which removes the guilt from between thee and God. That guilt cannot be cancelled save by the death of the sacrifice applied to thee. The application of that death by the sprinkling of the blood upon thee is that which at once takes away thy guilt, and makes thee wholly clean. Put yourself in the position which God asks thee to do; that is, *believe* the Father's testimony to the death of his Son. The moment that thou believest, the blood is sprinkled, the death is transferred, thou art counted as one who hast died, and so paid the penalty,—and thou art forgiven, accepted, *clean!*

5. *There is the sinner's new life thus received through death.* Aaron and his sons are marked with the symbol of death, and so accounted as dead men; yet they go away alive. The stains of the blood are washed off at the laver, though the legal and ceremonial effects of it remain indelible. They are

thus represented as men who have passed through death to a life beyond death,—who are alive from the dead. In other words, they are risen men; and as such, they go forth to the service of God.

Just so is it now with the saints,—God's kings and priests. They have been baptized with Christ's baptism, and have thus died with him. But having died with him, they also rise; and, as risen men, they go forth to serve Him who has done all for them. "I am crucified with Christ, nevertheless I live; yet not I, but Christ liveth in me; and the life I now live in the flesh, I live by the faith of him who loved me." Made partakers of Christ's resurrection and Christ's life, they go forth to do his will, in the strength of his risen life. It is as resurrection-men that they serve him; as men, partakers even here of the power of resurrection-life, and who are drawing from that resurrection-fountain daily treasures of life, wherewith to labour for him who died for them and who rose again. If ye then be risen with Christ, seek those things that are above, and make use of your risen life for duty, for temptation, for battle, for trial, for suffering. It will be sufficient for every time of need.

6. *There is the entire consecration of the whole man to God, in consequence of his having thus died and risen.* The solemn act of consecration described in our text brings out this very fully. The victim is called the "ram of consecration;" and it is the blood of this ram sprinkled upon Aaron and his

sons, which, while it symbolises their death and resurrection, represents their consecration to God, and to his service, by that same transaction. That which proclaimed them dead, in consequence of the applied death of the sacrifice, sets them apart for holy purposes in God's house.

Thus it is that the death and resurrection of our true ram of consecration, our better sacrifice, operate upon us. They "sanctify" us, as the apostle's expression is, in the Epistle to the Hebrews : "Jesus also, that he might *sanctify* the people with his own blood, suffered without the gate." Thus we are "sanctified," or set apart, or consecrated, by the application of the blood ; and hence the name of "saints," or "consecrated ones." God has thus taken special pains to shew us that it is by the application of Christ's death and resurrection to us that this consecration takes place. It is thus, through the blood of sprinkling, that we are separated unto God, as his true priests,—fitted to do his work here on earth, and hereafter more fully, more gloriously, in his kingdom. It is through death and resurrection that we pass to consecration for priestly service, in the temple and kingdom above.

But the ceremony described in our text is a peculiar one. The body of Aaron was not plunged in blood ; for the *quantity* of blood is of no consequence ; the blood was merely applied to three places of his body; and by this, the whole man was consecrated. The tip of the right ear was the first place, denoting that his hearing was now set apart for God, and that he was to be ever in the attitude of one listening to God alone,—hearing no words but his, heeding no instructions but his. The thumb of the right hand was the next place sprinkled, indicating the consecration of all bodily skill, and energy, and power, to the service of Jehovah, and telling him that that right hand and its "cunning" were to be used henceforth for no meaner employment than the work of the God of heaven. The great toe of the right foot was the third place touched with blood, signifying that his feet were to be ever ready for priestly service, that his limbs were to be employed for God, and their strength or swiftness solely dedicated to bearing his burdens or running his errands. The whole man, in all his faculties and powers of soul and body, was to be thus set apart for God.

It is this complete separation unto God that is effected by our participation in the death and resurrection of the Lord. In being made partakers of his baptism, nailed to his cross, buried in his grave, raised with his resurrection, we are totally consecrated to the service of him who raised up Christ from the dead, and who has thus raised us up with him, and made us sit with him in heavenly places. Our ears, our hands, our feet, are thus wholly his; not our own, not the world's, not Satan's. As those who have died with him and risen, we hear him always, and listen for his words and commands, ready to put forth hands and feet, every power and faculty of soul and body, in the service of him with whom we died, with whom we are risen, and to whom we are thus solemnly set apart. If the baptism of Christ, applied to us in believing, has any meaning at all, it sets before us these things respecting ourselves,—first, we are wholly sinners, wholly guilty, subject to wrath and death; secondly, we are wholly forgiven, in consequence of our Surety's sin-bearing baptism of death for us; for in His death we are dead. Next, we are wholly risen from death, in virtue of our Surety's resurrection; and lastly, we are wholly consecrated unto God, through means of this death and resurrection. The whole man, from head to feet, becomes a sacred thing, dedicated to the service of the living God.

Our ears are thus set apart to God. And if so, how wide open should they be to hear his voice; how thoroughly closed against all sinful sounds. They are the ears of risen men, and should have no sympathy with unholy words, or vain conversation, or earthly frivolities. Our hands are thus consecrated to God; let us use them for him alone, anxious not to profane the vessel thus set apart for the master's use. Our feet are set apart for him; let us run the errands of no other master, nor use our limbs in the service of the flesh, or the world, or the world's king. As God's consecrated priests, his true Aarons, his true Levites, his true Israel, let us reckon ourselves dead indeed unto sin, but alive unto righteousness through our Lord Jesus

Christ. Whether we eat or drink, or whatever we do, let us do all to the glory of God.

Follow the Master fully. Give him no divided heart. Serve him wholly. Give him no half-and-half service. Think of yourselves as alive from the dead, as partakers of Christ's baptism, and death, and resurrection, and act accordingly. Let not sin therefore reign in your mortal body, that ye should obey it in the lusts thereof; neither yield ye your members as instruments of unrighteousness unto sin; but "yield yourselves unto God, as those that are alive from the dead, and your members as instruments of righteousness unto God" (Rom. vi. 12, 13). "I beseech you," says the apostle, "by the mercies of God, that ye present your bodies a living sacrifice, holy, acceptable, unto God, which is your reasonable service; and be not conformed to this world, but be ye transformed by the renewing of your mind, that ye may prove what is that good, and acceptable, and perfect will of God (Rom. xii 1).

SERMON XXVIII.

A PRESENT SAVIOUR.

"Aud knew not that it was Jesus."—John xx. 14.

WHEN Jesus comes the second time there will be no mistake as to who he is. He comes in his own glory, and in his Father's glory, and with his mighty angels: in majesty, and power, and brightness. Every one shall know him then. The Jew shall know him, for he shall "look upon him whom he hath pierced, and mourn." The Gentile shall know him; for it is written, "Every eye shall see him, and all kindreds of the earth shall wail because of him." The saint shall know him,—for he comes "to be glorified in his saints, and to be admired in all them that believe." The sinner shall know him, for "he comes to take vengeance upon them that know not God, and that obey not his gospel. No one shall mistake him in that day; for it shall be either Jesus the bridegroom coming to be recognised and rejoiced in by his long-waiting bride, or it shall be Jesus the Judge and avenger coming to break his enemies in pieces with his iron rod.

But when he came the first time he was mistaken; few knew that it was Jesus. He passed in and out, yet was he unknown. He was in the world, and the world was made by him, and yet the world knew him not. "He came unto his own, and his own received him not." Nazareth, where he had been brought up, knew him not. Capernaum, where he dwelt, knew him not. Bethsaida knew him not, and even Jerusalem knew him not. He was full of grace and truth; He was the messenger of the Father's love, and the declarer of his own, yet men knew him not. He passed through this world unhonoured and unrecognised; One in whom man saw not the Mighty God, the Incarnate Word, the Eternal Son of the Father.

But even to his own chosen ones, who had received him, he was sometimes strangely unknown. The two Emmaus friends knew him not. Thomas knew him not. More than once we read that the disciples knew him not, and even Mary "knew not that it was Jesus." One would have thought this impossible in any circumstances, and yet here we find it so. Even Mary's eyes discerned him not. He stood before her, yet she knew him not. The keen eye of love, the quick-sighted eye of woman failed to recognise him. One wonders how it could be so. Could Jacob see his own Benjamin, his own Joseph, and yet not know them? Could Jonathan meet David, and yet not know him? Yet Mary met with Jesus, and knew not that it was he.

What hindered the recognition? It was nothing in Jesus himself. He was not unwilling to be known, nor reluctant to be saluted and recognised as of old. He did not veil himself. He did not stand aloof. What was it then?

1. *First, She was seeking the living among the dead.* She had gone to the tomb to find him: her only hope seemed there. She knew that he had died, and she expected to find him among the dead. She forgot that he was the living One, that death to him could be, at the most, but the matter of a day. She sought him where he was not to be found, and when he appeared, when she expected him not, she knew not that it was Jesus. Like the foolish child that would dig for the star in the little pool where it mirrors its beam, and does not recognise it shining in its living beauty above his head; thus Mary sought the living among the dead; the heavenly amid the earthly. No wonder that she knew him not. Beware of seeking, in like manner as Mary did, the living among the dead; a living Christ amid dead forms, and duties, and devotions, and rites; lest, when he does appear to you, you know him not.

2. *Secondly, She was laying too much stress on the mere body of the Lord.* She had known it in other days. She had seen him on the cross. She had helped to lay him in the sepulchre, and her whole thoughts were therefore occupied with the *body* of her Lord. When last she saw it, it was pale and cold, torn and bleeding, no life remaining. Her thoughts reverted to that scene. She could not realise anything else; and now this remembrance

of the body of her Lord came between her and the Lord himself. She was attaching too much value to his mere corporeal frame; here was a rebuke to her for so doing. She was so much occupied with the thought of his body, that the real Christ was hidden, the Christ himself, so that, when he appeared, she knew not that it was Jesus. Let us not allow anything pertaining to the outward form of Jesus,—in which sentimentalism may indulge, —to hinder our beholding the real, the living Saviour. Let us beware lest some particular aspect in which we expect to see him, be just the very thing that hinders us from seeing him at all. If we have made up our minds only to see him in one form, under one aspect, and in one way, it may be we shall not see him at all; or when he does stand before us, we shall be, like Mary, not knowing that it is Jesus.

3. *Thirdly, She was blinded by her overmuch sorrow.* Sorrow had filled her heart and absorbed her soul on one object; her dead Master. This blinded her to the living one. Sorrow dimmed her eye with tears, and she failed to recognise through those tears the very Christ whom she was seeking, the very being over whom she was weeping. Her excessive grief raised up a thick mist between her and her Lord. Let us beware of being blinded by overmuch sorrow. In the world we shall have tribulation; we may reckon upon that as our lot; yet, let us not be blinded by overmuch sorrow; or have our eyes so dimmed with tears as to be

unable to recognise or to realise a present Lord. Sorrow should produce a very different result. It should not veil, it should unveil Christ. It should not throw you to a distance from him, or bring in some mountain of separation between you and him; it should increase your nearness; it should bring you nearer to him and him to you. It should make him to be felt as more precious, more desirable, more entirely suitable, more indispensable. It should make you more quick-sighted in your love; instead of being, like Mary, less quick-sighted, so that you may know that it is Jesus when he appears.

4. *Fourthly, She was hindered by her unbelief.* Like the disciples, she was slow of heart to believe all that the prophets had spoken. The rising from the dead was a thing which she but darkly understood. Like the others, she could not believe that the Messiah would die, and now that he is dead, she does not believe that he can rise again. Her faith did indeed cling to his person; that person was precious to her, but all her need of him she did not know. Her need of his dying, her need of his rising she knew not. She knew enough of him for faith and love to rest upon; but not enough to keep her from falling into error or unbelief. It was unbelief that hindered her from prompt and full recognition of her beloved Lord. Is it not in our case still the same as in Mary's? Is it not unbelief still that comes between us and the Lord? He draws near to us; he stands before us, yet we know him not. Perhaps we seek him, seek him ear-

nestly, and he comes, yet, when he comes, we recognise him not; we know not that very Jesus whom we were seeking, if he comes not in the way that we expect. Unbelief has suggested that it is not thus that we are to expect him to appear, that it is not in this place, or in this way, or in this form, that we may expect to find him and to meet him. He presents himself to us as a risen Christ, an almighty Saviour, all that the sinner needs, full of grace and truth, with forgiveness upon his lips and eternal life in his hands; with every heavenly blessing held out to us; and yet we recognise him not; for unbelief has given another representation to him, and we are not prepared to recognise him, save in that form which we ourselves would prescribe to him, in that aspect that we have made ourselves think that he will surely appear to us in. Faith makes no such conditions as unbelief does. Faith does not attempt to prescribe to the Lord in what form, or at what time, or in what way, or in what circumstances he shall appear. It is ever ready to recognise him in any condition, and under any garb. It is glad to find him anywhere.

Mark then the peculiar position occupied by Mary. She thought that she was seeking an absent Lord, *whereas she was refusing to recognise a present one.* Most sinful mistake and full of evil to herself, robbing her of that fulness of blessing which was at her very side! Had you asked her what ailed her when she was weeping, she would have said, my Lord is absent, I have been seeking him and I cannot find him anywhere, whereas it should have been, my Lord is present and I do not know him. This was her sin. While professing to seek an absent Lord, *she was refusing to recognise a present one.* This was her sin, this was her calamity. "She knew not that it was Jesus." This kept her in sorrow, and in darkness.

Is not her position precisely that which we ourselves too often occupy ? Is not that sin of hers too often ours, and is not that calamity which overtook her just the very calamity which we so often bring upon ourselves ? Her case resembles ours. We thrust away blessings from us in the same way that she did ; we shut out the Lord just as she did. *Christ is present;* let us keep this in mind—" Lo, I am with you alway." He is no distant, no absent Saviour to any one, but ever nigh. He is at our very side, at the very side of each, so that no one can complain of distance in him any more than they can complain of estrangement or want of love. He is never absent, nor repulsive, nor unwilling to be recognised as Jesus, whether by saint or sinner. He does not veil himself to prevent our seeing him. He does not repel our advances. His grace never varies. Always is he the same. His ear is the same willing ear, his eye the same loving eye, and his hand stretched out,—the same gracious hand. To sinner and to saint, Jesus is near

This nearness of Christ is what faith recognises; for the office of faith is not to make him present, as so many seem to imagine ; it is not to bring him down from above. The office of faith is not to seek an absent, but *to recognise a present Lord*. And what a mighty difference there is between these two things! Unbelief seeks an absent, faith recognises a present Lord. *Recognition is faith's special office;* and the Saviour whom we preach is not far distant and inaccessible in yonder heaven, but near; and not only near, but the nearest of all near beings; the nearest thing to you on earth or in heaven. We preach a present Christ. Let faith simply recognise him as such, and all is well. And just as faith recognises this present Christ, instead of going in quest of him as if he were absent, unbelief blinds the eye to him. It cannot, indeed, thrust him away; that is impossible. It cannot, with all its efforts, make him the absent one; it cannot empty him of blessings, but it refuses to recognise him. It knows him not, it treats him as the distant one, in order thereby to be furnished with a ground for self-righteous efforts in seeking him. It treats him as an unloving one, as one hiding himself, one reluctant to appear; and thus it puts away that blessing which is at hand, in all its fulness. It keeps us in sorrow and in darkness; it prevents communication between us and the Lord. For, let us remember, that earnestness is not faith. There is an earnestness which is pure unbelief; and this earnestness of unbelief shews itself by going in quest of an absent Saviour while the earnestness of faith shews itself in recognising a present one.

Yes ; Christ is at our side, though unseen and unknown. When he works in us, effectually drawing the soul to himself, he cannot be hid ; but, for a time he may. A man does not always recognise him at first, even when he is really working in him, and drawing him to himself. Many things hide him, and yet he carries on his work though hid.

He has hidden ways of leading the sinner to the Father. It is, perhaps, sometimes a long way ; there are many windings in it, and it seems when we look at it, as if there was nothing but common events, common providences, common mercies, common trials ; and yet it was Jesus in each one, Jesus himself, though we knew him not. We saw the process, though we did not realise what it meant. We knew not that Jesus was in it, that he was in each of these events, in each of these providences, in each of these mercies, in each of these trials. There is danger in not giving Christ credit for his own work, but in taking the credit to ourselves for it, or giving the credit to chance, or to the common course of events. It is one thing to take to ourselves too much credit, and it is another thing not to ascribe enough to him, or not to realise him in certain things, because we think these things are not so remarkable as we should have expected him to work by ; but, how blessed does the discovery come, when at length we find that it was really he who was working, though we long refused to believe him, and that what we imagined to be just natural feeling, natural sentiment, was, after all, Jesus himself, carrying on his work in us.

He has hidden ways of giving peace to the troubled. The wounded spirit looks around for rest, and for healing; yet it comes not. It expects something outward, something visible, something striking, as Naaman did; and it is disappointed when there is nothing of this kind. It refuses to take peace in a way so simple; it refuses to taste and recognise the gift, because it is not presented to it in some striking way; till, at last, the soul is led to ask, What if, after all, I am putting away a present blessing, and refusing to recognise a present Christ? What if all these gleams of peace which I am putting away from me be real? What if it be the light of his countenance which I am refusing to receive? Thus, the soul begins to learn that it is really so, and that it has been Jesus all along, and yet we knew him not.

Again, he has hidden ways of comforting and gladdening the spirit of the afflicted. Trials ofttimes come strangely, very strangely, and we do not see Jesus in them. They are not the kind of trials we looked for, nor such as we should have thought best for us, and so we refuse to be comforted. But, perhaps, at some unexpected turn of the way we make the blessed discovery that it was really Jesus, and none but he! How much do we lose of consolation by failing to recognise Christ in each, even the commonest, even the unlikeliest, even the most untoward and adverse events that befall us. He is seeking to purify us. Each event, be it dark or light, be it sunshine or shadow; each event is tending to this. All is full of meaning, full of rich, deep meaning, though we know it not. We find, in spite of ourselves, a process moving onward, moving unaccountably, perhaps imperceptibly, on; and though, for a time, we discern it not fully, yet at length it unfolds itself in all its blessedness, and we see that the Lord was in it all, purifying us as silver. These changes that were taking place in us were not natural changes, the result of natural causes, but wrought by his own Almighty hand, though not in the way that we expected.

Let us learn, then, to recognise a present Lord! This is faith's especial office, and no amount of sin on our part, can reverse this state of things, this order which God has established. When we begin, because of felt guilt, or of conscious evil, and unworthiness, to seek an absent or a distant Saviour, we are giving way to unbelief in one of its worst forms. And never shall we return to our quiet rest again, until we have learned the sin of going in quest of an absent Lord, instead of doing what he desires we should at all times do, *recognise a present one.*

SERMON XXIX.

SELF OR CHRIST; WHICH IS IT?

"For none of us liveth to himself, and no man dieth to himself. For whether we live, we live unto the Lord; and whether we die, we die unto the Lord: whether we live therefore, or die, we are the Lord's. For to this end Christ both died, and rose, and revived, that he might be Lord both of the dead and living."—ROM. xiv. 7-9.

THE words "none of *us*" shew that the apostle is speaking of those who have been delivered from a present evil world. He is contrasting *them* with the men of earth. Once, our life, he means to say, was the same as theirs; now all is changed; and instead of resemblance, there is unlikeness in every feature. He does not count it pride to say, we are unselfish, they are selfish; we are of God, and the whole world lieth in wickedness.

Each of these verses brings out a distinct truth. In the seventh verse we have the setting aside of self; in the eighth, the substitute for self; in the ninth, the way in which this substitution has come about.

I. *The setting aside of self.*—I do not mean *annihilating* self, as some speak. There is no such thing, save in the dreams of a vain philosophy, or a self-righteous mysticism. I speak of giving self its proper place,—the place recognised by our Lord, when he said, "Thou shalt love thy neighbour *as thyself.*" Lawful self-love is not selfishness; yet we may say that selfishness is diseased self-love; and, as such, is the master-sin, the master-curse of man. He lives for self; his estimate of everything is its bearing upon self; the colour which he casts over everything is one derived from self. Self is the horizon which limits all his views. He is not like a man looking round on a noble landscape, and forgetting himself in the beauty of the wide expanse; but he is like a man carrying a mirror with him, into which he is continually looking, that he may see and admire himself; so that every object is seen in connection with self, and is only admired as it helps to set off self. The apostle's statement presents the reversal of all this. It shews us the mirror broken, into which we looked so complacently; the eye turned outward instead of inward; the horizon thrown back into the far distance, self-forgotten, lost sight of—"None of us liveth to himself, and none of us dieth to himself." We have done with self, at least, in the way in which we have hitherto been connected with it. It is displaced. It is brought down to its true position and level; it is set aside entirely as an end, or motive; and this, not in one thing, but in everything; for we may take the words, life and death, not merely as expressive of the very things that they mean, but as bringing before us the two extremes of man's being, and including, of course, everything between these two extremities. This displacement of self, then, is carried through man's whole being, from one extremity to the other. From his life and from his death, as well as from all between, this self has been displaced.

Now, mark how this process is carried out. The first setting aside of self is in the matter of justification before God; for, previously, self was the main ingredient in man's theory of justification. His object was to amend self, to improve self, or it might be, to mortify self, in order that thereby he might recommend himself to God. Thus self, in the matter of his justification before God, occupied the chief place. The first thing which the Holy Spirit does, when he convinces a man of sin, is to shew that this cannot be; that self can contribute nothing towards his acceptance with God. What is conviction of sin but just the setting aside of self; a negative, but still an important, step; shewing a man what cannot justify him before shewing him what can. Thus it is, then, in the matter of justification before God, that the setting aside of self begins. From that point it proceeds onwards throughout a man's whole life. From life, in all its parts and movements, great and small, his inner life, his outer life, his domestic life, his social life, self is displaced. Life is no longer tinged or shaded, or discoloured by self as it had once been. And then the close of his life, in like manner, exhibits the setting aside of self. On a sick-bed self is set aside; in dying, self is not allowed to come in. Nor in dying, are we to exhibit self or turn the eye either of ourselves or others to it; or to think merely of enjoyment, or comfort, or reputation among men, our good name, our fame after death,—posthumous fame, as men vainly call it. In reference to all these points self is set aside,—" None of us liveth to himself, and no man dieth to himself." Others may live to themselves, but not we who have been "bought with a price." Others may die to themselves, but not we who have been " redeemed with the precious blood of Christ."

How this *elevates* life! What was that which degraded life? It was the introduction of self. Now, this element of degradation is set aside, and life is lifted up into its true glory,—the true position which God originally designed for man. It is no longer the degraded thing that self has made it, but a glorious thing such as God meant it to be.

How this takes away life's littlenesses! What was it that introduced so much of narrowness into life, into every part of life, and its daily transactions? It was the infusion of self. It was this that made life feeble and little; that shrivelled it up, and contracted its original greatness. But now that this element is set aside and expelled, life expands to its true dimensions. Its littlenesses are gone.

How this establishes and strengthens life! What was the element of our weakness? It was self. Yes; self is the great element of weakness, for it disconnects us with the foundation of strength. It cuts us off from God. It isolates and makes us stand alone. But now, when this is set aside, life assumes the strength which God meant it to possess. It is "stablished, strengthened, settled."

How this secures us against all failure and disappointment! Why was it that we failed so often in our schemes? Because we lived for self. Why was it that we were often disappointed? It was because we were seeking self; but now that this is gone we cannot fail, we cannot be disappointed in anything, for we know that, though our plans and wills are crossed, yet God's good purpose is carried out, his ends are secured, his will is done. There can be no failure now; no disappointment now; for that which made failure and disappointment necessary and certain has been wholly set aside. Now we go forward as men who feel that, let whatever may come upon us, upon our land, or upon our world, we cannot fail, nor be disappointed. All must succeed, all must be well.

II. *The Substitute for self.*—It is the Lord Jesus Christ who has come into the place of self, filling up its room. In turning from self we do not leave ourselves without an object to live for, or to die for: we get one infinitely more worthy than we possessed before. Instead of self we get the Son of God; the glorious one. He fills us, occupies us, engrosses us henceforth. He is all to us what self was before. He takes the place of self in everything from first to last, great or small. He is the Substitute for self, first of all, in the matter of our standing before God. As the first thing the Holy Spirit does is to set aside self, in the matter of justification and acceptance, so his next is to present to us the Son of God as the true ground of our acceptance. We no longer seek to be justified by self in any sense, or on account of anything done to self; on account of amended self, or improved self; or mortified self, but solely on account of our Lord Jesus Christ, who died for us and who rose again. Having taken him in the place of self, we find ourselves at once accepted of the Father, "accepted in the beloved," accepted, not because self has been improved, but because self has been set aside and the Son of God substituted in its room. And in this Son of God, whom we take as a substitute for self, in the matter of our acceptance, we find an object worth living for, an object that we can carry through everything, through every part of life, into every region of life. We make him our Alpha and Omega, our first and our last. On a sickbed our object is, that Christ should be glorified whatever becomes of us. On a deathbed our desire is, that Christ should be magnified, and in all that may happen to our name after death, in anticipation either of good report or of bad report among men, our sole wish is, that the name of Christ should be exalted. Thus, in living and in dying, Christ is all. He has come in the room of self, and fills that room entirely. Our life is thus full of Christ, and so is our death; "Whether we live, we live unto the Lord; and whether we die, we die unto the Lord: so that living or dying we are the Lord's." You are not your own at any time, nor in any circumstances, but his, his only.

What *solemnity* is thus thrown over life! All its parts, all its movements, are now consecrated to the Lord. Up till the time when this substitution takes place our life is a wasted one, utterly thrown away. It is dedicated to self, just as some of Egypt's magnificent temples of old were consecrated to the worship of some reptile. But now that self has been cast out, and Christ introduced, our life has become a sacred thing; every part of it is consecrated,— made "holy unto the Lord."

What *dignity* this imparts, both to life and death! Let it be the life or death of the poorest, if he be a believing man, a man in Christ Jesus, what a dignity attaches to him; a dignity that attaches to no other being upon earth, not even to its mightiest kings. From the moment that he became a man in Christ Jesus, living not to himself but to Christ, all littleness vanished, all narrowness and meanness were gone, and in the place thereof grandeur, glory, and heavenly magnificence thrown around his person. What a change!

What *importance* now attaches to life! All triviality has passed out of it. It has now become an important thing either to live or to die. We have got something worth living for, and something worth dying for; and in circumstances such as these, there can be nothing unimportant about life.

The end we live for, the end we speak for, the end we act for, raises life up to an importance which nothing else could have done. There can be nothing little now about anything that we think, speak, or do.

What an *imperishable* character is thus imparted to life! Everything we do, whether in living or in dying, becomes imperishable, now that we live unto the Lord and die unto the Lord. It was self formerly that ruined everything, that made everything connected with us to crumble down and waste away. But now it is entirely different. The Lord has come in to occupy the place of self. He is come in, who is "the same yesterday, to-day, and for ever," and he imparts his immortality to us, in all we are and do. Now nothing dies, but everything lives, and that for ever, for it is done unto the Lord. Every word spoken for him has an eternal being. Every action done for him carries its results forward into eternity; and every step we take, if taken for him, is a step whose effects are immortal, as is our being, and as is the being of him who is, by his oneness with us, attached to all we do his own imperishable character.

What an *incentive to zeal* this gives us! We have now got something to do that is really worth doing; an object worth living for and worth dying for. There is nothing so heartless as to have no object in life, or a poor object; and, on the contrary, there is nothing so quickening, so animating, as to have a worthy object. How mighty, then, must be the impulse, when we can feel that our life is a life to the Lord, that our death is a death to the Lord.

What a reason for consistency and holiness of life! Everything we do tells, not merely upon our comfort, on our earthly prospects, on our good name, but upon the glory of Christ. We have now become so connected with him that everything we speak or do bears upon him and his cause. The consistency of a holy life honours him, and brings a good report of him to our fellow-men. How watchful, then, ought we to be; how jealous over ourselves, lest self should assume the place that belongs only to the Lord; how anxious to adorn the doctrine of God our Saviour in all things; how desirous that our life should be a consistent witness-bearing for Christ, that our light should shine before men!

Man out of Christ, I speak to you now. What art thou living for? What has thy past life been? what is thy present life? What are thy ends in living? What is thy hope in dying? The very utmost, I fear, is this,—to enjoy present things as much as possible, and to escape hell at last. Have your ideas, your hopes, your aspirings, ever risen beyond these two things? Man out of Christ, what art thou living for? For self! Is that all? What a poor object, what a mean and narrow aim; and what, in such a case, must thy end be but utter disappointment and eternal failure? Man out of Christ, what a poor life must thine be, and what a poor death! What an unmeaning, empty being is thine, and to what a more unmeaning, more empty departure out of it art thou hastening. And yet how different it might be. Why should not thou, even thou, begin to live unto the Lord? What a rich, noble life might thine become. Instead of a wasted, shrivelled, useless, perishable thing, thou mightest have a life filled up *for* God, and filled up *with* God; filled up *for* Christ, filled up *with* Christ; a life which, though in so far as this world is concerned, may be a life of poverty and obscurity, yet would be, in all other respects, a foretaste of everlasting life, the earnest of the endless glory. And what stands between thee and that life? It is self, the accursed thing. What separates thee from God? It is self, thy love of self, thy admiration of self, thy confidence in self. What is it that stands between thee and the forgiveness of thy sins? It is self; thy confidence in self. What is it that comes between that eye of thine and the vision of the eternal glory? It is self. It is self that is blinding and bewildering thee. What is it that is dragging thee down, and making thee cleave to the dust? It is self. And what is it that will ere long be thine everlasting ruin? It is self. Oh, that thou wouldest begin to make the great substitution of Christ for self. Put Christ where self is, in the matter of thy justification before God, and all is well. Put Christ in the place of self, in regard to the forgiveness of thy sins, and thou art straightway forgiven.

III. *The manner in which this substitution is*

effected—"For to this end Christ both died, and rose, and revived, that he might be Lord both of the dead and the living." Christ's claim over us *as Jehovah* is eternal, and nothing can be added to it. As the Eternal Son he has always been Lord both of the dead and living, of heaven, earth, and hell. But his claim over us as the *Christ* is different from his Lordship over us as *Jehovah*. His claim over us as the Christ is a superadded claim. It is not something which derogates from, or which neutralizes his former claim; it is simply something added to it. This claim of headship over us he has made good by his death and resurrection. "He died, and rose, and revived." He received the resurrection-life that he might have a legal claim to Lordship both over the dead and living; so that there might be no part of a man's being, whether pertaining to his life or his death, over which the Christ might not have the right of Sovereignty. Nor can any one dispute his claim or present a rival one, for no other has done what he did to secure it. He died and rose again; may he not demand entire Lordship over us in living and in dying? Does not every part of our being thus owe him allegiance? To whom do we owe homage save to him? Who has done for us what Christ has done? Has self done the like? Has the flesh done the like? Has the world done the like? Has any angel done the like? Has any fallen man done the like, that we should serve them, and that they should have lordship over any part of our being?

No one of these. He alone can ask homage and headship; for He only has the divine and indefeasible right. He has won the dominion, which none can now dispute, by dying and by rising.

Self, then, has no claims upon us, for it has done nothing for us,—nothing either for soul or for body. It has been a wall of iron between us and Christ. Is that a reason that we should serve it? It has been a mountain of ice between us and the world to come. Is that a ground of claim over us? Nay, brethren, self has done nothing to make us either live to it or die to it. It never can do anything; shall we then own it; shall we serve it; shall we do it homage?

The Lord has every claim. We have asked, What has self done? We ask on the other hand, What has the Lord not done? What indissoluble, innumerable bonds are there between us and him, as the living, the dying, and the rising one. He claims to be loved, to be served. Have we satisfied ourselves as to the ground upon which that claim rests? Have we acknowledged it, and is our whole life in every point an acknowledgment of this claim? The whole of our life is to be his, as his life was for us. Surely he has earned this, if he has earned anything at all. The least that we can give him is our life; the undivided service of our being, in every part; in our doing, in our speaking, in our planning, and in all our daily round of business, so that every part of our life shall be a witness-bearing for him.

Our death is to be his. In dying he thought on

us; so in dying let us think on him. Our death is to be for his glory. Our last testimony is to be a testimony for Christ. Do we not often, in looking upon death-beds, forget this? We desire from the dying, satisfaction as to their hope, as to their peace, but that is all. How rarely do we go beyond that, and remember that there is to be no dying for self, even as there is to be no living for self; and that there is something beyond getting satisfaction of our friend's state, and that something is, that Christ be glorified, that the saint's testimony be not merely as to his own peace, or as to his own prospects, but as to the glory of him who "died for us, and rose again."

Our eternity is to be his. He ever liveth for us; let us anticipate the ever living for him. It is not merely that we shall be for ever with the Lord; though that is well; but it is that we shall for ever glorify him, for ever live to him. Our whole eternity is to be one of obedience, love, service,—all for his glory, for "Christ is all and in all," whether in heaven or on earth. He is so, even here, in some poor measure, to those who have tasted that the Lord is gracious, but in the eternal kingdom he is to be still more fully so. Our life here, and still more our eternity hereafter, are to be for him. He is the Alpha and Omega of our life here; still more the Alpha and Omega of the life to come.

O man of earth, what is thy eternity to be? If thy life here is life without Christ, is thy eternity to be the same? Think what such an eternity will be to thee. Even if there were no hell, what will be an eternity without Christ? Perhaps thou thinkest little of that; and thou sayest to thyself, "I can do without Christ here, and I shall be able to do without him hereafter." Nay, my friend, it is not so. Thou canst do without him here, because thou canst contrive to forget him,—to forget him in the world, in pleasure, and in business; and this makes thee to do without him here. But hereafter there shall be no drowning of thy senses in such things as these, so as to prevent the conviction of thy infinite loss. Then the full knowledge of thy loss shall come up before thee, and it will not be a lost heaven merely, a lost kingdom, a lost inheritance, but it will be A LOST CHRIST. *That* will be the eternal sting; the sense of what thou hast lost in losing Christ. It will be the very bitterness of the cup of gall and wormwood that shall then be given thee to drink. The everlasting sense of *what thou hast lost* in losing Christ shall be the very sting of the undying worm, and the very torment of the ever burning fire.

SERMON XXX.

PRIMITIVE DOUBTINGS, AND THEIR CURE.

"When the Lord had thus spoken, he shewed them his hands and his feet."—LUKE xxiv. 40.

THERE are two special points which I ask you to notice here: first, the doubts of the disciples; secondly, the Lord's way of meeting them.

1. *The doubts of the disciples.*—There were some things respecting their Master which these disciples strangely doubted; and there were other things, which they as strangely, as it seems to us, did not doubt at all. They doubted whether he were risen, as some had reported; but they had no doubt that, if he were risen, all was well with them. They doubted whether those who said that they had seen him were correct in their statement; but they had no doubt that, if these witnesses were correct in their report, *they* had no further ground for sorrow, or doubt, or fear. They doubted whether this person, who now stood in the midst of them, were really their old Master, Jesus of Nazareth; but they had no doubt that, if this were really he, they had abundant cause of rejoicing.

This state of things is now in a great measure altered, or rather reversed. There are doubts now as to points on which there were no doubts then; and there are no doubts now upon points which, among the first disciples, were the only subjects of doubt. Seeing that this is the case, may we not suspect that there is something wrong with many of us; wrong at the very root? We do not doubt, it seems, whether Christ has risen; but we doubt whether this resurrection can be of any use to us personally, or wear any kindly aspect towards us, till we have succeeded in doing or feeling something to make it available and beneficial; as if the great virtue of his resurrection did not flow out of that event itself, but out of those acts of our own which we may have been enabled to put forth in connection with it. We do not doubt that the risen and ascended Jesus is actually the Christ of God, the Saviour of the world; but we doubt whether this is of any importance to us, till we have ascertained, according to the most approved tests, whether our knowledge and faith be of the right *kind;* that is, of such a *quality* as to warrant us to expect that this risen One will condescend to bless us because of it. We do not doubt that this Son of God is near us, within our reach, so that a touch, a word, a look, may in a moment connect us with him; but we doubt whether this nearness be in itself a matter of rejoicing, until we, by working ourselves into the consciousness of "acting faith" on this truth, have made it a blessing: as if the use of faith were not at once and directly to draw joy out of a thing of joy; to take and use, for purposes of immediate peace and comfort, the simple fact, that Christ is risen; but to put gladness into a fact which otherwise possesses none.

This surely is unnatural, and founded upon a misapprehension of the real meaning of the fact presented to us. The doubts of the first disciples, strange as they seem to us, were natural, in their circumstances. It needed no small amount of proof to convince them, that he whom they had seen crucified on Golgotha, and had buried with their own hands in Joseph's tomb, was actually risen; but, that proof having been fully given, there lay nothing beyond it to prevent them enjoying the divine fact, and rejoicing in the risen One. The position of many among his disciples now is by no means so intelligible. We admit the proof of his resurrection; we own him as the Prince of Life, and the Conqueror of death; but we say that all this is nothing to us, so long as we are not sure what our own feelings are, or what the quality of that faith of ours is, by which we believe in this resurrection.

This mode of dealing with the facts of the Bible, ascribes to faith what belongs to Christ. By all means let us render to faith what is due to faith; but let us not forget to render to Christ what is due to him alone. Let us beware of ascribing a virtue to *our faith*, which belongs to *His resurrection*.

Our method of treating Christ's resurrection leads us to concentrate our expectations upon *self*, and on the changes to be wrought on self. It makes our joy, to come, not at once from the *certain* good news of what the Father did for Christ when he raised him from the dead, but from the yet *uncertain* consciousness of what the Holy Spirit is to do for us and within us. It says that the sinner is not warranted in tasting the full cup of blessing which the resurrection of Christ presents, till he has wrought or prayed himself into a more suitable, more receptive frame of spirit; forgetting that nothing save the direct drinking of this cup can bring about this better and more blessed frame.

The way in which many of us treat the death and resurrection of Christ, always raises questions as to personal acceptance and fitness. The way in which the early disciples treated these, never raised any question pertaining to self at all. Conscious of no goodness, in word, or deed, or feeling; aware that no length of time nor earnestness of effort could make them more fit or more acceptable to Christ; knowing that it was the *lost* that Christ came to save, the very last thing that could have entered their minds was, that their Master would hesitate about receiving any sinner that would apply to him. They knew well about men refusing to follow him; they never heard of his refusing to receive one. Altogether satisfied as to his grace and power on the one hand, and as to their own poverty and emptiness on the other, there was no room for any question, about *self*, to be raised at all. If he were the Christ, as they believed him to be; and if they were the lost ones, as they knew themselves to be, then the whole matter was decided at once and for ever. Thoughts about self, and faith, and goodness, could have no place. They were excluded. By what law? Of works? No. But by that divine testimony, which, ages before, had announced, "he was wounded for our transgressions, he was bruised for our iniquities."

The only question which, during his lifetime, these disciples felt that they needed to have settled was, " Is our Master really the Christ ?" The only question which, after his death, they hesitated about, was, " Is our Master really risen, and is he, who now appears in the midst of us, the same as he who formerly went out and in among us, doing the mighty wonders which demonstrated that he was truly the Christ ?"

And, after all that has been said, and written, and disputed ; after all that has been advanced as to inward evidences and preparatory experiences, this is the one great question still, Is Jesus of Nazareth in very deed the Christ of God ? Has he died ? Was he buried ? Has he risen ? These are the questions which we should still feel to be the vital and the lawful ones, had we any right apprehension of the state of matters between us and God.

But did the disciples make of no account the question of their own acceptance ? They did not. But they saw it as so entirely included in, or at least so inseparably connected with, the question of his resurrection, that if the one were conclusively settled, the settlement of the other followed, as a matter of course, without difficulty or delay.

Not that they were accepted before they believed, or whether they believed or not ; not that they were to believe themselves accepted and forgiven, in order to be accepted and forgiven, as some would frame the Gospel. No ; but the *knowledge* of Christ, in his person and propitiatory work, was understood to be so necessarily and inevitably the introduction to acceptance and pardon, that they did not suppose it possible to *know* the Divine testimony concerning Christ, without being, thereupon and thereby, justified and blest. To know him, as crucified for sin, was to be "crucified with Christ." To know him as dead, was to be "dead with Christ." To know him as buried, was to be "buried with Christ." To know him as risen, was to be "risen with Christ." To receive the Father's testimony respecting him, as crucified, dead, buried, risen, and ascended, was, in the very act of receiving it, to enter into the state of "no condemnation," to get possession of eternal life, to be "accepted in the Beloved." The object of the Holy Spirit's work was, not to concentrate their thoughts upon themselves, or introduce them to the knowledge of their own acts of faith and love, but to fix their eye upon another, to introduce them directly to the knowledge of the risen Son of God. The saving vision was one, into which no element of self could enter : it was the vision of "the glory of God in the face of Jesus Christ."

SERMON XXXI.

PRIMITIVE DOUBTINGS, AND THEIR CURE.

"When the Lord had thus spoken, he shewed them his hands and his feet."—LUKE xxiv. 40.

THE light in which the disciples viewed the great facts respecting this dead and risen Substitute, never raised the question of their own acceptance; or at least, in raising it, settled it at once and for ever. Our way of regarding these, seems only to *raise* the question, not to *settle* it; nay, it makes the settlement of it one of the most subtle, prolonged, and intricate processes which a tried soul ever undertook. According to the apostles, the adjustment of the *personal* question was the simple and immediate result of their knowledge of the risen Christ. According to many of us, peace with God can only be the result of the knowledge of self, or rather of the begun improvement of self, in addition to the knowledge of Christ; the fruit of a lifetime's hard experience; the inference from an algebraic summation of doubtings and believings; the termination of one of the most tedious and painful processes of metaphysical analysis and mental scrutiny ever attempted by man. Strange, that the knowledge of a risen Christ, which, in apostolic days, was the *ending* of all doubt, and suspicion, and perplexity, should, in our day, with so many, be only the *beginning* of these. Strange, that that which was once the settlement of every personal question between the soul and God, should now be the signal for letting loose all such questions, and letting them loose in a way which makes it impossible that they can ever be conclusively adjusted. Strange, that that which was meant to throw men entirely out of self, either righteous or unrighteous self, by handing them over to the Divine Substitute, should be the very thing which now is employed for throwing them into self; thus degrading the Sinbearer, and converting into a secondary remedy his completed propitiation on the cross.

God's plan, in his glorious gospel, was to reach self by means of Christ; our plan is, to reach Christ by means of self. To be satisfied with Christ, was the primitive way of peace and forgiveness; to be satisfied with self, in addition to Christ, is the modern plan of many: as if the other were too free and too simple; as if the peace obtained in the primitive way were too liable to abuse, and therefore needing a check and safeguard, to protect the threatened interests of holiness.

To be *satisfied with Christ*, is surely, of itself, life and gladness, as well as the destruction of sin. To be satisfied with self, in addition to this, is to add to the finished propitiation of the Son of God, and to cast doubts upon the efficacy of his cross. To seek to be satisfied with self, in order to be satisfied with Christ, or to make Christ satisfied with us, is the introduction of one of the subtlest forms of self-righteousness, by means of which, combined Popery and Arminianism ever subverted the free grace of God, and rebuilt the barrier between the sinner and the kingdom, which the Son of God had thrown down. To be satisfied with Christ, is the simplest, purest, brightest form of faith. To be satisfied with self, is the darkest and deadliest form of self-righteous unbelief. To recognise the completeness, personal and vicarious, of the Christ of God, dying and rising for sinners,—this is peace, this is life, this is sunshine. To begin to think about our own act of recognition, in order to ascertain its completeness and perfection,—this is the entrance of gloom, and trouble, and doubt; nay, this is, in many cases, the first step of apostasy; this is to renounce the cross, and to fall from grace.

II. *The Lord's way of meeting the doubts of the disciples.*—" He shewed them his hands and his feet." That which they doubted was, whether this Stranger who had come to them, and who looked so like their old Master, were in very deed himself. If he were, then he must have risen from the dead; for they saw him die, nay, they had buried him. If this were he, then all had come true which he had spoken of himself, and which the prophets had spoken concerning him. He was now doubly demonstrated to be the Christ. That which he had spoken to them concerning his rising from the dead was no vain thing; and now they saw in him, not only all that they had seen before, but much more. As the *dying* Christ, he was much more to them than the *living* Christ; but as the *risen* Christ, he was more than the *dying* Christ. The seed had not only been sown and taken root, but was now springing up into a glorious tree.

His object, then, in shewing them his hands and his feet, was not only to convince them that he was no spectre, no shadow; but that he was the very Christ who had been crucified. The nail-prints were the proof, not only that he had died, but that he had triumphed over death; that, though "crucified through weakness, he lived again by the power of God." The sin had been borne; the blood had been shed; the sacrifice offered up; the penalty paid; the law satisfied; righteousness honoured; Satan baffled; death overcome. Of all these things the nail-prints assured them. They were the chief of the "many infallible proofs" (Acts i. 3) given to his disciples of his true resurrection.

Strange as this kind of recognition, this way of fixing the doubted identity, may seem, it was satisfactory. The mother in the story knew her long-lost child by the scar on the shoulder received in infancy; so was the Son of God recognised by the nail-prints and the bruises of the cross. But did the disciples need this? Were the loved features not the same as ever? Were the eyes that wept over Jerusalem not the same as before; or had the grave robbed them of their tenderness and lustre? Were the lips, from which came the gracious words of parting love, not the same as in the upper chamber at the Last Supper? Was the voice so altered, that they did not know its tones? No. These resemblances might all be recognised; but so many things threw doubt upon these recognitions, and they were so slow of heart to believe what the prophets had spoken, that, instead of reasoning in favour of his identity from the fact that he professed to be risen from the dead, they stumbled at this stumbling-stone, and raised doubts out of the very events which ought to have dissipated all. It was not till they had seen him die that they would believe that he could die; and now not even their own eyes will convince them that he is risen; so little did they understand what Messiah was to be, and to do, and to suffer. Their one redeeming point was attachment to his person. Of his sacrificial work they knew but little; of his blood-shedding they had but slenderly felt their need; into the profound significance of his death they had not yet entered. But to his *person* they were attached, with all the warmth of true-hearted friendship. And it is of this personal attachment that the Lord is making use, to lead them into the deeper, truer knowledge of his mighty work.

They were to be made to recognise him *by his wounds;* his healed, but still visible wounds; the scars of the cross, the marks of suffering and death. Their unbelief was to be allowed so to come out, that nothing would remove it, but that which proved him to be the very kind of person they had all along shrunk from acknowledging,—One who must *die* in order to bless them. Their former faith in his person had been shaken (founded as it was on very imperfect knowledge); and that which was to reassure them was *his wounds*. The old chords that fastened them to his person had been shaken and strained, till they had almost snapped; and the new link, which was to knit them more firmly than ever to his person, was that which fastened itself, not so much to his person, as to his *work* as the Substitute. They had known him as the seed of the woman; they were now to know him as the Man with the bruised heel, "the Lamb as it had been slain."

It was with this same blessed evidence that the staggering faith of Thomas was held up, when nothing save the sight of the nail-prints could reassure him; and it was on similar ground that the beloved John was comforted in Patmos, when he fell at the feet of the glorious one. This same Jesus laid his right hand on him, and said, "Fear not, I am the First and the Last; I am he that liveth and was dead." It is thus that he approaches us still, and shews us his hands and his feet, that by these scars we may be made to feel that he is in very deed the Christ that we need. And in in doing so, he shews us the true way of dispelling doubt, of whatever kind it may be, viz., the fuller knowledge of himself, as the dead, the buried, the risen, and living Christ. It is this that is the cure of all unbelief, the death of doubting, the cherisher of faith, the perpetual source of stability and peace; for the real cause of all doubting is imperfect knowledge of the Lord.

Nor let any one say, I know all that I can know, both of himself and of his work. He that says this, knows nothing yet as he ought to know. When doubt arises, and unbelief gets the mastery, and estrangement comes in, let the first thought be,—Could this have taken place, had I fully known him whom I profess to have received; and will not another look at him, another glimpse at his glorious person and deep-scarred wounds, fully reassure me, and rebuke all alarm or distrust?

He shews you once more his hands and his feet, that through them you may know him, by these "infallible proofs," to be the very Christ you need, both for heart and for conscience. The Christ we need is such a Christ as will not only reveal the immeasurable love of God, but convince our consciences as to the *lawfulness* of that love, by shewing us the life, the death, the resurrection of a divine *Substitute*, through means of whom this love to the sinner is enabled to give itself out *lawfully and righteously* to man.

He is the Christ of Bethlehem; the Child that was born, the Son that was given. But this is not enough. Mere incarnation falls short of our wants, and fails to pacify the conscience.

He is the Christ of Nazareth; the Man that

dwelt among sinners, and shewed the love of God to sinners. But this is not enough.

He is the Christ of Capernaum ; the great worker of miracles, the healer of the sick, the raiser of the dead, the feeder of the hungry, the utterer of the most gracious words that ever fell on the ear of man. But this will not purge the conscience, or secure our peace with God.

Accordingly, he shews himself as the Christ of Gethsemane, the Christ of Golgotha, the Christ of Joseph's tomb. And what shall we more say ? Who, after the proof that is given of death and resurrection, can persist in doubting, or refuse to be comforted ? And, if these gracious facts will not cheer and revive, what is there that will do it in earth or heaven ? Look at him with prolonged gaze. See him as he was and is ; as the dead, the buried, the risen One. Look at his hands, his feet, his side. These scars, though healed, are allowed to remain, just on purpose to meet your doubts, and banish your distrust. He who raised him from the dead, left these scars still visible, these marks of death and weakness, these memorials of the cross and its nails, in order, by means of them, to speak to you, to give you demonstration of his true death and true resurrection, that thereby you might be comforted exceedingly, nay, be like those of whom it is written, " Then were the disciples glad when they saw the Lord."

SERMON XXXII.

CHRIST AND THE WORLD.

"What fellowship hath righteousness with unrighteousness?"—2 Cor. vi. 14.
"The friendship of the world is enmity with God."—Jas. iv. 4.

WORLDLY people seem to be well aware that it is only in this life that they will be able to get vent to their worldliness. They quite count upon death putting an end to it all; and this is one of the main reasons for their dread of death, and their dislike even of the thoughts of it.

They know that there will be no "worldliness" in "the world to come;" that there will be no money-making, nor pleasure-finding, nor feasting, nor revelling; no balls, nor races, nor theatres, in heaven or in hell. Hence their eagerness to taste "life's glad moments," to take their fill of mirth, to make the best of this life while it lasts; and hence the origin of their motto, "Let us eat and drink, for to-morrow we die."

Such are the out-and-out "lovers of pleasure," the worshippers of the god of this world, the admirers of vanity, the indulgers of the flesh. They do not profess to be "religious;" but rather take pains to shew that they are not so, and boast that *they* are not hypocrites.

But pleasure won't do always; and this world will not last for ever; and vanity will soon pass away; and the flesh will cease to satisfy. And when all these things come to an end, what will be the condition of those whose gods they were? Cheated, befooled, despairing, their blossom shall go up as dust, and they themselves shall lie down in sorrow. Their idols are broken in pieces, and they find at last that they have trusted in a lie, and that now, when most they needed succour, they have none to succour them; they are left without a god, without light, without help, without even so much as the hope of a hope, or the faintest glimmer of a dawn, in that long night which, after their merry day of pleasure, has fallen so thickly over them.

Ah, yes; the fashion of this world passeth away; and they who have followed that fashion, and identified themselves with that world, will find too late that, in gaining the world, they have lost their souls; that, in filling up time with vanity, they have filled eternity with gloom; that, in snatching at the pleasures of earth, they have lost the joys of heaven, and the glories of the everlasting inheritance. Yes, life is brief, and time is swift; generations come and go; graves open and close each day; old and young vanish out of sight; riches depart, and honours fade; autumn follows summer, and winter soon wipes out every trace of leaf and blossom; nothing abides, or remains unchanging, but the blue sky and the everlasting hills! O man, dying man, dweller on a dying earth, living amid sickbeds and deathbeds, and funerals and graves, surrounded by fallen leaves and faded blossoms, the sport of broken hopes, and fruitless joys, and empty dreams, and fervent longings, and never-healing, never-ending heartaches;—O man, dying man, wilt thou still follow vanity and lies; still chase pleasure and gaiety; still sow the wind, and reap the whirlwind? After all that has been told thee of earth's weariness, and pleasure's emptiness; after all that thou thyself hast experienced of the poverty of all things here below; after having been so often disappointed, mocked, and made miserable by that world which thou worshippest; wilt thou still pursue the lusts of the flesh, the lust of the eye, and the pride of life?

> "Who has felt the desolation
> Of the earthquake's dreadful reign,
> And would seek the same foundation
> For his peaceful bower again?"

O follower of the world, consider thy ways and ponder thy prospects. Look behind thee, and see the utter emptiness of the past. Look before thee, and make sure of something better and more substantial. Look on the right hand and on the left, and see the weary crowds, seeking rest, and finding none. Look beneath thee, to that eternal fire which is preparing for all that forget God. Look above thee, and see that bright heaven, with all its unutterable gladness, which thou art so madly despising. Think, too, of thy brief time on earth, lent thee, in God's special love, to accomplish thy preparation for the eternal kingdom. And, when thou considerest these things, rouse thyself from thy dream of pleasure, and rest not till thou hast made good the entrance at the strait gate which leadeth unto life.

But these out-and-out lovers of pleasure are, after all, not the most mysterious class, nor the most difficult to deal with: for we know exactly what they are, and what they are seeking; for they do not disguise their worldliness, nor treat it as a thing to be cloaked or apologised for.

There are other classes of a much more uncertain and indefinite kind, whose object seems to be to get hold of both worlds. They want to infuse as much religion into their life, their doings, their conversation, as will make them be reckoned religious men; at least, save them from the imputation of being worldly men. But they want also as much of worldly comfort and pleasure as will gratify the tastes of a still unrenewed nature. Their life is a compromise; and their object is to balance between two adverse interests, to adjust the conflicting claims of this world and of the world to come; to please and to serve two masters, to gratify two tastes, to walk in two opposite ways at once, to secure the friendship of the world without losing the friendship of God.

The character as well as the life of these men is

undecided and feeble. They are not decided in their worldliness, and they are not decided in their religion. If they were compelled to choose between their two masters, the probability is that they would prefer the world; for their heart is not in their religion, and religion is not in their heart. Religion is irksome to them; it is a yoke, not a pleasant service. They don't want to part with it, for several good reasons; but they have no delight in it. Their consciences would not allow them to throw it off; but it occupies a very small part of their thoughts and affections. They are, in fact, worldly men varnished over with religion; that is all. They are made up of two parts, a dead and a living; the living part is the world, the dead is religion.

There are many of these in our day, when religion is fashionable. When religion is unfashionable, there are few; when it is scoffed at, still fewer; when it is persecuted, hardly any. But when it is in fashion, they are numerous. They may go under many names,—formalists, externalists, half-hearted Christians, half-and-half disciples; they may put on more or less of religion; they may indulge more or less in worldliness; still, the class I speak of is, in all circumstances, substantially the same. They have never broken with sin, nor crucified self, nor taken up the cross. Whatever their lives or their words may be, their *heart* is not right with God.

Some of these are men who have been brought

up in worldliness, and who have, as they grew up, added a little religion to their worldliness, to make it respectable. Others have been religiously brought up from childhood; they have been well taught in the things of Christ; they have had their religious impressions, some deeper, some shallower; and these have remained for a season, so as to mould their character and life considerably. But such feelings have never gone deep enough; they never led to the new birth; they issue in no lasting spiritual life, so that, instead of leading to the transformation of the whole man, inner and outer, they have merely religionized the outer being, leaving the inner man unmelted, unbroken, and unrenewed. The persons thus moved have gone a considerable way, but not the whole. They have been roused, but not converted. They have passed through a certain religious process, but not experienced the heavenly change, without which they cannot enter the kingdom. They have *felt* a good deal, *read* a good deal, *prayed* a good deal; they have not been without their earnestness and solemnity, perhaps their sighs and tears. They have been moved under sermons; roused by searching books; done many things and taken many steps which seemed to be religious. Yet, after all, there has been no broken-heartedness, no opening of the eye, no breaking off from sin, no surrender of the soul to God, no crucifixion of the old man, no resurrection to newness of life.

After a while, in such cases, a deep and settled

formalism has supervened. Earnestness has faded away, and left nothing but its dregs. The soul has become sapless and insensible. The edge of feeling, both upon heart and conscience, has become blunted. The routine of religion is still gone through, and the profession still kept up; but all within is dried up and withered; there is no enjoyment of spiritual things; the service of God is a burden; praise and prayer are irksome; sermons and sacraments are wearisome; and the poor professor moves on in his heartless career; outwardly still religious, but at heart as unspiritual and worldly as if he had never at any time been touched or awakened at all.

In such a case, with a religion in which he has no enjoyment, and with a profession which brings him no liberty and no comfort, it is not wonderful that he should have recourse to the world, to fill up the dreary void within. His carnal tastes never having been radically changed, but simply overborne for a season, by a rush of religious earnestness, he returns naturally to their gratification in their old objects, and his only restraints are the dread of a dark future, which he cannot shake off, and the desire to maintain a religious character, to stand well with religious men, and to maintain his place in the church. How many of this class there may be in our day, God only knows. We are warned that, in the last days, there will be multitudes having the form of godliness, but denying the power thereof.

These are the ambiguous disciples of our age,

who belong to Christ but in name. These are the stony-ground or thorny-ground hearers; men who have a place at our communion tables, who figure at religious committees, who make speeches on religious platforms, yet are, after all, "wells of water," "trees without root," stars without either heat or light.

The *religion* of such is but a half-and-half religion; without depth, or decision, or vigour, or self-sacrifice. It is but a picture or a statue, not a living man.

The *conversion* of such has been but a half-and-half conversion; it has not gone down to the lowest depths of the man's nature. I do not say it is a pretence or a hypocrisy; but still, I say it is an unreality. It has been a movement, a shaking, a change, but it has not been a being "begotten of God," a being "born from above."

The *discipleship* of such is but a half-and-half discipleship. It has some of the aspects of discipleship; but it is not a forsaking all, and taking up the cross and following Christ. We do not count genuine the discipleship of the man who is to-day with Christ, to-morrow with the world; to-day in the sanctuary, to-morrow in the ball-room. There must be suspicion attaching to all such inconsistent discipleship; it is both cold and hot; it is both worldly and unworldly; it is both Christian and un-Christian;—what can it be?—what can it mean?

In speaking of such inconsistencies, we must be

faithful and direct. We are not to prophesy smooth things, and hint at certain evils, as if they were but minor imperfections, the quiet removal of which would set all to rights. No; we must strike deeper than this. We must lay the axe to the root of the tree, and say at once, that such inconsistencies betray the utter unsoundness of the man's whole religious profession. It is not that there are some flaws in his religious life; it is that his religion itself is *hollow*,—without foundation, without root or soil. I will not say it is all a *lie*; for there is sometimes a certain amount of good intention in it; but it is all a mistake,—a mighty and terrible mistake; a mistake which, if not rectified at once, must issue in the fearful darkness and woeful disappointment of an undone eternity!

Such a man's whole religious life is one grand misconception; and every step he takes in it is a blunder, and a stumble, and a snare. Let such a man know that, in his present half-worldly, half-religious condition, he has no real religion at all. It is a fiction, a delusion. It will stand no test of law or gospel, of conscience or of discipline, of time or of eternity. It will go to pieces with the first touch. It is all hollow, and must be begun again, from the very first stone of the foundation.

If, then, O worldly formalist, thou wouldst make sure thy hope, and obtain a discipleship that will stand all tests, begin this day at the beginning. Count all the past but loss. Fling away thy vain hopes and self-righteous confidences. Give up thy fond idea of securing both earth and heaven. Go straight to Calvary; there be thou crucified to the world, and the world to thee, by the cross of Christ. Go straight to the grave of Christ; there bring all thy sins, thy worldliness, thy half-heartedness, and all pertaining to thy old self, that being made partaker of Christ's death and burial, thou mayest be sharer of his resurrection too. Go at once to Him who died and rose again, and drink into his love. One draught, nay, one drop of that love will for ever quench your love of sin, and be the death of that worldliness which threatens to be your eternal ruin. The love of Christ will not only make you an out and out Christian, a thorough-going, decided man in all the things of God, but it will pour in a peace which you have never known, which you cannot know, save in simple faith in the heavenly Peacemaker, and in entire surrender of soul to him who gave himself for us, that he might deliver us from a present evil world, according to the will of God our Father.

SERMON XXXIII.

THE GOD OF GRACE.

"That in the ages to come he might shew the exceeding riches of his grace, in his kindness toward us through Christ Jesus."—Eph. ii. 7.

The history of God's "grace," or free love, goes back into eternity. Our earth's six thousand years mark neither its beginning nor its end. It dates immeasurably backward among the ages that are past, and it stretches immeasurably forward into "the ages to come." It is like Him in whose bosom it dwells, unbeginning and unending; so that, as he is from everlasting to everlasting "God," so is he from everlasting to everlasting the "God of all grace."

This grace must give vent to itself and be manifested, for it is the very law of the divine nature,—not merely *to be*, but to *manifest itself*. This is the law of all being,—to bring forth that which it contains; in other words, to manifest *itself;* as in the case of the seed sown in the ground; a law which, in the creature, is the finite copy or image of that which has its seat and origin in the infinite Creator himself. The sun cannot but shine; the fountain cannot but pour forth its waters; the seed cannot but shoot up and bear fruit after its kind; so, **divine goodness cannot but spread itself out, divine holiness cannot but come forth, divine wisdom cannot but give utterance to itself, and divine grace cannot but unfold its riches.**

But, for this unfolding of grace, this manifestation of what is gracious in the divine character, there must be a *purpose;* for grace is not to manifest itself at random, or without due regard being had to time, and place, and objects, and circumstances, and final issues. It is this " purpose of grace," as the apostle calls it, that is needed for giving shape and direction to the divine self-manifestation. It is this purpose of grace that adjusts the awful question,—a question which no finite being can ever solve or ought to entertain,—of how far a certain amount of permitted evil may so be overruled for far greater good as to warrant that evil being allowed to enter. It is this purpose of grace that defines the objects towards whom this grace is to direct itself; the circumstances in which it is to find them; the time or times at which, and during which, it is to reveal itself; the channel through which it can righteously flow; the amount of obstacles which it can righteously overcome; the nature, as well as the extent and duration, of the results which it is to accomplish. All these, as so many preliminaries, God's purpose of grace must define; leaving nothing to chance, trusting nothing to the caprice of creature-will or the uncertainties of creature-mutability; embracing all conceivable contingencies, and regulating the exact amount of evil that righteousness can tolerate, and that grace can undertake to deal with.

The details of this purpose are to be found in the history of our race. That story, which in so many of its parts seems to us tangled and unmeaning, is no random assemblage of events, but, in all its processes, as well as all its issues, is the deliberate unrolling, fold after fold, of that purpose of grace, which, transmuting the indefinite into the definite, the contingent into the certain, and anticipating the permitted entrance of evil, proposed to deal with this evil, not by swift expulsion or extinction, not by immediate and unrepealable judgment on the transgressors, but in a way more transcendently glorious, and more fitted to draw forth the hitherto unknown wonders of Jehovah's character, and the unimaginable resources of his wisdom and grace.

This purpose selected the channel through which this divine manifestation was to come, and in selecting it settled, at once and for ever, the vain question that has been so often raised, Could there not have been another channel equally efficacious? There could not. The divine selection of *one* is the setting aside of all the rest as inadequate to accomplish the design. This purpose, then, gave definite shape to the future, arranging its endless movements, as certainly as the motions of each starry orb in the firmament are adjusted, by the hand of the Creator. It regulated the *time* when grace was first to come forth, the *place* where it was first to be proclaimed, and the *race* in reference to whom the manifestation was to be made. It was not to shew itself at the first irruption of sin. In that case, righteousness was alone to triumph, and the transgressors consigned to everlasting chains. But at the second irruption, after it had been proved that vengeance executed on the criminal could not deter others, and that thus righteousness *alone* was insufficient to deal effectually with sin, *grace* was to be introduced, to deal with it in a way such as would render any future outburst of it for ever impossible. Immediately on man's fall, grace was to come in, and undertake the mighty work; a work in which righteousness had been baffled. On the very spot where sin had burst in upon the new-made world, grace was to plant its standard, and at the very commencement of the conflict proclaim its certain victory. It was to meet sin face to face, choosing for its battle-field the very territory where sin had displayed itself. It was to begin its actings on the soil where the blight had fallen and the ruin been wrought. Confronting both the tempter and the tempted, interposing between the spoiler and the victim, bidding the law stand by and see itself vindicated to the full, though in a new way; calling on righteousness to forego its prey, under the promise of a far nobler and more satisfying victim, it proclaimed "glory to God in the highest" out of that event which seemed most to dishonour his name, "peace on earth" out of that disaster which seemed to have driven peace out of the world, "good-will to man" out of that sin which threatened to make God man's enemy for ever. Hard by the forbidden tree of Eden, God opened the well-spring of grace, and, out of the fountain there opened, have flowed to us all the manifold streams of grace which have, since that, watered our parched and cursed soil.

This grace is something wholly *new*, and, as such, difficult for man to apprehend. The very idea of grace is strange, and, we may say, unnatural to man. He understands the meaning of righteousness, but not of grace, save in the sense of mere indifference to sin. His thoughts are not God's thoughts; and hence the difficulty of making the sinner comprehend what grace really is, or, having comprehended it, to *act* upon it. To know what grace is, and to act upon it,—to know what grace is, and to go to God, simply as one who has heard that he is gracious,—this is salvation,—this is eternal life! Yet thus to teach the sinner what grace means is strangely difficult; and to persuade him to trust his soul for eternity to that God who has thus made known his grace, is a thing so impossible, that as nothing but the infinite skill of the divine Spirit is sufficient to overcome man's unteachableness in this thing, so nothing save the almightiness of the same Spirit is able to conquer his determination not to allow himself to be dealt with in any such way by God. To the grace which consists in indifference to sin he offers no objections; the grace that would allow him to work his own way back to God, and accept his doings at what he conceives them to be worth, he comprehends: to the grace that would make him partner in the work of salvation he would submit; but to the grace which sets out with the total condemnation both of himself and his sin, which allows him no standing before God save that of the sentenced criminal, and no plea save that of worthlessness, which treats himself as one thoroughly lost, and his case as absolutely desperate, and which, while doing all this, presents him with a complete, an immediate, an eternal salvation, —without preparation or prerequisite, as the purchase of the great redemption on the cross, and the gift of God's free and boundless love,—to this grace he has insuperable objections, and would perish rather than take life upon such terms, nay, would turn round upon God and accuse him of unfairness in such treatment of himself, and of disregard to the interests of morality and virtue, in disallowing what he calls the honourable competition for eternal life.

From the hour that God proclaimed this grace upon the earth, he gave man to understand that there was grace enough to meet his case as a sinner. The first promise embodies this as its essence; and upon the strength of this simple assurance, sinners in those early days drew nigh to God, and saints walked with him in holy companionship. They knew but little then; for God's purpose of grace dawned slowly on the world; but what they knew gave rest to their souls, for they could say this much at least, "There is enough of grace in God to meet my case." Thus they tasted that the Lord was gracious, and went upon their way rejoicing, to keep the commandments of their God.

But as the world went on, sin went on; and it might be doubted whether this grace of God that was sufficient at first was sufficient still, or whether man's sin might not exhaust it, or whether it could continue to widen its circle, and embrace yet larger and larger measures of unworthiness. Grant that the rays of the sun can pierce a certain amount of darkness, is there light enough to pierce all darkness whatsoever, though it were to deepen and thicken beyond measure? Grant that the light has proved itself sufficient to absorb the darkness of the world's first sad night, is it adequate to swallow up the darkness of ten thousand midnights gloomier and more sorrowful than these? Will grace last? Will it expand itself to take in greater guilt? Will not God be wearied with receiving so many sinners, and forgiving so many sins? All these questions required to be answered, and God proceeded to answer them age after age, by shewing that "where sin abounded, grace did much more abound."

He not merely allowed sin to enter, but to spread; not only to spread, but to increase in heinousness; not only to increase in heinousness, but to vary itself, and take every conceivable shape that man's spirit could undergo,—all in order to demonstrate that his resources of grace were adequate to meet it all. Sin might widen its circle age after age, but grace widened its circle and still went far beyond man's transgression. Age after age sin ascended a higher pinnacle of rebellious ungodliness; but grace ascended along with it, and took its station far above it, like a bright canopy of heavenly azure. Age after age descended to lower and lower depths of hateful pollution; grace went down along with it, and when the soul found itself at the very bottom of the horrible pit, and expected to meet nothing there but hell itself, it found the hand of grace still beneath it, as mighty to save, as willing to bless as ever. Just as sin abounded, so grace did much more abound.

Such has been the history of our world, and such the way in which God's purpose of grace has unfolded itself, and widened its circle just as sin continued to widen,—so that every part of it has been a story of abounding sin, and far more abounding grace. We know that Adam's case was such, and such has been the case of each saved one to this hour. What was Abraham's history but one of abounding sin and superabounding grace? What was Rahab's, but a history of abounding sin and superabounding grace? What was David's, but a history of abounding sin and superabounding grace? What was Manasseh's, but a history of abounding sin and superabounding grace? What was the history of Saul of Tarsus, but one of abounding sin and superabounding grace, as he himself declares, "The grace of our Lord was exceeding abundant towards me with faith and love, which is in Christ Jesus?" What has all Israel's history been, but the history of abounding sin and superabounding grace? Nay, what is all this world's long history, protracted to its utmost length by God's marvellous long-suffering, not willing that any should perish, but that all should come to repentance;—what is it but a history of abounding sin and superabounding grace? O the infinite dimensions of this immeasurable grace! It has a breadth and length, a depth and height, that pass all knowledge. And it is this wondrous grace, in all its exceeding riches, that God is presenting to each sinner here, that they may take it and live for ever. There was enough for Rahab, and Manasseh, and Saul; be assured that there is enough for you.

SERMON XXXIV.

THE GOD OF GRACE.

"That in the ages to come he might shew the exceeding riches of his grace, in his kindness toward us through Christ Jesus."—EPH. ii. 7.

BUT the *past* has not exhausted this grace; the future is as much connected with it as is the past. It is in "the ages to come" that he is "to shew the exceeding riches of his grace." The Lord's first coming displayed much of these exceeding riches, his second coming is to bring them to light in yet larger fulness. From the foot of the cross the fountain of free love poured itself plenteously forth; but from the foot of the throne this same fountain is again to break out and send abroad its unexhausted abundance. Of the many ways in which grace shall then get vent to itself, I do not mean here to speak; yet this much may be said, that in a thousand forms and ways shall grace yet unfold itself,—in bringing back the captivity of Zion, in converting the world, in binding the strong man, in removing the curse, in making all things new, so that God's last demonstration of grace shall be the strongest and the fullest,—proving that where sin has abounded grace has much more abounded.

Of these, however, I do not speak further, as the Apostle's words in the passage before us speak more especially of the Church, and of what grace is yet to do for her in the ages to come. To this same thing and time refer the words of the apostle Peter, when he speaks of "the grace that is to be brought unto us at the revelation of Jesus Christ" (1 Pet. i. 13). Both passages point us forward to the day of Christ's appearing, as the day in which new treasures of grace shall be unlocked to us, and God's free love have a new manifestation which shall shew that the past has not exhausted it; nay, that the past has merely been the earnest of the wonders yet to come. It is grace that strives with the sinner, grace that renews him, grace that leads him to the cross, grace that forgives him, grace that heals all his diseases, grace that bears with him after forgiveness, grace that guides him along, grace that fights for him, grace that comforts him, grace that trains him for the kingdom and makes all things work together for his good, grace that keeps his soul in peace amid the tumults of a stormy world, grace that maintains his unbroken fellowship with the Lord, grace that lays him down quietly to sleep in Jesus, with the blessed hope of soon rising again and putting on immortality;—it is grace that does all these marvels for him and in him. In experiencing these things, he feels oftentimes as if grace had gone to its utmost stretch, as if it were not possible nor conceivable that grace could do more for him than it has done.

Its past dealings with him have been so marvellous, that it seems ingratitude as well as presumption to anticipate more. Yet that which he is afraid even to imagine, is that which God has in store for him. Grace, nay, riches of grace, nay, exceeding riches of grace, are yet to be unfolded to him in the ages to come. Eye hath not seen them, ear hath not heard them, the heart has not conceived them; yet they are not the less surely provided for him.

There is, of course, a difference in the ages to come. There are no more sins to be forgiven, and no more perversity and unbelief to be borne with; but still the man is the same man that was once in the miry clay, that was once a sinner and an alien, and accordingly he can only be dealt with, even hereafter, by *grace*. It was only grace that could meet his case here in his sins; and it is only grace that can deal with him hereafter, even when made perfect. All that shall be done for him in the ages to come, shall be the result of grace. Here it is grace seen in justifying; hereafter it is grace seen in glorifying the justified. The amount of grace given out here is just the amount needed for the forgiveness of his sins, and the new-moulding of his nature, and the helping of his infirmities; but the amount of grace to flow forth in the ages to come, is to be measured by the excellency of the inheritance which is then to be bestowed. That which man calls " exceeding riches of grace " is just that extent of grace which he needs here, when fighting his way to the kingdom, for his finite soul can hardly conceive of anything larger; but that which God calls the " exceeding riches of grace" is that which is measured by "the exceeding and eternal weight of glory."

We often feel as if grace had done its utmost when it has carried us safely through the desert, and set us down at the gate of the kingdom. We feel as if, when grace has landed us there, it has done all for us that we are to expect. But God's thoughts are not our thoughts. He does exceeding abundantly above all we ask or think. It is just when we reach the threshold of the prepared city, that grace meets us in new and more abundant measures, presenting us with the recompence of the reward. The love that shall meet us then to bid us welcome to the many mansions, shall be love beyond what we were here able to comprehend; for then shall we fully realise, as if for the first time, the meaning of these words, "The love of God which is in Christ Jesus our Lord;" and then shall we have that prayer of Christ fulfilled in us, "That the love wherewith thou hast loved me may be in them, and I in them." It is grace that bestows the inheritance; and the greatness of that inheritance will be the measure of the grace. It is grace that crowns and enthrones us; and the crown and throne, which shall then be ours, will be the measure of the grace. It is grace that provides for us the New Jerusalem, with its bright beauty and divine magnificence; and that celestial city will be the measure of the grace. It is grace that spreads for us the Lamb's marriage-supper, and clothes us with the bridal-dress; and that marriage-supper, that bridal-dress, will be the measure of the grace. It was grace that on earth said to us, "Come unto Me, and I will give you rest;" and it will be grace, in all its exceeding riches, that will hereafter say to us, "Come, ye blessed of my Father, inherit the kingdom prepared for you from the foundation of the world."

No doubt, in one sense, we might say that God's Son, his unspeakable gift, is the measure, even as he is the pledge of the grace; and, speaking generally, we might say, the grace must be boundless, seeing the gift is infinite, so that we do not need to wait for the ages to come to disclose the riches of the grace. But let us remember that it is one thing to know that a friend's bountifulness is large, and another thing to know in what gifts that large bountifulness will display itself. God's gift of his own Son assures us that there is nothing too costly for him to bestow on us; so that, applying this measurement generally, we may say, "He that spared not his own Son, how shall he not, with him, freely give us all things?" But not until these "all things" are made ours in the ages to come, can we realise all the grace that the "unspeakable gift" includes and implies. Faith uses this as the great standard of measurement when calculating the extent of its anticipated possessions; hope assures itself by means of it that it shall not be put to shame. But all this is only seeing things "in a glass darkly." Possessing Christ, we feel assured that we can possess nothing of greater value; but still the things which we receive in him and through him, will most marvellously contribute to make us understand the grace which is given us in him. In giving us Christ, the Father traces round us, as it were, an illimitable circle; but then our exact appreciation of its wide dimensions depends much upon its contents, upon the nature of the things which it comprehends. To say that our treasure-house is infinite, is one thing, and to bring forth its treasures and spread them out before us, is another. It is one thing to tell us that there is over our heads a vast and all-including firmament, bright with the glory and the love of God; and it is another to withdraw the clouds that veil it, and to present us with a whole sky of stars. And just as, in receiving our daily forgivenesses at his hand, God made us to understand the riches of his grace, while here, in a way such as we never could by any mere statement of their greatness; so, in conferring on us the incorruptible inheritance hereafter, he will give us conceptions of his unutterable grace such as, till then, we could not realise. The truth is, though it may seem almost a contradiction, that while we measure the greatness of the coming glories by the unspeakable gift, we are also to measure the greatness of the unspeakable gift by the glories which shall then be revealed. We stand at the cross just now, and, realising the love of which that cross gives us the happy pledge, we look forward into the ages to come and say, What will not God give? so hereafter, when these ages shall have begun, we shall turn our eye backward to the cross, and, encircled with the glory of the kingdom that shall then be ours, we shall exclaim, "Oh, what hath God given us in giving us his Son!"

This glance into "the ages to come," with all their "exceeding riches of grace," is plentiful in lessons, as practical as they are precious. It opens out so largely, in all its breadth and length, in all its depth and height, the infinitely gracious character of "the God of all grace," that we cannot give it admission for a moment without feeling what a new intensity of light it casts upon "the gospel of the grace of God."

Pointing to these "ages to come," we can reason with the man of *this* age, the man who is walking "according to the course of this age," and who, if Christ were coming now to introduce the age to come, would be found all unready; we can reason with him and say, Behold these riches of grace! are they not enough to startle even *your* heedlessness into solemnity, and to convince you that there is a better portion, than this poor world, for that empty soul of yours? Is that boundless store of love, which the eternal ages are to unfold, not more satisfying, more gladdening to the spirit than this present evil world? And does it not assure you, though you be the guiltiest and most alienated that earth contains, that there is grace enough in God to receive you, save you, pardon you, bless you, and make *you*, even *you*, an heir of God and joint-heir with Jesus Christ.

Again, pointing to these ages to come, we can reason with the troubled spirit, weary of its burdens, yet doubting whether its wounds can be healed or its sins forgiven :—These "ages to come," my friend, with all their exceeding riches of grace, do they not speak peace to your sorrowful spirit ? Do they not tell you of grace so free and ample that it is not within the bounds of possibility that your sins can exceed it ? You do not need to vex yourself with the thought, "But what are these riches of grace, so long as I am not assured of my portion in that kingdom ?" This is not the point with which you have more immediately to do. The question on which the commencement of your peace depends is not, "What is your ascertained participation in that promised heritage ?" but, What is the character of the God with whom you have to do, and what is the light which these future ages cast upon his *character* as the God of all grace ? His past dealings with sinners reveal his graciousness, and is not that enough to make you feel that there is a welcome for you ? The cross of his Son ; where the great pacification was accomplished, in virtue of which his grace has got righteous vent to itself; that cross makes known his graciousness, and is it not sufficient to pacify your conscience and win your reluctant confidence ? But, as if all that were still inadequate, he gives you a prophetic glance into the fountainhead of his immeasurable grace, and disclosing to you the gracious bosom out of which all grace has come, he shews you such a vastness of love, and such an infinite magnitude of resources ready to be poured forth at the bidding of that love, that it seems as if he would not allow the very shadow of an excuse to remain for one distrustful imagination, one suspicious thought. This God of all grace, the God of these coming ages, is he not just such a God as even *you* may go to, with the whole outcry of your complaints, the whole burden of your wants and sins? Whether it be your sense of sin or your want of a sense of sin that is saddening you; whether it be a new and sudden rising of doubts within you, or a long-protracted course of unbelief, and insensibility, and darkness; whatever it be, know this, that there is grace enough in this God of all grace even for such a case as yours. And if you would but be persuaded to give yourselves at once to the blessed impression which the simple announcement of these tidings of grace is fitted to make, you would know, ere you were aware, the divine peace that calms every tumult within; and, tasting that the Lord is gracious, you would go upon your way rejoicing, the Lord directing your heart into the love of God and into the patient waiting for Christ.

Lastly, pointing to these ages to come, we can reason with the struggling saint and say, Look at these exceeding riches of grace which are to be unfolded at the revelation of Jesus Christ, and then ask yourself, Is there any room for that faintness and oppressive despondency which sometimes weighs you down? Is there room for care, and anxiety, and dread, and sadness? Is there room for anything save joy in the Lord, and exultation in the hope of his appearing? It was thus that our Lord reasoned with his disciples, "Fear not, little flock; for it is your Father's good pleasure to give you the kingdom;" the meaning of which passage is not, as some take it, "Be not afraid, for you shall soon have a kingdom that will make up for all poverty and privation here;" but, "Fear not, neither despond respecting your present lot; he who is about to give you a kingdom will assuredly supply all your need according to his riches in glory; the kingdom which you have in prospect is a pledge that he will deny you nothing here." So we say, He that has made you heirs of his kingdom, will *he* withhold anything from you? Nay, what will he not fully give, whether pertaining to the soul or the body? Is his grace large enough to give you a kingdom, and yet not large enough to provide for you on the way to it? Are not these exceeding riches of grace, which are to be unrolled in the ages to come, the pledge of all present grace which your case requires? That which God purposes to do hereafter tells you how much he is willing to do just now. What sin is he not willing to forgive? What want is he not willing to supply? What infirmity is he not willing to help? What enemy is he not willing to bruise under your feet? What evil in you is he not willing to uproot? What fruits of his Spirit will he not ripen in you? What fear is he not willing to remove? What burden is he not willing to bear? What desire of your heart is he not willing to grant? What trial is he not willing to alleviate? What wound is he not willing to heal? What sorrow is he not willing to turn into joy? Ah, these exceeding riches of grace in the ages to come,—these are the Church's pledge for all needed blessings now! If we may expect these hereafter, what may we not count upon now? He that has prepared for us a crown of righteousness, will he not uphold our goings here? He that has built for us the New Jerusalem with all its glory, will he not give us a place on earth whereon to lay our head? He that has provided the white raiment of the bridal feast, will he not give us clothing for our bodies in the days of our pilgrimage? He that is to spread for us the table with the hidden manna and the fruit of the tree of life, will he not give us bread to eat, while passing onwards to the kingdom? He that is ere long to give us the bright and morning star, will he not shed light upon the darkness of our dreary path, till the day break and the shadows flee away?

SERMON XXXV.

THE SINCERITY OF THE DIVINE COMPASSION.

"It repented the Lord that he had made man on the earth, and it grieved him at his heart."—GEN. vi. 6.

THE manner in which God here acknowledges man as his handiwork is specially to be noted. The words are, "It repented the Lord that he had made man upon earth." It is not said generally, "that man had been made;" but definitely, that "he *had made* man." He had spoken of man in his primeval goodness, as coming from his hand; so now he does not fail to remind us that it is this same man, this very race, that has now become so worthless and hateful.

He might have drawn a veil over this point, so as to prevent our being so vividly reminded that man was truly his own workmanship. But he does not. Nay, he brings the sad fact before us,—a fact that seems to reflect upon his own skill and power. He does not disavow creation. He does not disown man. He does not speak or act as one ashamed to be known as the Maker of one so miserably apostate, so incurably depraved. Even when making known man's extremity of guilt, he openly owns him as his creature. He does not keep silence on the matter, as one desirous that it should be forgotten or unnoticed. He brings it directly forward, as if to call attention to the fact.

When man fails in some great or favourite project,—as when an architect plans and builds a palace, which, by reason of some essential defect, almost immediately tumbles down,—he is anxious that its failure should not be proclaimed, and that the work thus ruined should never be known as his. He cannot bear the reproach which is sure to fall upon him; he shrinks from the responsibility which has been incurred; he cannot afford to lose the reputation he may have gained.

But with God there are no such feelings; no such desire of concealment; no desire to shake off the responsibility devolving on him as Creator. He can afford to bear man's petty censure; he can afford to have it said, "Behold the work of thy hands." He is not concerned to keep back anything from his creatures, as if their blame or praise could affect him. Hence it is that we discern something altogether unlike man, something truly God-like, in that simple form of expression here, "It repented the Lord that *he had made* man upon the earth."

Marvellous words indeed; words such as no *man* could have ventured to use respecting God; words too strong and bold for any one to have employed but God himself! Let us look calmly into them, for they are too full of solemn meaning to be lightly passed over, or generalised into a vague expression of God's hatred of sin, or explained away into a mere figure used by God after the manner of men.

In endeavouring to discover what the words *do* mean, let us first inquire what they do *not* mean.

1. *They do not mean that God's purpose had been frustrated.* That purpose shall stand, for it is the perfect combination of infinite wisdom and power. It is not within the limits of possibility that the creature should thwart the purpose of the Creator. It cannot fail. It must be carried out, though at times its movements may seem checked, or even become apparently retrogressive. To suppose aught else, would be to say that the will of the creature was stronger than the will of the Creator; and that the folly of the creature had baffled the wisdom of the Creator.

2. *They do not mean that an unexpected crisis had arisen.* With man it may be so. A crisis may come to him unexpectedly, so as entirely to disconcert himself and defeat his schemes. With God there can be nothing unexpected, nothing sudden, nothing unforeseen or unprovided for. The whole future, with its endless turns and intricacies, lies before him, as open and as clear as the past. No evil, however great, shoots up unpermitted or unlooked for. Neither Satan's wiles nor man's apostasy; neither the rejection of Noah's warnings, nor the spread of sin, nor the ruin of the race, were unexpected evils.

3. *They do not mean that God is subject to like passions and changes as we are.* He does not vary

as we vary, nor repent as we repent. Instability is the property of the creature, not of the Creator. Frailty is for man, not for God. There is no vacillation, no fluctuation in him. That he does *feel*, we know. If he did not, he would not be God. But his feeling is not weakness. That he alters his procedure we know, but not as we alter ours. There is no caprice in his emotion or his acting. All is the serenity of highest wisdom, which cannot be taken by surprise, nor blinded by anger, nor rendered unavailing by fickleness, or facility, or arbitrary will.

4. *They do not mean that He has ceased to care for his creatures.* Wrath, indeed, has gone out against the transgressor; the righteous wrath of the righteous, though loving, God; and "the soul that sinneth it shall die." Yet, neither man himself, nor his habitation, the earth, has been overlooked by God, far less hated and spurned. The words intimate neither the coldness nor the dislike of the Creator toward the creature. It is something very widely different which they convey; a sadder, tenderer feeling; a feeling in which, not indifference, but profound compassion, is the prevailing element. They do not intimate the quenching of his love, nor even imply coldness or distance. They are not the utterance of resentment, as if pity had now been extinguished, and the fondness of affection been supplanted by the fierceness of revenge.

But still, it may be asked, How are the words to be reconciled with the character of God as the all-knowing Jehovah, seeing the end from the beginning, and ordering everything from eternity, according to the counsel of his will? To clear up this, let me remark—

1. That God is represented to us here, as looking at events or facts, simply *as they are*, without reference to the past or future at all. He isolates or separates them from all connection with his own purpose; and looking at them simply as they stand alone, he declares what he thinks and feels. In so far as they stood connected with his own vast purpose, which age after age was evolving, he did not repent, or change his mind, or wish them undone; but, in so far as they were exhibitions of human wickedness or wretchedness, he did grieve, and he did repent. For let us remember that there must ever be two kinds of feelings in such matters,—one called up by looking at each event by itself, and another by looking at it as part of a mighty plan, which, in its origination and developments, is from eternity to eternity.

2. That God's purposes do not alter God's estimate of events, or his feelings respecting individuals and their conduct. It was by the "determinate counsel and foreknowledge of God" that Christ was betrayed and slain, yet that did not affect God's estimate of the crime committed by them that slew him. God's allowing man to fall did not make God the approver of his sin; it did not make him the less to hate and to grieve over the sin whose permission had been foreseen and

decreed. Each action or event is a link in God's mighty purpose, yet it must be weighed *separately* in the balances, and judged according to the perfect standard of right and wrong.

3. That God is looking at the scene just as a man would look at it, and expressing himself just as a man would have done, in such circumstances. He takes the place of a *finite* being; hears with *finite* ears, looks with *finite* eyes, and utters the sentiments of a *finite* heart. He sees all the present misery and ruin which the scene presents, and they affect him according to their nature; and as they affect him, so does he speak, in the words of man. For the feelings implanted in man must, to some extent, be the same as those existing in the bosom of God. Man was made in God's image in respect of his *feelings* as truly as in respect of his *understanding*; the human heart is the counterpart of the divine, just as Israel's earthly tabernacle was the copy of that which is above. Hence it is that God so often uses the language of human feeling. It is not merely that God is condescending to man (though this is true), but it is also because the heart of man, being fashioned after that of God, the language that gives utterance to the feelings of the former, will, in a greater or less degree, according to circumstances, give utterance to the feelings of the latter. God's love, hatred, wrath, pity, joy, grief, are all *real;* and they are, *in kind*, the same as man's, only there is no sin in them; so that we may say, that all the feelings of man that

are *holy*, or that can be called forth *without* sin, do exist in God.

But now let us look at the words of our text,— "repenting,"—"grieving at the heart."

1. *Repent.*—The word frequently occurs in the same connection as in our text; Ex. xxxii. 14, "The Lord *repented* of the evil which he thought to do unto his people" (see also 1 Sam. xv. 11, 35 ; Jer. xxvi. 13, 19). In these and other like passages, it denotes that change of mind which is produced towards an object by an alteration of circumstances. Nor is this inconsistent with unchangeableness in God. It is true that he is without variableness or shadow of turning ; there is no caprice or vacillation in him. But his unchangeableness is not a mere arbitrary principle,—a thing which makes him feel the same towards a person, however he may change from good to evil, or from bad to worse. It does not mean that his proceedings are unchangeable, though it does mean that his purposes are so ; nay, the very change of his *proceedings* may be the result and manifestation of the unchangeableness of his *purposes*. When Adam fell, God changed his mind towards him from favour to displeasure ; yet that was just the result of his unchangeableness. When a sinner repents, God changes his mind toward him ; yet, this is not changeableness ; nay, it is the carrying out of his unchangeableness. His "changing," in such cases, is the display of his holiness and wisdom. Were he not to change, it would be mere arbitrariness,

—it would not be wisdom, but foolishness. His "repentance" is not only the true and necessary expression of holy feeling, but it is part of his unchangeable purpose.

2. *Grieve.*—The word used in reference to *man*, is found in such places as the following: 2 Sam. xix. 2, " The king was *grieved* for his Son ;" and, in reference to God, in such as the following: Ps. lxxviii. 40, " How oft did they provoke him in the wilderness, and *grieve* him in the desert !" and Isa. lxiii. 10, " They rebelled and *vexed*" (Heb. *grieved*) " his Holy Spirit." In these passages the word denotes simply and truly what we call " grief ;" and then, in the passage before us, as if to deepen the intensity of the expression, and to shew how thoroughly *real* was the feeling indicated, it is added, " at his heart." The grief spoken of is as true as it is profound. It is not the grief of words. It is not the grief of fancy or sentiment. It is true sorrow of heart. How this can be, in the bosom of the blessed One, it is not easy to shew. How he can remain unruffled and unbroken, in his infinite tranquillity of being, while " grieved at heart" because of his rebellious creatures, is difficult to explain. How his heaven can abide as bright as ever, without a shade over its dwellings, or sackcloth upon its dwellers, while he is mourning over the ruin of a world and the wretchedness of a guilty child, we cannot say. We take the words as we find them,—especially as it is but one out of the many similar utterances of which Scrip-

ture is full,—utterances all confirmed and reiterated by the Son of God, when he wept over the doomed and apostate Jerusalem.

Yet, after all, what greater difficulty should we find in understanding this sorrowful commiseration for the lost, than in comprehending the joy with which all heaven is made to resound because of even *one* sinner saved ? Shall heaven ring with gladness when one soul is plucked from the devouring fire; and must it be passive when millions plunge into the everlasting burnings ? Is salvation a thing so very blessed as to occasion new joy in the bosom of God, and be the occasion of a new song ; and is damnation such a trifle as to be beheld unmoved ? Is the saved soul's deliverance, and recovery of sonship, so glorious, as to draw forth the utterance of the divine complacency " in the presence of the angels ;" and shall the sinner's ruin, the lost soul's funeral, call forth no feeling at all ? Would this be true perfection ? Passivity and insensibility were not the perfection of Him who wept over doomed Jerusalem ; can they be the perfection of Godhead ?

SERMON XXXVI.

THE SINCERITY OF THE DIVINE COMPASSION.

"It repented the Lord that he had made man on the earth, and it grieved him at his heart.—GEN. vi. 6.

WE come now to ask, why did the Lord thus grieve at his heart?

1. He grieved to see the change which sin had made in the work of his hands. Once it was "very good," and in this he had rejoiced. Now, how altered! So altered that it could hardly be recognised as the same. Creation was a wreck. The world lay in ruins. Man's glory had departed. The fair image of his Maker was gone! How could the Creator behold so sad a change, and not be "grieved at his heart!" How could he look upon the sin, the ruin, the darkness, the defilement, and not *feel?* God cannot be indifferent to the desolation which sin produces, even when righteousness constrains him not to interfere for its prevention, but only for its punishment. Yes, he feels it, he mourns over it, all the more, because mercy has reached its utmost limit, and righteousness demands the forthputting of his almightiness to avenge, and not to save. It may seem strange that a being of infinite power should

grieve over that which the exercise of almightiness could have prevented. But let us not forget that there is *righteousness* as well as *almightiness* in God, and that, while his power can be limited or restrained by nothing out of himself, it is and must be limited by his other perfections, so that his almightiness cannot accomplish anything that is unrighteous. When, therefore, his power has reached its righteous limits, and can no longer be put forth towards the sinner, then it is that he is grieved at heart. He is grieved that sin has got to such a height that the works of his own hands must be destroyed, that they must be put away from his sight as an unclean thing.

2. He grieved at the dishonour thus brought upon himself. It was, indeed, but a temporary dishonour; it was one which he would soon repair; but still, it was an obscuration of his own fair character; it was a clouding of his glory; it was an eclipse, however transient. It was like a wound inflicted by a most unlooked for hand, which, however quickly healed, could not but be sorely felt. How could he but be grieved at heart at being thus dishonoured by those whom he had made to glorify him,—dishonoured by a favourite child,—dishonoured by those who, he might well expect, would have been specially sensitive on such a point, peculiarly tender and jealous of his honour.

3. He grieved at man's misery. Man had not been made for misery. Happiness, like a rich

jewel, had been entrusted to him. He had flung it away, as worthless and undesirable. Not only had he taken no pains to retain the treasure, but he had laboured to alienate it. He had offered it for sale to every passer by; nay, he had cast it from him as vile. He had plunged himself into misery; he had refused to be happy; he had not only said to evil, "Evil, be thou my good;" but he had said to sorrow, "Sorrow, be thou my joy." This wretchedness filled his soul, and overshadowed this once blessed earth. How, then, could God but grieve? He is the infinitely *blessed* God; he knows what blessedness is, and what the want of it must be. Could he, then, fail to be grieved at his heart? He grieves over the sinner's wretchedness, as Jesus wept over Jerusalem. These fears and that grief are the same. "How often would I have gathered thee!" "If thou hadst known." "O that thou hadst hearkened to my commandments!" "Ye will not come to me that ye might have life." Such are some of the utterances of this divine grief. And then he saw the *eternity* of man's wretchedness. It was no *lifetime's* sorrow that lay before man. It was an *eternal* woe. The infinite eye of Jehovah looked through that whole eternity, realised its bitterness and anguish,—saw the torment, the darkness, the worm, the fire, the second death; and seeing these, he was grieved at his heart. For he has no pleasure in man's sorrow, either the sorrow of an hour, or the sorrow of a whole eternity. It is no joy to him that man should be wretched. Nay, it grieves him at his heart. Fury is not in him. Vengeance is his strange work. His joy is to bless, not to curse; to save, not to destroy. He takes oath before the universe that he has no pleasure in the death of the wicked, but rather that they should turn and live.

4. He grieved that now he must be the inflictor of man's misery. No alternative remains. There had, for long years, been an alternative. He could be gracious; he could be long-suffering; he could pardon; or, if not actually pardon, he could suspend the gathering vengeance, he could delay the stroke. But now this alternative is denied. Such was the accumulation of sin; such was its hatefulness; such were its aggravations, that grace can no longer hold out against righteousness; long-suffering has exhausted itself, and judgment must take its course. If matters are allowed to go on as they have been going, the law will become a dead letter, the divine holiness will be called in question, the faithfulness of God in his threatenings will be suspected; nay, the very power of Jehovah will be denied,—as if it were insufficient either to restrain the evil from arising, or to crush it when it has risen to such a pitch. Mercy had long prevailed against judgment; now judgment prevails against mercy. Grace had done wonders for the sinner. To do more would be to subvert righteousness, and to tamper with the awfulness of law.

As the gracious Father, he had hitherto delayed the vengeance; but now, as the righteous Judge, he *must* interpose. He has long lingered in his love, yearning over his rebellious children; he can linger no more. His strange work must be done, at whatever sacrifice, either to himself or to man. He must not only withhold the good, he must visit with the evil, and he must do it *himself*. He, the Maker, must be the destroyer too. Man must be given up! He has gone beyond the limit within which grace can be righteously exercised. He has made it impossible for God to bless him. He has put it out of God's power to do anything more in his behalf. He has made it a matter of *righteous necessity* that God should execute vengeance upon him. God wanted to bless, man has compelled him to curse. God wanted to save, man has compelled him to destroy. Condemnation, wrath, ruin, wretchedness for ever, must now be man's portion! The vessel which God had made, and meant for honour and for gladness, must become a vessel of shame, eternal shame, filled with gall and wormwood! No wonder that it grieved him at his heart!

However incomprehensible the subject may be; still these words of our text are plain. We would not explain them away. We would not dilute them, or rob them of that solemn tenderness, to which they give such mournful utterance. We would not add to them; but neither would we take from them. And surely they do affirm that God's grief is both sincere and deep. It is a Creator's grief. It is a Father's grief. It is grief such as afterwards uttered itself, over Israel, in such words as, "How shall I give thee up, O Ephraim? how shall I deliver thee up, O Israel? how shall I make thee as Admah, how shall I set thee as Zeboim? mine heart is turned within me; my repentings are kindled together." It is grief such as, at a still later day, gave vent to itself in Christ's tears over Jerusalem. And is not all that *reality?* Was there ever reality like it? Yet all this does not make hell less true, nor the everlasting burnings less terrible.

Many seem to suppose that, because God has not passions such as we have; that because he is not liable to emotions like ours; that because there are no such swellings and subsidings of feverish excitement, interfering with the infinite serenity and blessedness of his divine being, that therefore *God does not feel;* that it would be degrading him to suppose that he can be affected, in the remotest degree, by the alternations of joy or sorrow,—especially in so far as the condition of his creatures can be conceived as being the source of either.

It is not so. This would be indifference, not serenity. It would make Jehovah not the God who is revealed to us in the man Christ Jesus. It would make him inferior to his creatures in all those tender affections which constitute so noble a part of our being. It would invest him with the insensibility of Stoicism. But with him whom we call our God, there is no such insensibility, no such Stoicism. He is love. He is the God of all grace. He is merciful and gracious, long-suffering, slow to anger, keeping mercy for thousands, forgiving iniquity, transgression, and sin. He so loved the world as to give his only-begotten Son. It is written of him, that "his soul was grieved for the miseries of Israel;" that "in all their affliction he was afflicted." He stoops over us in the fondness of parental love. He yearns over us. He longs to see us happy. He delights to bless. His strange work is to curse. Nay, he is the very fountainhead of love. All the affections of man's soul are but the copy of his; faint indeed and dim, yet truly the copy, the counterpart, the earthly likeness of the heavenly reality. Man's heart is, in all the affections that are holy, the very transcript of God's. In God is the birthplace of all feeling, and shall *he* not feel? With him is the well-spring of all affection, and shall *he* be cold, and divested of all loving sympathies? Shall he give to man such powers of emotion, constituting the divinest part of our nature, and shall he himself be unmoved and immoveable? He is the Father of spirits, and shall he so entirely differ from the spirits that he has made? He made them in his own image; and is that image nothing but unsympathising callousness? Is it but the ice, or the rock, or the iron? He sent his Son to be the revelation of his mind and heart; and do we not see, from that Son, how deeply the Father feels? Do we not see in *him*, who is his perfect image, what is the Creator's sympathy for his creatures in their joys and sorrows?

Do we not see in him, with what strength he can hate the sin, and yet love, nay, weep over, the sinner? Ay, and does not the Holy Spirit also unfold his feelings? And do we not read of that Spirit being resisted, *vexed, grieved*, as if sorrowing over our coldness, our neglect, our unbelief, our ungodliness?

What, then, can these things mean, but that our God truly and deeply *feels?* There can, indeed, be nothing carnal, nothing allied to imperfection or weakness, in such sensibility; but to suppose him to be devoid of feeling, as we too often do, is to deny him to be perfectly and truly God! Ah! it is only when we learn how profoundly he feels, that we know aright the character of that God with whom we have to do. It is only when we realise how sincerely he yearns, and pities, and joys, and grieves, and loves, that we understand that revelation which he has made of himself in the gospel of his grace, and in the person of his Incarnate Son. Nor till then do we feel the unutterable malignity of sin, as being a grieving of God, a vexing of his loving Spirit, and become rightly alive to the depravity of our own rebellious natures. It is only then that we can cordially enter into God's condemnation of the evil, and sympathise with him in that which makes him grieve. Never, till we give him credit for *feeling* as he says he does, can we really long for deliverance from that which is not only the abominable thing which he hates, but that thing of evil and sorrow over which he so sincerely mourns.

It is this which gives such power to God's expostulations with the sinner, and his appeals to the sinner's conscience and heart. We are apt to treat these utterances of God as mere words of course, or, at least, as words which, however gracious in themselves, could not be supposed to embody the *feelings* of him from whom they come. It is far otherwise. God not only *means* what he says, but he *feels* what he says. He is not unconcerned about our condition, or indifferent to the reception or rejection of his messages. When he says, "I have no pleasure in the death of the wicked," he utters the deep feeling of his heart. When he says, "How shall I give thee up?" he shews us how he *feels*. When he says, "O that thou hadst hearkened to my commandments," he tells us how he *feels*. And when his only-begotten Son, in the days of his flesh, said to the unbelieving Jews, "Ye will not come unto me, that ye might have life," he shewed us how truly, in this respect, the Father and the Son are one, and that to each poor child of earth, however erring, however dark, however unbelieving, however rebellious, he is stretching out his hands in love, and, not the less sincerely, because, to tens of thousands, he is stretching out these hands in vain.

SERMON XXXVII.

THE SINCERITY OF DIVINE EXPOSTULATIONS.

"Therefore, O thou son of man, speak unto the house of Israel, Thus ye speak, saying, If our transgressions and our sins be upon us, and we pine away in them, how should we then live? Say unto them, As I live, saith the Lord God, I have no pleasure in the death of the wicked; but that the wicked turn from his way and live: turn ye, turn ye from your evil ways; for why will ye die, O house of Israel."—EZEK. xxxiii. 10, 11.

LET us beware of putting a human and finite construction upon things divine and infinite. We need to keep these words in mind, "My thoughts are not your thoughts, neither are your ways my ways." God's character stands out as the contrast of man's, even as light is the contrast of darkness, as paradise is the contrast of the waste howling wilderness.

1. What a contrast are God's *thoughts* of man to man's thoughts of God! God is seen yearning over his poor wanderer with the profoundest compassion, cherishing thoughts of peace and friendship towards him; man is seen suspecting God, looking on him as a hard master, an austere man, reaping where he has not sown, and gathering where he has not strawed.

2. How opposite are God's *feelings* towards man to man's feelings respecting God! The one love, the other hatred; the one kindness and goodwill, the other enmity!

3. How different God's *estimate* of man from man's estimate of God! God's estimate of the value of man is the price he paid for him,—his own Son; man's estimate of God is the price he offered for the Son of God,—thirty pieces of silver.

4. How unlike God's *purposes* to man's! God says to man, "Live;" man says to God, Let him die the death; crucify him; this is the heir; come, let us kill him.

5. How far asunder are God's *ways* from man's! God's are all *towards* man, in the direction of reconciliation; man's are all *away* from God, repelling his fellowship, and heedless of his favour.

Such is the contrast presented in these two verses. In the former (10th), we have the state of man's heart in reference to God; in the latter, the state of God's heart in reference to man. Let us take up in succession these two points.

I. *The state of man's heart in reference to God.* This 10th verse clearly refers to Israel's revengeful murmurings against Jehovah. God had visited them both with warning and entreaty, with threats and invitations. These being utterly slighted, judgment smote them. Still God continues entreating and inviting. The judgments are not removed, but the gracious messages remain; nay, are multiplied. This was the state of things which drew forth the rebellious mutterings of our text. Messages of mercy, *in the midst of judgments*, were what they could neither comprehend nor endure. It was this that raised their enmity to its utmost pitch of blasphemous defiance. They did not, they would not, see how perfectly consistent these were with each other; the grace not contradicting the judgment, nor the judgment cancelling the grace, but both together forming a blessed and marvellous combination of goodness and severity. But they set the one against the other as if they were irreconcilable, and the one the mockery of the other. They murmured, they fretted, they cavilled, they sneered: "If our transgressions be upon us, and we are pining away under them, how should we then live! That is, You tell us of life; you promise us life; yet we find judgment lying on us in full weight; we find ourselves pining, perishing, consuming away; is it not mockery to speak to us of life? Is not the message of life a falsehood; and is not God insincere in sending it? Surely, if we do perish, *we* are not to blame; let him bear the blame who is wounding us to death, and yet mocking us with the promise of life!" Desperate and daring words! How fearful to hear the creature thus blaspheming, to see him fighting against the God that made him, especially when that God is entreating him in all the tenderness of divine love, yearning over him in all the lingering fondness of paternal pity and unextinguished grace!

It is in this way that the sinner murmurs still. It is thus that he reasons against God, struggling with the Almighty, contending with his power, rushing against the thick bosses of his buckler.

He murmurs against God for not giving him life. He hears the promise of life, yet feels that he has none; and he asks, Why am I thus? God promises life. He proclaims his willingness to give it. I have no life. Is he not mocking me? Christ promises rest. I have none. Can he be sincere? I have been doing all I can,—striving, praying, reading books, amending my ways, using means; still there is no peace, no life for me. Can the message be a true one?

Nay, more, he casts the whole blame of his death on God. He says, I see that I must just die; there is no help for it; the blame is not mine, but God's. Death may be my portion hereafter; but how can I help dying? how can I help sinning? If sin and death are my lot, let God see to it. My fallen nature, my education, my circumstances, my temptations,—these are my excuses. Thus he accuses God of his sin, and of his doom. He has done all he can, and God will not give him life; must not God be the sole author of his ruin? To this we answer, No; God is not the author of a man's sin, or of his death. He is pure of their blood. The evil is not of God, but of man. If they perish, the guilt is all their own. For mark, the sin is their own, wholly their own. No one forces them to sin. God does not force them to sin, and Satan cannot force them. Their sin is their own, in the fullest sense. But more: it is wholly they who are to blame for their not being delivered; for the real and true reason why they are not delivered is, that they will not take life in God's way, and upon God's terms. They may be willing enough to have it, but not in God's way. They insist on paying for it, or meriting it, or doing something towards its attainment, or at least towards rendering themselves not wholly unworthy of its being conferred upon them. And when God tells them that it is bought already, and cannot be bought over by them, that it cannot be earned by them, that if they will not take it *free* they cannot have it at all, they turn round upon him, and, in the fierce rage and dark rebellion of disappointed pride, urged on and embittered by the deep anguish of their wretched souls, exclaim, It is all a mockery, a deception! As if it were some relief to them, in their anguish, to find God insincere, and to be able to fling upon him the blame of their perdition.

There may be some here thus putting life away from them. You feel your need of it; you are wretched under a sense of the want of it; and yet you are refusing it. You will not have it after all; for the terms do not please you. This life becomes yours, not by toiling or struggling, but simply by receiving the divine testimony concerning it,—by listening to the voice of Him who, while he says, "Ye will not come to me that ye might have life," says, "I am the way, the truth, and the life;" "He that believeth on me, though he were dead, yet shall he live." Could the blessing be cheaper? Could it be had on easier, simpler terms? Could it be brought nearer, or could you be made more entirely welcome to it? It is not by climbing some inaccessible hill, or treading your darksome way through some tangled forest; it is just by sitting down where you are at this moment, and drinking of that well of living water that is bursting up freshly at your side.

The life of a sinner, as such, can only end in the second death. If it is to end in gladness, and to run on into the life everlasting, it must be *begun over again*. The evil does not lie merely in the leaves and branches of the tree, but in the stem and root; the sap is tainted, and unless that is healed, all efforts at improvement are vain. It was this, evidently, that the Lord meant to tell Nicodemus, when he startled him with the awful words, " Ye must be born again." Our whole life must be treated as utterly evil, our spiritual life-blood thoroughly corrupted; and no remedy can be of any use save that which goes to the very source. The sinner's life must be recommenced from its very first outset. It is not merely to be gone over and retouched; but it is begun anew, as if it had never existed before. " Verily, verily, I say unto thee, EXCEPT A MAN BE BORN AGAIN, he cannot see the kingdom of God" (John iii. 3).

It is the disbelief or forgetfulness of this that produces so much false religion, so many abortions, so many half-discipleships, so many shipwrecks of faith. The religion of form and rite, of lukewarmness and compromise, of sentiment and fashion, of intellect and philosophy, has begun somewhere short of this,—short of the birth from above. It may have gone back a considerable way, but not to the very beginning. It may have dug a little way down, to reach some kind of foundation, but not deep enough to reach the one sure foundation laid in Zion. In this it falls short, and therefore totally fails. It does not matter how long the cable may be ; if it be but one foot too short, it is useless. So it does not matter how greatly a man may change his life, or how religious he may make it. Unless he begin it all over again ; unless we be "BORN of the Spirit," it profits nothing. The one authentic commencement of religion in the soul of a man, is the being born again, "not of corruptible seed, but of incorruptible, by the word of God which liveth and abideth for ever" (1 Pet. i. 23). And, as it was connection with the death of the first Adam that wrought our ruin, so it is connection with the resurrection of the second Adam that works restoration and blessedness. "We are begotten again unto a lively hope, by the resurrection of Jesus Christ from the dead" (1 Pet. i. 3).

That well-known apostle of the last century, John Berridge, wrote his own epitaph some years before his death ; and in it he left his solemn testimony on this point. It is a sermon in itself. "Here lie the earthly remains of John Berridge, late vicar of Everton, an itinerant servant of Jesus Christ, who loved his Master and his work ; and after running on his errands many years, was called up to wait on him above. Reader! ART THOU BORN AGAIN? *No salvation without a new birth."*

Unready sinner! yonder is the Judge, and the throne, and the gathering crowd, waiting their sentence! Hear the shout, and the trumpet, and the thunder, and the voice of Majesty! Are you looking out, or are you asleep? Are you preparing, or are you resolved to risk everything, and brave the Judge of all? What is time worth? What is gain, or pleasure, or sin, or earth worth? Nothing. What is the soul worth? What are heaven, and God, and Christ, and the kingdom, and the glory, worth? Everything. And yet these are nothing to you! One piece of earth's gold, one acre of land, one smile of gay companionship, one wreath of the world's honour, one day of time's power and greatness, you would prefer to all that is divine and eternal! O madness of the human heart, how unsearchable and incurable! O spell of sin, how potent and enthralling! O snare of the evil one, how blinding, how fatal, how successful!

SERMON XXXVIII.

THE SINCERITY OF DIVINE EXPOSTULATIONS.

" Therefore, O thou son of man, speak unto the house of Israel, Thus ye speak, saying, If our transgressions and our sins be upon us, and we pine away in them, how should we then live? Say unto them, As I live, saith the Lord God, I have no pleasure in the death of the wicked; but that the wicked turn from his way and live: turn ye, turn ye from your evil ways; for why will ye die, O house of Israel?"—EZEK. xxxiii. 10, 11.

II. HAVING thus seen, from the tenth verse, the state of man's heart in reference to God, let us mark *the state of God's heart in reference to man*, as we find it brought out in the eleventh verse: "As I live, saith the Lord God, I have no pleasure in the death of the wicked; but that the wicked turn from his way and live : turn ye, turn ye from your evil ways; for why will ye die, O house of Israel?"

It is thus that God meets Israel's hard thoughts concerning him. Instead of being provoked to anger by this most daring rebelliousness, he answers their suspicious unbelief by a reiteration of his words of grace. How patient, how longsuffering, how condescending! Instead of executing vengeance, he renews the assurances of his most unfeigned and affectionate interest in their welfare. Unmoved by their horrid taunts and charges of insincerity, he approaches them in the posture of a friend; he repeats the declaration of his gracious mind; he adds new, and larger, and fuller asseverations of his unwearied and inexhaustible compassion. Nay, in order to efface every suspicion, and anticipate every form and shade of unbelief, he adds his oath,—his oath as the living God,—that by two immutable things in which it was impossible for God to lie, they might have the most deliberate assurance of his gracious mind, and the remotest possibility of such a charge against himself as that of insincerity to be provided against.

God has thus in the most solemn way declared to us his loving intentions. He has laid bare the inmost thoughts of his heart. He tells us that these thoughts are the very opposite of ours; that his desire is not to curse, but to bless; not to destroy, but to save. And what an oath is this! It is not the oath of a man, but of the eternal God; of him who liveth for ever and ever. As if his word might be called in question, he adds his oath. He swears by himself, because he could swear by no greater; he swears by his own *life*,—the greatest of all realities, the most certain of all certainties. "As surely as I am,—as surely as I am Jehovah,—so certainly I have no pleasure in the death of the wicked." What an infinite certainty is this! "An oath for confirmation is," the apostle says, "an end of all strife." So should this oath be to the sinner an end of all suspicion, of all doubt, as to the gracious mind of God. How anxious must Jehovah be to meet and remove all your jealous fears,—to convince you that he is not the false being which you take him to be,—that he is sincere in his desires to bless you! O sinner, what could you have more than this? If this will not make you ashamed of your unbelief, what will? If this will not convince you of God's honesty and true-hearted yearning over you, what will or can? Ah, how unfeigned, as well as how infinite, are his thoughts of grace towards you! And is there not something in this gracious commiseration, so solemnly affirmed upon oath, fitted irresistibly to attract and win the most jealous and unbelieving heart?

Let us consider now the substance of this divine declaration, thus made on oath, and recorded for the sinner's use in all ages. It is a twofold declaration: In the first part of it God denies the imputation cast upon him, of seeking the sinner's death; in the second, he declares himself to be most sincerely desirous of his life.

1. *He has no pleasure in their death.* This does not imply that the wicked shall not die. No. The wicked shall be turned into hell. Millions have already perished; millions more shall perish. There is the second death, the death beyond which there is no life for the impenitent,—the unquenchable fire, the everlasting burnings. But still it remains true that God has no pleasure in man's death. He did not kindle hell in order to gratify his revenge. He does not cast sinners headlong into its endless flames in order to get vent to his blind fury. No. He has no pleasure in their

death. He will finally condemn the unbelieving, but not because he delights to do so, but because he is the righteous Lord that loveth righteousness. Whatever your treacherous heart may say, whatever your jealous suspicions may whisper, it remains a truth for ever true,—a truth affirmed upon oath, —that God has no pleasure in your death! Are you seeking to escape eternal death? It is well. But do you think that God is trying to thwart you? Nay, he is as desirous of this as you can be, only his desires run in a righteous channel, and he can only give vent to them in a righteous way. He is not bent upon your ruin. Was the father bent upon the ruin of his prodigal? Was the shepherd intent upon the destruction of his stray sheep? Was the Son of God delighting in the desolation of Jerusalem when he wept over it? Or was the God of Israel bent upon the misery of his people when he said, "How shall I give thee up, Ephraim? how shall I deliver thee up, Israel? how shall I make thee as Admah? how shall I set thee as Zeboim? Mine heart is turned within me, my repentings are kindled together." The God that made you is not your deadly enemy. The God in whom you live, and move, and have your being, has no pleasure in your death. He did not send his Son to destroy, but to save; he did not nail him to the tree that you might die, but live; he did not send his Holy Spirit to seal your perdition, but to pluck you as a brand from the burning.

2. *His desire is, that the wicked should turn and*

live. As in the first clause of this oath he denied the imputation cast upon him, that he had pleasure in the sinner's death, so, in this second part, he declares his wish that they should turn and live. This declaration is the expression of a thoroughly honest desire on the part of God. It is not the language of insincere profession, or of feigned earnestness. There is nothing here of exaggeration or random utterance. Each word bears the impress of ingenuous truthfulness. God means what he says when he affirms, "I have no pleasure in the death of the wicked, but rather that they should turn and live." It is to life,—life everlasting,—that he points your eye, sinner. It is of life that he desires to make you partaker. And surely it is *life* that you need. For what one word more fully or more terribly describes your present state than *death?* You are *dead!* Dead, not like the stone or the rock; that would at least be freedom from torment. Dead, not like the withered leaf or the uprooted tree; that would at least be unconsciousness of loss, and ignorance of what might have been won. But you are dead to all that is worth living for, and yet alive to all that makes life a burden and a woe. Yours is a death whose present form is the utter absence of everything that God calls peace or blessedness, whose future form is the undying worm, the weeping, and the wailing, and the gnashing of teeth. You are dead to that which you were created for, as well as to him who created you. You live in pleasure on the earth, yet you are *dead!* You smile, and sport, and dance, and revel, and make merry; yet you are *dead!* For the life in which God is not; the life of which he is not the spring and centre, is utter *death!* And that is misery to you,—misery now, misery in the long, long ages to come!

Ah! surely, then, it is *life* that you need,—such a life as will fill that soul of yours with gladness,—such a life as shall not merely shed sunshine around you, but shall pour its joyous freshness into every region of your spirit, and fill every recess of your immortal being with the joy unspeakable and full of glory.

It is such a life that God desires you to possess. It was to bestow upon you such a life that he gave up his Son. It is that such a life might find entrance into you, that he is striving with you by his Spirit. And it is that, without another hour's delay, you might become possessors of such a life, that he sends to you once more this message of life,—so unequivocal, so genuine, so pitiful.

Do you say, If God wants me to live, why does he not at once give me life? In other words, why does he not *force* life upon my acceptance, and burst through every barrier? I ask in return, Is God bound to take *your* way in giving life? I ask again, Do you really suppose that a person is not sincere in his kindness, because he does not carry out that kindness by every means, lawful or unlawful? Is it not possible that there may be a limit to that kindness compatible with the most perfect sincerity ? You admit that God does not wish you to be ungodly; yet you are ungodly; might you not as well say, God must really desire me to be ungodly, else I should not be so? Nay, you admit that God wishes you to be holy, just as he wishes all his creatures to be holy. Should you think of saying, God does not desire me to be holy, else he would make me holy; God must have pleasure in my unholiness, else he would not permit me to remain in it Surely this would be false reasoning as well as daring profanity: not less so is it when you argue, God cannot really desire to bless me, else he would bless me; God cannot desire me to live, else he would give me life.

There may be difficulty for finite man to reconcile the two things,—our want of life and God's desire that we should possess it; but there is no difficulty and no doubt as to the blessed fact itself. God's desire is, that we should turn and live! Not all the sophistry of unbelief, nor all the malignant falsehoods of the evil one, can shake or alter this mighty, this most glorious truth. God's desire, his undisguised and cordial wish, is, that the wicked should not die, but live! He has spoken it, he has repeated it; he has sealed it with his own most solemn oath; and woe be to the sinner who, giving way to the subtile suggestions of his own jealous heart, refuses to take God at his word, hesitates to give him credit for speaking the plain truth when he lifts up his hand to heaven and swears, "As I live, saith the Lord, I have no pleasure in the death of the wicked; but rather that he should turn from his ways and live.

The expostulation, with which all this closes, is one of the most urgent importunity on the part of God, proving yet more fully his real desire to bless. It is like one vehemently enforcing an invitation upon an unwilling listener,—making a last effort to save the heedless or resisting sinner. He lifts up his voice, he stretches out his hand, he exhorts, he commands, he expostulates, he entreats, "Turn ye, turn ye, from your evil ways; for why will ye die?" must not he who thus reasons and remonstrates with the sinner, repeating and re-repeating his entreaties, enforcing and urging home his message with every kind of loving argument, as well as with every form of solemn appeal,—must not he be truly in earnest? Is it within the remotest bounds of possibility or conceivability that he is insincere; that he does not really mean what he says?

The ways from which he calls on them to turn are named by him "evil ways;" and what he calls evil must be truly so,—hateful in his eyes, as well as ruinous to the soul. The end of these ways he pronounces to be *death;* so that sinners must either turn or die. It is the broad way which leadeth down to death on which they are walking, and there is no hope of escaping unless they retrace their steps. As certainly as their bodies shall return to dust, so certainly shall their souls have their portion in the second death, and their dwelling-place in the eternal tomb of the fiery lake ; where, instead of the worm of earth preying upon their lifeless flesh, there shall be the worm that never dies, gnawing their spirits, and making them feel that all that has hitherto been known of death on earth,—its pangs, its throes, its horrors, its separations,—has been but a type of what is coming, and that the reality contained in that word DEATH had never before been imagined,—nor, indeed, can be,—till the Judge's sentence has cut them off from God for ever, and flung around them the darkness of the endless midnight ; till hell has closed its gate upon them, and made damnation sure !

But then there is another way, whose end is life ; and the life, which forms the termination of the one, is as certain as the death which forms the termination of the other. It is on this way that God so earnestly desires to see them walking. However wide astray they have gone, and however near the confines of the second death they may have come, he beckons them back with his gracious hand, and beseeches them with his most loving voice, " Come now, and let us reason together." Nay, more, he *commands* them to turn. It is not mere liberty to retrace your steps that he gives you ; he lays his command upon you ; and it is at your peril if you disobey. " Am I at liberty to come to God ?" you ask perhaps. At liberty to come ! Is that the way you put it ? At liberty to obey his direct command ! Do you ask, Am I at liberty to keep the Sabbath ? Am I at liberty to honour my father and mother ? Am I at liberty to forbear swearing, or stealing, or coveting ? Who asks such questions as these ? And shall any sinner upon earth,—even the ungodliest that ever forsook God and walked in his lusts, and trampled on the cross, and quenched the Spirit,—shall any on this side of the second death presume to ask, Am I at liberty to return to God ? At liberty ! YOU DARE NOT DO OTHERWISE. There is all the obligation that a command can give ; there is a necessity laid upon you, an immediate necessity, a necessity from which nothing can loose you, a necessity arising out of the very righteousness of that God who is commanding you to quit your unrighteousness, a necessity springing from the certain doom that awaits you if you turn not. Yes ; there is a necessity, one of the greatest of all necessities, laid on you by God, to turn and live !

God expostulates with you, and asks, Why will ye die ? Have you any reason to give for preferring death, or for supposing that you must just die, and that you cannot help it, and that the blame is not yours, but God's ? *Must* you die ? Must you really die ? Is there no help ? There was, indeed, once a reason for your dying, a reason which made dying inevitable,—the ancient law of the universe, "The soul that sinneth, it shall die." But now the Son of God has come, and he has taken up that law, and has so fulfilled and honoured it by dying himself, that the same inevitable necessity for *your* dying no longer exists. It was once only righteous that you should die; now it is as righteous that you should live. Righteous death;—that was once your doom; now righteous life is the gift which God presents to you. Life upon righteous terms; life in a way that honours righteousness; life through a channel as holy as it is free: it is this that is now announced to you, and it is in reference to this that God asks, Why will ye die?

Is life not desirable? Can a soul be in love with death? Or is death so inevitable that it is vain for you to flee from it? Or is there some barrier in your way? Or is God not really willing to remove the death, and to bestow the life? Are these the reasons? Or what answer do you mean to make to God's question, so urgently, so importunately put and pressed home on you, "Why will ye die?"

SERMON XXXIX.

THE SIN AGAINST THE HOLY GHOST.

"Verily I say unto you, All sins shall be forgiven unto the sons of men, and blasphemies wherewith soever they shall blaspheme; but he that shall blaspheme against the Holy Ghost hath never forgiveness, but is in danger of eternal damnation: because they said, He hath an unclean spirit."—MARK iii. 28–30.

It would serve no purpose to discuss or enumerate the various opinions that have been held respecting this sin. Let us just take the passage itself, and try to find out what the narrative really is meant to teach us.

The key to the passage is contained in the 30th verse,—"Because they said" (were saying), "He hath an unclean spirit." This is the Evangelist's remark for the clearing up of the statement; or rather, I should say, it is the Holy Spirit's own comment on a declaration made specially respecting himself. In the 28th and 29th verses, the Son is speaking of the Spirit, and of the sin against him; in the 30th, the Spirit interprets the words of the Son, and shews that the sin against himself is in reality a sin against the Son. In reading these three verses, in this connection, as spoken successively by the Son of God and the Spirit of God, we see how jealous the one is for the honour of the other. The Holy Spirit will not put upon record this testimony of the Son regarding himself without adding his own testimony to the Son, and shewing how sin committed against himself is committed against the Son, and dishonour cast upon himself is dishonour cast upon the Son.

It was in Galilee that these words were spoken; for Jesus was, at this time "going through every city and village preaching, and shewing the glad tidings of the kingdom of God" (Luke viii. 1). He was opposed, reviled, and threatened, as he went along, teaching and healing. The opposition, however, did not come from the Galileans, but from the Scribes and Pharisees who came down from Jerusalem (Matt. xii. 24, Mark iii. 22). There might be among the inhabitants of that half-Gentile region, ignorance and unbelief; but they did not go so far in their malignity as the more intellectual, better educated, and (in the common acceptation of the word) more "religious" citizens of Jerusalem, as represented by their leaders, the Scribes, and Pharisees, and Priests. These, though better read in the Prophets, and professing to be waiting for Messiah, were foremost in the rejection of Christ; setting themselves against himself and his Messiahship with a persevering and desperate malignity, such as we might have reckoned impossible.

Not only did these Jewish leaders shew their unbelief, in Jerusalem and Judea; but they went everywhere, tracking the Lord's footsteps, endeavouring to provoke and entrap him; misrepresenting all that he said and did ; maligning him as a wine-bibber and a keeper of the worst company ; nay, as possessed of a devil ; nay, more, as doing and saying all that he said and did under the influence of this possession. In the present narrative we find them in Galilee, many days' journey from Jerusalem. What were they doing there ? They did not come to listen, nor to be taught, nor to be convinced, nor to admire. They had travelled all this distance out of pure malignity. Like demons from hell, they followed the Lord in order to assail him or plot against him. They grudged no toil, no travel, no cost, in order to carry out their hatred of Christ. They watched, with hellish eagerness, every word and motion ; misconstruing all his doings ; abusing him both for what he did and for what he did not do ; and seizing every opportunity for poisoning the minds of the people against him.

In the scene to which our narrative refers, we find him working a miracle ; a miracle of no ordinary kind. The case is a very desperate one. The man is both dumb and blind,—perhaps deaf too ; and more than this, he is possessed with a devil. He is a signal monument of Satan's power. He is one of Satan's best fortified and best garrisoned fortresses. There could hardly be a clearer or more explicit exhibition of Satan's infernal enmity to man, and of his horrid character as the marrer of God's workmanship, the inflicter of darkness and disease. Seldom had the seed of the serpent been so exhibited in his hatefulness and enmity ; and seldom had he been so directly and gloriously confronted with the woman's Seed, in all his loveableness of character and his kindness to man. If ever, therefore, human unbelief were utterly inexcusable, it was here. If ever man's enmity might have been expected to give way, it was here. If ever, in the awful halting between two opinions, a better choice might have been *forced* upon man, and even the Pharisee made ashamed of siding against Christ, it was here. God had brought heaven and hell face to face, before man; he had brought the Prince of light and the prince of darkness into close and direct collision; and that in circumstances most likely to enlist man's sympathies with heaven against hell, with the Son of God against the devil and his angels. It might have been expected that man would, at least for once, have taken the side of God; and that the Scribes and Pharisees, the most enlightened and best educated of the land, would have given way in their prejudice and hatred. But it is just here that the greatness of their hostility comes out; and as afterwards the cry arose in Jerusalem, "Not this man, but Barabbas," so here, in Galilee, a like cry is heard, from the lips of the same men, "Not the Holy Spirit, but the devil!"

Thus it was that these Scribes and Pharisees sinned against the Holy Spirit, by imputing to the devil the works of Christ, which he did by the power of the Holy Ghost in him. They did not do this in ignorance; for they were not half-enlightened Galileans, but men well-read in their Scriptures; they did it knowingly. They did not do it hastily, and under the influence of passing excitement; they did it deliberately, and resolutely, and continuously. They did it with their eyes open; they did it maliciously, in the desperate hatred of their hearts. They did it without one extenuating circumstance,—without anything either to excuse or to account for their malignity. This is the sin which our Lord here declares to be unpardonable. To have said that this marvellous universe was created by the devil, and not by God, would have been a *kindred* crime; a sin of awful daring. To have said that the miracles of Egypt, the dividing of the Red Sea, the manna, the water, the healing of the serpents' deadly bite, the drying up of Jordan, the overthrow of Jericho, the arrest of sun and moon in Gibeon, were all the work of the devil, would have been sins *like in kind* to this of the Pharisees; but not, by many degrees, equal to it in dark malignity. For, in this miracle of Christ, thus misinterpreted, we have more of divine love and power,—more of God himself, than in all these other miracles together. One of the fullest and brightest manifestations of God's character, as our loving, healing, pardoning, redeeming God, is in this miracle; and hence the peculiarly aggravated guilt of those who reviled it as the work of the devil. It was a work done by the special power of the Holy Ghost,—a work in which might have been clearly read the Father's love and power, the Son's love and power, the Spirit's love and power.

Yet this work of the Holy Spirit, this miracle of Godhead's love and power, is ascribed to Satan! It was calling God the devil, and the devil God; it was calling hell heaven, and heaven hell. It was not mere rejection of Christ; it was not mere disbelief of his miracles; it was not mere refusal of the divine testimony to his Messiahship. It was something beyond all these phases of unbelief. It was the substitution and preference of the evil for the good, of the darkness for the light, of the seed of the serpent for the Seed of the woman. Nay, more, it was the deliberate declaration, not that the works of God the Holy Ghost were unreal and untrue,—but that they were not his works at all, but those of the devil. It was the admission of their reality, but the ascription of them to the devil. It was carrying out hatred of Christ to such an extreme, as to be willing to acknowledge Satan as the worker of miracles rather than Christ; nay, it was so hating the Holy Spirit, because of his thus witnessing for Christ, as to call him "an unclean spirit," Beelzebub, the prince of the devils!

Such is the sin against the Holy Ghost; a sin which originates in very peculiar circumstances; which can only be committed by those who sin wilfully, daringly, and maliciously; and which, in all probability, could only be committed when the Lord was upon the earth, working miracles by the power of the Spirit.

It is worthy of notice, that our Lord does not affirm that even these blasphemous Pharisees had *actually committed* the sin. The awful words regarding the sin that has no pardon are spoken as words of warning In them the Lord is pointing to the horrible gulf which these Pharisees were approaching, and warning them off. He sees them like a vessel drawing nearer some raging whirlpool, and he speaks that they may be alarmed and turn back. In this there is a blessed mixture of grace and righteousness. He would warn even the Pharisees! He would sound the alarm even to those who were on the very point of plunging into hell!

The sin is thus a peculiar sin. It is not the same as rejection of Christ and final unbelief. It is not even blasphemy against Christ and his work. It is not simply sin against light and knowledge. It is not repeated, or prolonged, or outrageous backsliding. It is something special; something open and before others; it is something deliberate and malicious; it is something which would render the man's state quite hopeless, and seal his doom at once. It is something connected directly with the Spirit, and which involves daring blasphemy against him and his doings. It must, then, be a greater sin than that of **Judas**, for his sin was pardonable to the last. It must be a greater sin than scourging, buffeting, reviling, crucifying the **Lord of glory**. Oh, how unutterably hateful must that sin be, of which we thus read, "Wherefore I say unto you, All manner of sin and blasphemy shall be forgiven unto men; but the blasphemy against the Holy Ghost shall never be forgiven him. And whosoever speaketh a word against the Son of Man, it shall be forgiven him; but whosoever speaketh against the Holy Ghost, it shall never be forgiven him, neither in this world, neither in the world to come. He that shall blaspheme against the Holy Ghost hath never forgiveness, but is in danger of eternal damnation; BECAUSE THEY SAID, HE HATH AN UNCLEAN SPIRIT!"

But, while this sin is a very peculiar one, and, possibly, only committed when our Lord was here, and that by those who ascribed to the devil the miracles which Christ did, by the Holy Ghost, there are approximations to it, in all ages, of which men need to be warned. The way in which many attack Revivals, and revile those engaged in them, and ascribe the conversions to mere excitement, or hypocrisy, or love of show, or *to Satan himself*, is a perilous approach to the blasphemy against the Holy Ghost. Let men beware how they speak of these religious awakenings. If you dislike them, or see no evidence for their genuineness, at least let them alone. Especially let those who, in their zeal for ecclesiastical order, have set themselves against such movements, and do not hesitate to throw out insinuations as to all these being the devil's work, beware lest they be found fighting against God, and reviling the Spirit of God. They may be nearer the sin of the Pharisees than they are willing to think; and their zeal for sound words, in which they pride themselves, only helps to identify them the more with these haters of the

Lord. The dislike of sudden conversions looks very like a denial of the Spirit's work ; just as the dislike of assurance looks like a questioning of the work of Christ,—a denial of its sufficiency to give immediate peace to the awakened conscience. Let the ungodly beware of scoffing at revivals; and let professing Christians beware of standing aloof from them, as if they were fanaticism, or excitement, or the work of Satan.

Let us gather, in closing, such lessons as these :—

I. *Honour the Holy Spirit and his work.*—As the the third person of the Godhead, equal with the Father and the Son, he is to be worshipped. Never let us overlook the Spirit, or undervalue either his power or his love. Nor let us lose sight of his great work in the Church and in individual souls. Without his almighty hand there is no conversion, no faith, no repentance, no light. Let those who deny his work, or explain it as a mere influence, or affirm that it is nothing but the effect of the word upon us, consider how much they are dishonouring the Spirit, and how near they may be approaching to the sin against the Holy Ghost.

II. *Prize him as the gift of the glorified Christ.*— He is the promise of the Father; he is the gift of the Son ; and in him are wrapped all other gifts for sinners. He is in the hand of Christ for us, let us go to Christ for him; for he is exalted a Prince and a Saviour to give repentance and forgiveness, through the shedding down of the Holy Spirit upon us. We need not fear a refusal from such a Saviour.

III. *Beware of grieving and quenching him.*—Israel's great sin was their "resisting the Holy Ghost" (Acts vii. 51). "They rebelled and vexed his Holy Spirit" (Isa. lxiii. 10). Let us beware of Israel's sin. O grieve not the Spirit, by your unbelief and hardness of heart! He will not always strive.

IV. *Receive that Christ of whom he testifies.*—His office is to *glorify* Christ; to *show* Christ. He is willing to do this for sinners. He wants to show you your need of Christ. He wants to show you Christ's sufficiency. He wants to give you true and high thoughts of Christ. Oh, turn not away!

V. *Be not scoffers.*—God's words are very awful ones—"Be ye not mockers, lest your bands be made strong." Do not ridicule religion; nor speak evil of Christians; nor circulate reports against the work of God; nor deny "sudden conversions." Beware of everything like irreverence, or levity, or flippancy, in speaking of the things of God or the transactions of eternity. Judge nothing before the time; or if you will judge, see that in your judgment you honour the Spirit of truth and holiness.

SERMON XL.

THE SIN UNTO DEATH.

"If any man see his brother sin a sin which is not unto death, he shall ask, and he shall give him life for them that sin not unto death. There is a sin unto death: I do not say that he shall pray for it. All unrighteousness is sin: and there is a sin not unto death."—1 JOHN v. 16, 17.

THE sin mentioned here is not the same as the "sin against the Holy Ghost." The persons spoken of, as respectively guilty, are very different from each other. In the latter sin, it is the Scribes and Pharisees. the malignant enemies of Christ, that are the criminals; in the former, that is, the case before us, it is a *Christian brother* that is the offender: "If any man see *his brother* sin." We must beware of confounding the two sins and the two parties. The sin unto death is spoken of as that which a believer could commit; but no believer could possibly be guilty of the blasphemy against the Holy Ghost.

This clears the way so far, or at least it narrows the ground, and so facilitates our inquiry.

But while removing one difficulty, does it not introduce another? Does it not assume the possibility of falling from grace, and deny the "perseverance of the saints?" We think not. But, as much depends on the meaning of the expression, "a sin unto death," we must first take up this.

Death may mean either temporal or eternal death; either the death of the soul, or that of the body. In the passage before us, it seems to me to mean the latter. The sin unto death, would mean a sin involving temporal death; such a sin as God would chastise with disease and death, though he would not exclude the doer of it from his kingdom. The difference between these two kinds of sins may be illustrated by the case of Israel in the desert. The generation that came out of Egypt died in the wilderness, because of their murmurings; yet many of these were believing men and women, who, though thus chastised, by the infliction of temporal death, and deprivation of the earthly Canaan, were not delivered over to eternal death. Moses himself (we might add, Aaron and Miriam) is an example of the same thing. In him we see a believing man suffering temporal death for his sin, yet still a child of God, and an heir of the heavenly Canaan.

But have we any cases of this kind in the New Testament? If we have, they will tend greatly to confirm our interpretation of the passage before us, and shew that, in all ages, God's way of dealing with his saints has been the same; and that, while in some instances there was chastisement, in the shape of pain, or disease, or loss of property, or loss of friends, in others there was chastisement in the shape of death. In the case of Moses, we have this paternal chastisement, involving death; in the case of Job, we see it involving loss of substance, loss of family, loss of health, but stopping short of death; but in the New Testament, we shall see it in the infliction of *death* upon the saint.

The most remarkable instance of the kind is in the Corinthian church. That church was in many respects noble and Christ-like, "coming behind in no gift." Yet there was much sin in it, and many of its members were not walking "as becometh saints." Specially in reference to the Lord's Supper, there was grievous sin, as the latter part of the eleventh chapter of the First Epistle to that church intimates. God could not suffer such sin in his saints. They are not indeed to be cast away, nor condemned with the unbelieving world; but they are not to be permitted to go on in evil, unrebuked. Accordingly, God interposes. He sends disease on some of these transgressing members, and death on others. "For this cause," says the apostle, "many are weak and sickly among you, and many sleep" (1 Cor. xi. 30). Weakness, sickliness, and death, were the three forms of chastisement with which the Corinthian church was visited. Some were sinning sins which require to be visited with weakness; others were sinning sins which required to be punished with sickness; while others were sinning sins which needed to be chastised with "death;" for this the word "sleep" evidently means (1 Cor. vii. 39, κοιμηθῇ,—xv. 18). Against these sins unto disease, these "sins unto death," the apostle warns these Corinthians, when he says, "If we would judge ourselves, *we should not be judged ;*" that is, we might have been spared these chastisements. If we had judged ourselves, and condemned our own sin, we should not have been thus judged by God. And then he adds, that even this judgment was in love, not in wrath : "When we are thus judged, it is the Lord chastising us, in order that we may not be condemned with the world."

We find the same solemn truth in the Epistle of James (v. 14, 15) : "The prayer of faith shall save the sick, and the Lord shall raise him up ; and if he have committed sins, they shall be forgiven him." Here sickness is spoken of as the consequence of sin,—sin in a saint. The sick and sinning one is to be prayed for ; and if his sin and sickness be not unto death, God will have mercy on him. The sin shall be forgiven, and the sickness taken away.

We find the same truth in 1 Cor. viii. 11, "Through thy knowledge shall the weak brother perish, for whom Christ died" where the "perishing" is the infliction of temporal death.

These passages shew the true meaning of our text. The sin unto death is a sin such as God chastises by the infliction of disease and death.

What this sin is, we do not know. It was not the same sin in all, but different in each. In the case of the Corinthian Church, unworthy communicating was "the sin unto death ;" but what it was in others, is not recorded.

Thus the passage in John and that in James correspond strikingly, the one illustrating the other. In the case of the sick brother, spoken of by James, we have the very thing referred to in the first clause of our text: "If any man see his brother sin a sin which is not unto death, he shall ask, and he (*i. e.*, God) shall give him life for them that sin not unto death." Thus the prayer of faith was to save the sick man from death, to raise him up, and to secure for him forgiveness of the sin which had produced the sickness.

But then the question would arise, How are we to know when a sin is unto death, and when it is not unto death, so that we may pray in faith? The last clause of the 16th verse answers this question. It admits that there is a sin unto death; which admission is thus put in the 17th verse: "All unrighteousness is sin; but all sin is not unto death." But what does the apostle mean by saying, in the end of the 16th verse, "I do not say that he shall pray for it?" If we cannot know when a sin is unto death, and when not, what is the use of saying, "I do not say that he shall pray for it?"

The word translated "pray" means also "inquire," and is elsewhere translated so: John i. 19, "The Jews sent priests and Levites from Jerusalem to *ask* him, Who art thou?" (See, also, John i. 21, 25, v. 12, ix. 2, xix. 21.) If thus rendered, the meaning would be, "I say he is to ask no questions about that." That is to say, if he sees a brother sick and ready to die, he is not to say,

Has he committed a sin unto death, or has he not? He is just to pray, letting alone all such inquiries, and leaving the matter in the hands of God, who, in answer to prayer, will raise him up, if he have not committed the sin unto death.

The passage now becomes plain; and while it remains as an unspeakably solemn warning, it does not teach us that there is some one mysterious sin which infers eternal damnation; still less, that a saint of God can commit such a sin. It may be thus paraphrased: "If any one see his brother in Christ sin a sin, and see him also laid upon a sick-bed in consequence of this, he shall pray for the sick brother; and if his sin be one of which the punishment is disease, not death, the sick man shall be raised up; for all sins that lead to sickness do not necessarily lead to death. And as to the difficulty, How shall we know when the sin is one which merely infers sickness, and when it is one which infers death? I say this, Ask no questions on this point, but pray, and leave the case to God."

Let us now come to the lessons of our text.

1. *Don't puzzle yourself with hard questions about the particular kind of sins committed.*—Be satisfied that it is sin, and deal with it as such. There are sins unto death, and there are sins not unto death. Do not trouble yourself or others with questions on this point, which no man can answer. Remember that all unrighteousness is sin; and that it is simply with sin, as sin, as a breach of the perfect law of righteousness, that you have to do. It is not the

nature or the measure of its punishment that you have to consider, but its own exceeding sinfulness.

2. *Be concerned about a brother's welfare.*—" Look not every man on his own things, but look also every man on the things of others," as said the apostle. If any of you see a brother sin, do not let him alone, as if it did not concern you. Do not say, "Am I my brother's keeper?" Desire the spiritual prosperity of all the saints. Seek, too, the salvation of the unsaved. They need your pity and your effort. Leave them not.

3. *Don't trifle with sin.*—Count no sin trivial, either in yourself or another. Do not dally with temptation. Do not extenuate guilt. Do not say, May I not keep my beloved sin a little longer? Part with it, or it will cost you dear. In what way it may do so I know not; but I can say this, that sooner or later it will cost you dear, both in soul and body.

4. *Take it at once to God.*—Don't puzzle yourself with useless questions as to its nature, but take it straight to God. In the case of a brother, do not raise evil reports against him because of it, but go and tell God about it. In your own case do the same. Do not let it remain unconfessed a moment after it is discovered. It is unrighteousness; it is sin; it is breach of law. God hates it; you must hate it too. You must bring it to that God who hates it; and who, just because he hates it, wants you to bring it to him. Give it at once to him. He knows how to keep it, and to deal with it. If

you keep it to yourself, it will be your ruin. It will be poison in your veins. It will eat as doth a canker. It is not too great for him to deal with or to cover. The blood of his only-begotten Son will cover it. Let that blood prove its divine efficacy by the cleansing which it can administer to *your* soul. Rest not without forgiveness through the great propitiation. An unforgiven man is an unhappy man. Blessedness is the portion only of the forgiven. If you have not yet found the pardon, this blessedness cannot be yours. And if you but felt the misery of the unpardoned, and the joy of the pardoned, you would not rest till you had *made sure* of the forgiveness that there is with God, and tasted the reconciliation that they only know, who have settled the great question for eternity, at the foot of the cross.

There is such a thing as THE SECOND DEATH. And who shall deliver the doomed one from it? Who shall pray him up out of hell? The second death! Ah, when it has come to that, all is over! No Christ will do then; no blood; no cross! Oh, wait not till your sins have landed you in that! Take the proffered pardon. God gives it to you in his Son. Take it, and live for ever. He who died and lives presents to you the gift of the everlasting life,—life that no second death can touch,—life in Himself,—life beyond the valley of the shadow of death, in the city of the Living One, from which no life departs, and into which no death can enter.

SERMON XLI.

THE THREE WITNESSES.

"Who is he that overcometh the world, but he that believeth that Jesus is the Son of God? This is he that came by water and blood, even Jesus Christ; not by water only, but by water and blood. And it is the Spirit that beareth witness, because the Spirit is truth."—1 JOHN v. 5, 6.

The world is not for us but against us. It lieth in wickedness, and must be our enemy. It is Satan's kingdom, and can afford us neither home nor friendly shelter. It was Christ's foe, and it is ours no less; seeking our ruin both by force and craft. It has always hated the Church; it does so still. It hated the Master, and it hates the servant too. The seed of the serpent and the seed of the woman must be at variance with each other.

It is to be fought against; not yielded to. There can only be warfare between it and us; not friendship, not peace, not truce, not alliance, not compromise. In this warfare, it is faith only that can give us the victory,—faith which shews us the shadowy vanity of things seen and temporal, and the abiding glory of things unseen and eternal. The BELIEVING MAN is the only conqueror. It is as a *believing man* that he fights and overcomes. Mere earnestness will not do; nothing but faith.

In what, then, or in whom is it, that he believes?

in Jesus as the Son of God. It is not faith in ideas, or principles, or opinions, or doctrines, that gives the victory. It is faith in Christ Jesus, the Son of the living God.

But what does this imply? And who is this Son of God? And how do we know that Jesus is the Son of God? To this the apostle answers, He "came by water and by blood;" that is, he was marked out by these two things;—and so proved to be "the coming one," the Messiah, the Son of God. These shewed him to be the Christ, and sealed him as such. Both of these things were needed, and both were given; the one at his baptism, the other at his crucifixion.

The Christ, revealed to Adam, was one who was to be truly the Son of man and the Son of God; who, as the seed of the woman, was to be bruised in his heel, when consummating his victory over the serpent. The Christ revealed to the patriarchs and prophets was the same. The Christ of type and sacrifice was the same. The Christ of the prophets was still the same. He was such a Christ as could have a twofold testimony borne to him; a testimony by water and a testimony by blood; so that, had either of these been awanting when he came, the evidence of his being the very Christ, the Son of God, would have been incomplete. To these two God adds a third witness, confirming the testimony of the previous two,—the Holy Spirit. *He also comes in as a witness-bearer, uniting his testimony to the others, and proclaiming the same* truth,—giving his evidence to the same facts. So that thus we have a threefold testimony on earth, a testimony directed to one great point,—that Jesus is the Christ, the Son of God, the Saviour of the world. Two witnesses under the law were sufficient to attest a matter; and God gives two witnesses, who are both most explicit in their testimony; but to make assurance yet surer, he adds a third, the Holy Spirit. And thus there are three that bear witness upon earth, the Spirit, the water, and the blood; and these three agree in one; or, literally, "are towards this one thing," or, are directed to, or converge in this one point, viz., that Jesus is the Christ, the Son of God.

This, then, is the way in which God lays the foundation for faith to rest upon. He not only sends his Son, but he accompanies his mission with convincing evidence as to who and what he is. He places a basis for faith, so sure and satisfactory, that a man, understanding it, can at once say, "Now I know of a truth that this is the Christ, the Seed of the woman, the Seed of Abraham, the Seed of David, the Son of Mary, the Son of God." It is in this way that God produces faith in us; not by calling on us to put forth some vast effort to accomplish an act which we call faith;" but by turning our eyes to the Person of the Messiah, and opening them to see it, and to see, at the same time, the evidence for Jesus of Nazareth being the Christ, the Son of the living God. You who complain of weak faith or no faith, and who are all the day crying, " Help my unbelief," yet turning your eye away from the object of faith, look here; look at God's testimony to his Son. Mark the divine evidence given, the threefold proof that Jesus is the Christ. Faith 'cometh by hearing, and hearing by the word of God.

Let us look at this threefold evidence.

I. *The* WATER *says Jesus is the Christ, the Son of God.*—That baptismal scene at Jordan means much. Not only by it did Jesus fulfil all righteousness, but by it he was declared to be the Son of God. In it we see the Father and the Spirit uniting in their testimony to that mighty fact, or truth, on which our faith rests,—that Jesus of Nazareth is the Christ, the Son of the living God. As the *voice* from heaven did *audibly*, as the descending Spirit, in his dove-like form, did *visibly*, so did the waters of baptism, *sensibly and palpably*, proclaim to us that Jesus was the Son of God. The announcement coming forth from that baptismal symbol, of which the *one* John made use, and of which the *other* John here reminds us, was most intelligible and explicit. It was neither ambiguous nor uncertain. It pointed out the person, while it proclaimed his character and office. And it came not from earth, but from heaven. It came from him who cannot be mistaken, and who will mislead no man; from him whose witness-bearing is the surest of all testimonies. Unbelief can no longer cavil or misdoubt; faith need no longer hesitate; here is God's own proclamation, that puts uncertainty aside, and sets all misgivings at rest. God himself, in that water, speaks to man, and says, "This is my beloved Son, in whom I am well pleased." What farther need have we of witnesses?

II. *The* BLOOD *says Jesus is the Christ, the Son of God.*—On four occasions was the blood poured forth, at his circumcision; in Gethsemane; in Pilate's hall, when he was scourged and crowned with thorns; and on the cross. But it is to the testimony of the cross that the apostle here refers. That testimony was given both before and after death. The nails of the cross drew forth his blood before death, and the soldier's spear drew out the remainder after death; thus completely pouring out the "blood which was the life," and announcing that he had thoroughly died, and that the evidence of that death was as *complete* as it was *visible.*

The blood is God's testimony that he is in very deed "the Christ;" the Seed of the woman; the Man with the bruised heel; the Messiah of the prophets; the Sin-offering of Israel; the Fulfiller of all types and promises. While the water says, "Unto us a Child is born;" the blood says, "He has borne our griefs and carried our sorrows, the chastisement of our peace was on him, and by his stripes we are healed." His baptism said to us, "The Word has been made flesh;" the cross proclaimed, "Behold the Lamb of God, that taketh away the sin of the world"

As, without the sacrificial life-taking on the cross, he would have been but half a Christ, nay, no Christ at all *to us;* so God has taken special pains to let us see that that life was really taken, and that he is in very deed the Christ of God. Hence the stress which John lays on the piercing of his side, and the issuing of the blood and water; "He that saw it bare record; and his record is true; and he knoweth that he saith true; THAT YE MIGHT BELIEVE" (John xix. 34, 35). And then he adds afterwards, "These are written that ye might BELIEVE THAT JESUS IS THE CHRIST, the Son of God; and that believing, ye might have life through his name" (John xx 31).

On this testimony, then, let our faith rest. The witness is divine, for it is "the blood of God;" and he who speaks to us in that blood is Jehovah himself. The blood is the proof which God has given us, that this Jesus of Nazareth is in very deed the Christ of God. False religion and vain philosophy gather round a Christ of their own fashioning; a golden calf of their own moulding; a Christ whose blood was never shed. But that which is true and divine, acknowledges, as its alpha and omega, a Christ who *died* as well as lived; a Christ who took upon him our curse; a Christ whose person, however glorious in itself, is nothing to us sinners, without the bloodshedding of his sacrificial work.

III. *The* SPIRIT *says Jesus is the Christ, the Son of God.* It was the Spirit that bore witness to Christ at his baptism, when he descended on him like a dove ; and it was the same Spirit who, at Pentecost, came down in such mighty power to sum up the testimony. As the Dove at Jordan, and as the tongue of fire in the upper chamber, he bore witness to the truth that Jesus is the Son of God. And still he carries on his testimony, though no longer by visible form, or audible sound. He testifies of Christ ; he glorifies Christ. He points at once to his person and his cross ; he takes us to his cradle at Bethlehem, and to his tomb at Golgotha. All that he now is doing bears reference to the Son of God. He tells us what the water means, and confirms its testimony. Thus is the evidence completed ; nay, more than completed ; for though *two* witnesses would have sufficed, according to the law, God has added this third one, — one in all respects *divine*,— to confirm the truth beyond the possibility of doubt. And now we know of a truth that Jesus is the Christ, the Son of God, the sacrifice for sin, the Saviour of the world.

Now we know that the Son of God is come ; and this is the resting-place of faith. The water says, " He is come ;" the blood says, " He is come ;" the Spirit says, " He is come." Here faith rests ; and, resting here, it " overcomes the world." No other faith can give us the victory save that which roots itself in the truth, that Jesus is the Son of God, and in the evidence of this, supplied to us by these three witnesses. " A faithful witness will not lie ;"

and here are three faithful witnesses, furnished by God himself. A "true witness delivereth souls;" and here we have three true witnesses, on whose testimony we rest for the deliverance of our souls.

If, then, we would be conquerors, let us cast ourselves more absolutely on this threefold testimony, and drink in its spirit and meaning. It is only in proportion as we do so that we shall prove victorious. Nothing else can give victory but faith; and no faith can do this save that which leans on divine testimony. Every other will give way or break down. This only will stand, and, in standing, prove itself an "overcoming" faith; a world-overcoming faith, because a faith in Him who has overcome the world for us. The more that we know of him who lived that he might do battle with the world, and died that he might vanquish it, the more shall we ourselves prove conquerors, "more than conquerors, through him who loved us."

The reason why so many are weak and sickly among us, so unable either to fight or to stand, is that they do not believe that which these three witnesses testify, that Jesus is the Christ, the Son of God; or, if they believe it, they do not think it enough. They must have something added to this great truth before it will yield them either confidence or strength! But if God be true, it is, of itself, enough. If what the water says be true; if what the blood says be true; if what the Spirit says is true, we are provided with all we need, for the warfare and the victory. "Who is he that overcometh the world, but he that believeth that Jesus is the Christ?" In all our battles let us take this as our watchword, the mighty, the divine spell, with which we overcome the enemy. There is nothing like it. And just as it is written, "Who is he that overcometh the world but he that believeth that Jesus is the Christ," so it is also written, "Whosoever believeth that Jesus is the Christ, is born of God." Can words be more explicit? If this great fact be true; if there be enough of evidence for it, and if it be, in its own large fulness, sufficient to bring you blessing, as God says it is, then why should we doubt, or why refuse, to take the gladness which this fact of facts embodies and presents? Most assuredly it does contain, as in a golden urn, all the peace, and the hope, and the joy, which a human soul can possess; and he who has not received this joy and peace, has not yet understood the meaning of this mighty fact. Is Jesus really the Christ? Is this proved and established beyond a doubt? Do you receive it as true, not upon the report of men, but upon the testimony of these three witnesses? Then is it not written that "whosoever believeth that Jesus is the Christ is born of God?" and what, then, should shake your peace or your confidence, save that which shakes the evidence of this blessed fact, —the evidence that Jesus of Nazareth is the Christ, and that this Christ of God died and rose from the dead?

Is this truth, this event, which God accounts so excellent and so momentous, a dubious thing? Or, even though certain, is it a small thing in your eyes;—a trivial and subordinate piece of knowledge which a man may accept, and yet not be the better for it, or reject, and yet be none the worse? Nay; it is no poor, no common thing. It is the greatest fact which our earth has yet witnessed; it is the most powerful, the most pregnant, the most vital, the most transforming of all. Take it gladly in. Bid it welcome. Let it have free course throughout your whole being, unchecked by any wretched surmises, as to its not being sufficient to do such great things for you. Take it in all its rich and boundless meaning, as at once the vindication of God's righteousness, and the exposition of his love; and you will find what peace, what life, what healing it can diffuse throughout your whole being. Like a goodly vessel, laden with the riches, the fruit, the fragrance, of a hundred climes, —nay, with the very glory of the heaven of heavens—it will enter your port and unload its divine freight, filling your soul,—were you the most sorrowful of earth's sons,—with the joy unspeakable and full of glory.

SERMON XLII.

THE DIVINE BANQUET.

"He shall eat the bread of his God, both of the most holy, and of the holy."—Lev. xxi. 22.

It is not easy to say whether the words, "bread of his God," refer generally to the sacrifices and offerings, or specially to the "shew-bread." We take them as pointing to the latter; as, indeed, in any interpretation of the expression, the shew-bread must be *included*, if not mainly intended.

It was called the "shew-bread;" or, more properly, "the bread of the presence;" the bread that stood on the King's table, and in the King's presence; the bread which was therefore intimately connected with him who is called "the Angel of the Presence" (Isa. lxii. 9); the bread which was associated with him whose "presence" went with Israel whithersoever they went (Ex. xxxiii. 14).

The name of itself marked it as something different from the *manna*. That was "angels' food" (Ps. lxxviii. 25); it was the bread of heaven (Ps. cv. 40); but this was "presence-bread," the King's own loaf; "royal dainties;" taken each Sabbath morning from the King's table, and given to the "royal priesthood" who ministered to the Mighty

King. Yet was it made of common wheat, the fruit of the curse-laden soil; ground in the mill; mixed with water; kneaded by the hands of a man; baked by fire,—and this not altar-fire, but common fire from man's hearth,—like other bread. And though, in after times, all this was done by the Levites or Kohathites, yet at first it is enjoined on Moses himself, as the representative of the great King, whose bread it was. Such was the typical bread; the "bread of the presence;" bread setting forth something truer, and more substantial, more spiritual, more royal, more divine; the "true bread;" the bread of God; that "flesh which is meat indeed." For the food of the Church, in each age, has been the same; "they did all eat the same spiritual meat" (1 Cor. x. 3); and thus all along faith realised "the communion of the body of Christ" (1 Cor. x. 16), and even before he came, led Israel to see, that, "though many, they are one bread and one body, being all partakers of that one bread" (1 Cor. x. 17).

Let us examine this true "presence-bread," set before God's kings and priests as their true and eternal food.

I. *It is provided by God.*—As in carrying out his purpose in the old creation, he provided every fruit-bearing tree for man; so, in accomplishing the new creation, he has supplied the "food convenient." He gave the tree of life for the paradise of the first Adam; and he has not forgotten it in that of the second. He has made the provision for his house; and he has also blessed it. For the sustaining the life which he imparts, he provides the food required. Therefore was the "presence-bread" of old called "the bread of our God," because both itself, and that which it symbolised, were provided by God himself. To clothe the lilies and to feed the ravens, was to give us the pledge of fullest blessing for the souls of those who were more precious by far than lilies or ravens; and to place the twelve weekly loaves on the sanctuary table for the representatives of the twelve tribes of Israel, was to give to his whole Church, in all coming ages, the thousand times repeated assurance, that he would provide for each member of that vast but scattered company, the true bread, even the flesh of Him who was given for the life of the world.

II. *It is prepared by God himself.*—Moses, as representing God, prepared the twelve loaves; and God himself has prepared the better bread, the flesh of the Son of Man. "A body hast thou prepared me." As it was not mere fruit, the simple growth of the soil, that was to be laid on the sanctuary table as God's bread, but loaves carefully prepared of certain materials, so was it in the case of him whose "flesh is meat indeed." Very careful was the preparation of this bread of God. It was committed to "the Holy Ghost," and it was accomplished by "the power of the highest" (Luke i. 35). Various were the earthly processes through which it had to pass, before it could be laid on God's table and become proper food for God's royal priesthood; and, in the growth of the wheat in Israel's fields for Israel's shew-bread,—its cutting down, its grinding, its kneading, its firing,—in all these we have a symbol of the processes, by means of which the bread of God was prepared for us. In the history of the birth, the life, the sorrows, the hardships, the blood-shedding, the death of the incarnate Son of God, we have a description of the way in which the "shew-bread" or "presence-bread" of the Church was prepared, according to God's own method, for our everlasting food. A fragment of our common humanity, separated from the mass by God's own hand, is united to Godhead in the person of the Eternal Son. This God-man, very man and very God, is subjected to poverty and want, to hunger and thirst, to weariness and sleeplessness, to pain and sorrow, to the persecution of man and the fire of God's anger, till being "made perfect through suffering," he becomes "the bread of God." Israel's shew-bread was not eaten raw, nor unkneaded, nor unbaked, nor unfired; so, neither could our bread be fit for our use till it had passed through similar processes of preparation. Ah! how little we realise the truth, that a Christ not made perfect through sufferings, would have been no Christ to us; and that every grief he bore, every change he passed through, was fitting him to be more fully and more truly the "bread of life" for us.

III. *It is given to us by God.*—God causes it to be provided for us; nay, he prepares it himself; and then having thus provided and prepared it, he *gives* it. "God so loved the world that he *gave* his only-begotten Son" (John iii. 16); "the bread that I will *give* is my flesh, which I will *give* for the life of the world" (John vi. 51); "this is my body which is *given* for you" (Luke xxii. 19). "My Father *giveth* you the true bread from heaven" (John vi. 32). There is no buying on our part, or selling on his; it is all *a gift* from first to last; the gift of divine love, the donation of royal munificence; the liberality of him who, as he would not have us bought with anything but blood divine, or clothed with anything but heavenly raiment, so would he not have us fed on anything save "the finest of the wheat." Yes, "this is the record that God hath given to us eternal life, and this life is in his Son." He that hath the Son hath life; and he that believes the Father's testimony hath the Son. "All things are ready, come ye to the feast." "Eat, O friends; drink, yea, drink abundantly, O beloved." And to the sinner it says, "Wherefore will ye spend your money for that which is not bread and your labour for that which satisfieth not? hearken unto me, and (ye shall) eat that which is good, and your soul shall delight itself in fatness" (Isa. lv. 2). "This is the true bread, of which if a man eat he shall live for ever."

IV. *Who they are who feast on it.*—Perhaps the

answer to such a question will be,—God's priesthood, his church. Nor would this be incorrect; yet it would be defective. No doubt this heavenly bread is for them, just as the tree of life was for Adam, or the temple shew-bread was for the sons of Aaron. But it is so specially called "the bread of our God;" and the table on which it is set is so specially God's own table; and the place where it is to be eaten is so manifestly the royal banquet-hall of heaven, that we come to the conclusion that *God himself is partaker of this feast as well as we.* The King, sitting at his own table, in his own festal chamber, not only feeds his guests, but himself partakes of that which is set before them. Of wine it is said (no doubt in reference to the drink-offering), "it cheereth God and man" (Judges ix. 13); as if God himself were refreshed by those offerings by which the souls of his people were refreshed. In reference to the meat-offering and the drink-offering, it is said that they are "of a sweet savour unto the Lord" (Num. xxviii. 8), shewing us that the thing in which his people delighted was the same with which he himself was satisfied. It was not the mere wine, nor the bread, nor the lamb, nor the frankincense, which was thus so acceptable to God, and in which his soul delighted; it was that which these all symbolised and embodied; that which in the fulness of time was to be unfolded in its manifold excellence,—the unsearchable riches of Christ, the fulness of him "in whom it pleased the Father that all fulness should dwell."

It was for himself, then, no less than for us, that the Father was preparing this divine feast; it is for himself, as truly as for us, that he has furnished this table, and set on it that divine bread which is to be his repast, and ours as his priesthood, throughout that eternal Sabbath in which we are both to rest and feast with him. The sacrifice is over, but the feast remains, for it is eternal; standing perpetually upon God's table, and not needing, like Israel's perishable shew-bread, to be removed and renewed, but abiding the same for ever; not consumed, though ever fed upon by numbers without number, but, like the five Bethsaida loaves, leaving more behind at the end than it had at the beginning!

Israel's various sacrifices and offerings of all kinds were the various dishes set upon the great temple-table; each of them full of meaning; each of them containing that which would satisfy and comfort; every one of them setting forth some part of the glorious fulness of the God-man, as the true food of souls; and all of them together representing that complete and blessed feast of "fat things" partaken of by God and by his redeemed, in some measure now, but hereafter to be more fully enjoyed at the great marriage-supper in the New Jerusalem, when that shall be fulfilled, so long realised but in parts and fragments, "I will come in to him, and will sup with him, and he with me" (Rev. iii. 20).

Thus God in preparing Christ, in making him what he is, in filling him with the divine fulness, was not only providing bread for us to all eternity, but for himself; for with nothing less than this could he be satisfied. There is that in Christ which affords infinite and unutterable satisfaction to the Father; and if, over the creation of heaven and earth, he could rejoice, pronouncing it very good, and feasting on the wondrous workmanship of his own hands, how much more will he delight in him who is infinitely more glorious, more excellent, more perfect than all heaven and earth together; how much more truly and satisfyingly will he feast on him who is the infinity of created and uncreated excellence, the vast treasure-house of all that God, or man, or angels, can desire, the perfection of all perfection, the beauty of all beauty, the glory of all glory.

Israel's bread was called "shew-bread" or "presence-bread," because set before the presence of Jehovah, and eaten in his holy place. So is it with Christ. He is specially the bread of the Presence, the bread set before the King, and eaten in his palace. As it is said of the feast in Ezekiel's temple, "The prince, he shall sit in it, to eat bread before the Lord" (Ezek. xliv. 3); and so do we sit down at a communion-table to eat the true presence-bread before the Lord, the Lord himself, in whose presence we sit, feasting along with us.

Israel's shew-bread was for the priesthood; no others were to eat it. So the bread of God is for God's true priesthood, his church. It is not for angels, at least in the way that it is for the redeemed. Angels' food was, indeed, once given to man; but man's food is not to be given to angels. It is something of which only redeemed men can partake, and in partaking of which they are associated with God.

Israel's shew-bread was specially for the Sabbath feast of the priesthood. So, as we have seen, is Christ the food, not only of our Sabbaths here, but of the eternal Sabbath in reserve for us, when we shall enter into the temple of our God, to go out no more.

Israel's shew-bread is called the "continual" bread. Though the symbolic loaves were of necessity changed every week, yet there were always loaves on the table, and always loaves for the priest's repasts, so that the bread seemed always to be in the process of being eaten, and yet never diminished nor consumed. Our better shew-bread is "continual;" it is "everlasting;" and as the bush burned with fire, yet was never consumed, so the bread is always being eaten, yet never wasted. It is everlasting bread.

This, then, is the "true bread;" the "bread of God, the bread of life;" that which God calls "the bread of their God;" "My bread" (Num. xxviii. 2); the eternal food of the soul; that on which we feed, and on which God feeds; that, in feeding on which, we have communion with God, and God with us, both sitting at the one table and partaking of the one bread. As it is at the cross of Christ that we first meet with God in peace, so it is round the eternal table where the great shew-bread is placed that we meet continually, and carry on the intercourse begun at the cross, "The bread which we break, is it not the communion of the body of Christ? so that we, though one body and one bread, are all partakers of that one bread." We have thus found a common centre, a true and congenial meeting place. We feed on that which God calls his bread; and with that bread we are satisfied, even as he is satisfied; well-pleased with that with which he is well-pleased. We sit down at the same table, and partake of the same food; and the Lamb slain, the broken body of the eternal Son of God, is at once the centre of our fellowship, the substance of our repast, and the fountain of our joy.

SERMON XLIII.

BETHANY AND ITS FEAST.

"Then Jesus, six days before the passover, came to Bethany, where Lazarus was which had been dead, whom he raised from the dead. There they made him a supper; and Martha served: but Lazarus was one of them that sat at the table with him. Then took Mary a pound of ointment of spikenard, very costly, and anointed the feet of Jesus, and wiped his feet with her hair: and the house was filled with the odour of the ointment."—JOHN xii. 1–3.

WE find ourselves here at Bethany, amid fig-trees, and olives, and sycamores. In its quiet hollow, on the eastern slope of Olivet,—there it lies, encircled with its orchards, out of the reach of the city din. It has been noted for many things in the life of Christ, but specially for the resurrection of Lazarus. The like could not be said of Jerusalem, though so nigh at hand. And with what an eye of solemn wonder would men look on it, as they passed on their way to or from Jericho, saying to each each other,—In yon village a man was raised from the dead.

The house at which we find ourselves is that of Simon the leper (Matt. xxvi., Mark xiv.); a house that had once been shunned, and would still be looked upon with a suspicious eye. To this house Jesus had been invited; and he goes. What matters the name of a leprous house to one who has come to heal; to one whom no infection can touch, and all diseases obey. The feast is a great one; and many are there; some to see Jesus, and some Lazarus, the risen man. It is Jesus, however, who is the centre of the circle; and round him the group is gathered. The persons mentioned here are only spoken of in connection with Him: Lazarus, Mary, Martha, are but subordinate parts, in a scene of which the Lord is the centre. From him it is that they derive all their interest and significance. Their names, their persons, their characters, their movements, are nothing to us, save in their relation to him.

Apart from him, too, the feast is but a common meal, such as is every day partaken of among men. It is *His* presence that sanctifies it, and turns it into something special, if not sacramental. When he comes in and sups with us, the room, the table, the food, the company undergo a transfiguration. Connection with him dignifies and ennobles, nay, consecrates them. Without him all things are low and tame. With him they become sacred and lofty. As his touch healed, so did his presence elevate and glorify.

Let us note each of the four personages here, in so far as they are linked with Him who gives meaning and importance to what they are, and what they do.

I. *Simon entertaining.*—He had known Christ before; though when and where we are not told.

It seems to have been his leprosy that first brought him to Christ, and Christ to him. His disease was his link of connection with the Lord; and had it not been for it, he might never have sought him. It is still so with us. Our first interview is respecting our sin, our moral leprosy. It is *conscience* that seeks the interview, even though filled with misgivings as to its result. We go to converse with him, not about the good that is in us, but the evil. The sense of *guilt* draws us to him as the pardoner, and the consciousness of *sin* constrains us to deal with him as the healer and renewer. And as we began, so also do we go on. Sin brought us to him, and him to us; and sin keeps us constantly at his side. Intercourse with him has become a necessity of our new being. It cannot break or end. It must not be loosened, but drawn closer every day; for the more that we get from him, the more we learn our need. Simon finds that he has much more to do with Jesus than merely for the cure of his leprosy; therefore he must have him under his roof, and at his table. So is it with us. We begin our intercourse by going to him with our sins; but we soon discover that it cannot be ended here. Our acquaintanceship must be a companionship; a constant interchange of thought and sympathy. We invite him to our house, and he comes. We ask him to dine with us, and he comes. For no invitation, whether from Pharisee or publican, did the Lord ever decline. He sits down to feast with us at our table here; and while sitting there as our guest, he invites us to sup with him at his table above, where we shall be the guests, and he the host. How great the honour enjoyed by Simon, of entertaining the Lord of glory; sitting at his own table, with Jesus at his side as his guest! And how marvellous the condescension of Christ, in thus sitting at the leper's table as one of his household! Here, then, is the Saviour that suits us;—the healer of the leper, and the guest of the healed one! We say to him, "Heal me," and he heals; "come in," and he comes; "sit down at my table," and he sits down straightway.

In this Bethany-feast, it is interesting to notice what we may call the sinner's side of the gospel. Here, it is not Christ inviting and receiving the sinner; but the sinner inviting and receiving Christ. It is not Christ saying, "Come to me, and I will give you rest;" it is the sinner saying to Christ, "Come to me, and I will feast you;" it is not Christ knocking at the sinner's door, but the sinner knocking at Christ's; it is not Christ supplying the sinner's wants, but the sinner supplying Christ's. In our dealings with the Lord we must not overlook either side. He is, no doubt, *first* with us in all things; but this should only make us the more anxious to remember the response,—the lifetime's response,—with which he expects to be met. The love and the embrace must be mutual, as also the invitation and the joy. It is not Joseph weeping on the neck of Benjamin; but Benjamin weeping on the neck of Joseph.

II. *Lazarus feasting.*—He is a fellow-guest, with the Lord himself, at Simon's board. When Simon sends his invitation to Christ to dine with him, he bids Lazarus also to the feast. And there this raised one sits, side by side with Jesus, at the leper's table. What a feast, and what a company! The like had not been seen before; Simon the healed one, and Christ the Healer; Lazarus the raised one, and Christ the Raiser; dipping in the same dish, drinking of the same cup, conversing together on the things of the kingdom.

How or when Lazarus first became acquainted with Christ we know not; but it was his *death* that had brought about the special closeness of contact; and it was at the *tomb*, not at the *table*, that the Lord and he had so wonderfully met. The living One had gone into the dwelling of death, and there saluted the dead man in his dark abode. What a meeting! Ah, surely, Lazarus then discovered that he needed Jesus in a way such as he had never done before. Back from the silent chamber Jesus had led him; and now he sits down with him, at a table of earth: type of the risen saints who are to take their places with the Lord at the marriage-supper of the Lamb. What has Lazarus now to do, but to gaze and listen? Simon entertains; Lazarus sits as guest, drinking in the everlasting words from heavenly lips, and holding fellowship with the blessed Speaker. This is our true posture, as those who have died and risen with Christ! *Listening;* yes, LISTENING; not bustling, nor talking;

but listening to the Lord. There is a time for working and for speaking; but there is a time for *listening.* Blessed are they that know it, in an impetuous age like ours. When shall we learn it; and, in so doing, taste the profound tranquillity with which it soothes the soul?

III. *Martha Serving.*—This is her usual employment. To serve the Lord of glory; to watch at the table; to observe all his motions; to anticipate his wishes and supply his wants; this is Martha's posture, both of body and soul. It was the lowest place, yet not the least blessed; more like his own than any other. He came to serve; and in this Martha imitates him. To resemble him in anything was to be partaker of his blessedness and to share his fellowship. To have in us any part of "that mind that was in Christ Jesus," is both honour and joy. Service to Christ in any form, how blessed! To loose his shoe-latchet; to wipe the dust from his feet or the sweat from his weary brow; to pour water upon his hands or to prepare his couch; to supply any of his commonest wants or render the simplest offices of happy love: these are things which angels might covet, even were it for nothing else than the near contact with himself into which they bring us; for anything that brings us within the sound of his voice, or the glance of his eye, or the touch of his hand, must be blessedness. And if any one asks, how this can be done now, seeing he is in heaven and we on earth:

we answer at once in his own gracious words, "inasmuch as ye have done it unto the least of these my brethren, ye have done it unto me." He serves us, and we serve him; and in this mutual service we have our mutual fellowship and common joy.

IV. *Mary anointing.*—Reverence, homage, love, are all embodied in this act. It was with desire to honour him; and also with a dim half-conscious reference to his coming death and burial that she did this. She grudges no cost; and as the Bride in the song says, " the best wine for my beloved," so said her heart, if not her lips, " the best spikenard for my beloved Lord." All to honour him whom she so reverently loved. She is not *entertaining*, like Simon; she is not *feasting*, like Lazarus; she is not *serving*, like Martha; she is doing what some would consider a very useless thing, pouring ointment on his feet! That is all! Oh, useless expense and waste of substance, that might have benefited the poor! Yet her act gets most notice from her Lord. He says nothing to Simon, nor Lazarus, nor Martha. It is Mary that he marks and commends. Her fervent love, pouring itself out in one single act of honour, gets the highest notice. Is there no silent lesson here for us? It is not labour, nor suffering, that get the fullest commendation; it is *love;* pure, warm, ungrudging, loyal love. It is this that gets the Master's " Well done." He can do without the others, but not without this.

Thus, these four are presented to us in connection with the Lord; and such are the different points at which the connection comes out. Simon's connection is that of entertaining Christ; Lazarus's is that of feasting with him; Martha's that of serving him; and Mary's that of anointing. In all these ways there is connection, living connection, the contact both of faith and love. There is nearness, there is communion; not once, but constantly; not for a day, but for ever. It matters little in which of these ways we may have this connection. They are all real and they are all blessed;—the entertaining, the feasting, the serving, the anointing. We may have each of them in turn; for a saint's life is an enjoyment of all the four. Yesterday he was Simon; to-day he is Lazarus; to-morrow he may be Martha; the day after, Mary!

It is but little indeed that we can taste here, even in the walk of happiest fellowship; for the best of earthly feasts are but foretastes of the marriage-supper. But the whole glad fulness we shall yet enjoy, when all things are made new; and when we shall meet a long absent Lord, not at *our* table, but at *his own;* not in Simon's house, but in the great hall of the new creation, when God shall have cleansed this old leprous earth and healed its leprous dwellers; not amid the fig-trees of Bethany, but under the shade of the eternal palms. That day shall be the day of the Master's joy, as well as of ours; he feasting with us, and we with him; he enjoying our fellowship, and we his, for evermore.

SERMON XLIV.

THE CHURCH'S WIDOWHOOD.

"And there was a widow in that city; and she came unto him, saying, Avenge me of mine adversary."—LUKE xviii. 3.

WITHOUT entering at length on an exposition of this parable, in either of its aspects, practical or prophetical, we may say this much, that it sets before us, under the figure of a widow,—a feeble and injured widow,—the true character and standing of the Church of God on earth, during the present age. In numbers she is few,—a mere election, a gathering out, no more; in power, slender; in honour, little set by; in alliances, little courted, nay, shunned; in relative position, unfit to sway the world's counsels; in political and social influence, save as the salt of the earth, incapable of what man calls great achievements or overawing combinations, seeing she is scattered and divided among all kingdoms; and that, not like some vast network of electrical wires encompassing the globe, and capable, by its union of parts, to act with simultaneous force upon the nations, but only like the separate dew-drops, which, though many and pure, and fitted to cheer the blossom on which they rest, have no power to turn the rock into a garden, or to make the wilderness blossom as the rose.

That such is the case, nay, that such *must be* the case, appears from such things as these :—

(1.) *The Father's purpose concerning her.*—That purpose has great things in store for her, in the ages to come; but at present her lot is to be weakness, poverty, hardship, and the endurance of wrong. Through much tribulation she must enter the kingdom. It is not the purpose of God that she should be numerous, or powerful, or honourable; but, like her Head, disesteemed, rejected, despised, treated oftentimes as the offscouring of all things. Her success is not to be measured by the extent to which she has been able to overawe, or to attract, or to dazzle the world,—to disarm its enmity, or to purchase its friendship; but simply, and only, by the manner in which she has been enabled to fulfil the Father's will; to manifest her sympathies with the Father's purpose; to be faithful to her calling and character; to testify for him whose blood has bought her, and to be separate from the evil that is in "this present evil world."

(2.) *Her conformity to her Lord.*—He is her pattern, not merely as to character, but as to the whole course of life. In him she learns what her lot on earth is to be. He the rejected one, even among his own, she must be rejected too. He the hated one, she must be hated too. Better treatment than he met with, she is not entitled to expect; nor should she wish to have. Union with him in reigning is her hope ; union with him in suffering is her experience here. Conformity to him in holy glory hereafter is what she looks for ; conformity to him in shame and sorrow now, is what she knows to be her lot. She feels that she could not be the true Bride of a suffering Bridegroom, if her path below were one all smiles and sunshine.

(3.) *Her standing by faith.*—It is the world's *unbelief* that so specially makes it the world; so it is the Church's *faith* that makes her what she is, the Church. All that she can say for herself is what the apostle did for himself and the saints of his day, "We have known and believed the love that God hath to us." Her connection with the testimony of God, with him of whom it speaks, and with the glory to which it points, is one simply of *faith*. It was faith in that record which first drew her out of the world, and which still keeps her separate from it. As one believing in a kingdom yet to come, she shakes herself free from the entanglements of time. She becomes a stranger here, having no continuing city, but satisfied with the tent of the desert, till she reach the city of habitation. The faith which realises the unseen and the eternal, displaces, both in her vision and in her heart, the things seen and temporal.

(4.) *The condition of the world out of which she is called.*—It is an evil world. It lieth in wickedness ; and her calling is to come out from it, and, like Noah, to condemn it. All belonging to that world is evil, and what has she to do with it? Satan is its prince and god, and what has she to do with him? It crucified her Lord, what can she have to do with it? Her mission is not to transform the world into the Church, but to be God's instrument in taking out of it a people for his glory. In such a world, how can she be other than a stranger? In its cities, how can she be other than a sojourner? She has nothing in common with it. All is uncongenial.

(5.) *Her prospects.*—She is an heir of God, and a joint heir with Christ Jesus. An everlasting kingdom, an unfading crown, an eternal weight of glory,—these are her prospects. What has she then to do with a world where all these are unrecognised, nay, despised or disowned? As the Bride of Christ, what sympathy can there be in her bosom, with the vanities of a world so vain as this? It doth not yet, indeed, appear what she shall be; but she knows that, when he shall appear, she shall be like him, for she shall see him as he is; and having this hope in him, she purifies herself, even as he is pure.

The Church, then, is thus, of necessity, a *widow*. Hence, while the Spirit of God uses various figures to describe her, they all, more or less, point to some such forlorn and helpless condition. Whether she is spoken of as a pilgrim, or a stranger, or an orphan, or a little flock, or a lily amongst thorns, still the leading thought is the same. In her orphanage, or strangership, or widowhood, she still moves before us as the separated, rejected, lonely one, in the midst of an unfriendly world, that far outnumbers her, and that feels itself strangely incommoded and made uncomfortable by the presence of one who sets light by all the precious and pleasurable things of earth, having her eye and her heart fixed upon something more glorious, of which the world knows nothing.

It is by acting out her character, fully and consistently, that she honours God, and bears witness to Christ, and condemns the world, and testifies to the glory of the promised kingdom. It is thus, too, that she wins the eye of the heedless worldling, pointing upwards to the incorruptible crown, and bidding men set their affection on things above, and seek their treasure and their joy in heaven. It is her widowhood that is her testimony. It is her widow's weeds, with which she dare not part, that make known beyond mistake, and yet without a voice, what she thinks of the world and the world's ways; how she disesteems the world and the world's joys; how thoroughly she has broken off from the world and the world's companionships, and taken the true measure of its fascinating gaieties; how wide she deems the difference between herself and the children of time; how stedfastly she has set her face towards the kingdom; and how completely the King in his beauty has absorbed her soul, and displaced the poor objects of admiration or affection with which the world would seek to win her steps back to itself, and recover her heart to the dreams of creature-love and creature-beauty. How solemnly does her widow's cry, "Avenge me of mine adversary,"—"How long, O Lord, how long!"—proclaim to the world a truth which it seems to have forgotten, that its King and Lord is absent; thus reminding it of the shade which that absence has thrown over creation, by telling of the blank which it has made in her own bosom, even though she knows that she is his, and that he is hers.

If, then, the Church forsake this position, and forego this character, she abandons her calling, she lowers her testimony, she destroys her usefulness, she becomes unfaithful to Christ, and, instead of preserving her purity, she becomes the mother of a spurious race of Christians, who are neither Christ's nor the world's; who think it possible to make the best of *both* worlds; in whose features one can find few traces of resemblance to the great Exemplar; in whose constitution and habits one can discover none of those elements of power, and hardness, and endurance, which primitive days exhibited; in whose doings, or darings, or sacrifices, one can detect nothing of that zeal, and self-denial, and decision, which led one of other days to say, "I count not my life dear unto me, that I may finish my course with joy."

A widow's proper raiment, as well as her true ornaments, are her *weeds*. Gold, and silver, and precious stones, she has put off. They are the symbols of mirth, and gaiety, and triumph; and what has she to do with these, in the absence of her Lord, and in the midst of a world that disowns him? It is in her *weeds* that she passes along the world's highway, as one who has little in common with it, whose sympathies have all gone upwards to One whom, having not seen, she loves. They speak of an absent Husband. They tell of faithful affection and constancy, as well as of indifference to all love save that of him whose memory she cherishes, and whose absence she mourns. They are expressive of indifference to the attractive scenes and objects of earth, not merely because of their uncongeniality, but because they cannot be truly enjoyed in separation from the Beloved One.

A "widow indeed" is thus described by the apostle :—" She that is a widow indeed, and desolate, trusteth in God, and continueth in supplications and prayers night and day" (1 Tim. v. 5). But a mere widow in name is one who "liveth in pleasure," and is thus "dead while she liveth." The true Church of God is the former; the false church, the harlot-bride of Satan, is the latter; for she openly repudiates the name of widow, while she lays aside the weeds of widowhood, saying, "I sit as a queen, and am no widow, and shall see no sorrow;" decking herself all the while "in gold, and silver, and precious stones, and pearls, and fine linen, and purple, and silk, and scarlet" (Rev. xviii. 12).

This contrast between these two not only shews

us the right standing of the one church, and the false and faithless character of the other, but it intimates this, that one of the church's most subtile temptations will be to lose sight of, if not to disown, her widowhood, and to live, and act, and speak, as if she were well content with the world as it is, and had no consciousness of any blank, either within her or without.

The world loves not the faithful widow, and would fain seduce her to a second marriage,—a marriage with itself. Decked in costly array, it would admire her, and give her its willing fellowship. But dressed only in the widow's mournful garb, it cannot tolerate her. Her faithfulness to her Lord condemns it. Her seclusion and separation rebuke it. Her continuing in supplication and prayers night and day it cannot away with. Her wistful eye, glancing eagerly upwards, as if to see the Unseen, and greet the absent One, is a continual reproof. The widow's cry sorely disturbs the world's peace, and, ringing nightly through its glittering halls of pleasure, turns all its music into discord.

Nor less does Satan dislike the widow's weeds and the widow's cry. For they remind him that his day is short, and that he who is to bind him in chains, and cast him out of his dominions, will soon be here. They torment him before his time. They proclaim the doom of his harlot-spouse, who sits now as queen, in that "one hour" when desolation shall overwhelm her (Rev. xviii. 19). They point to the glory of the now widowed church, in that day, when, instead of her attire of sackcloth, she shall be arrayed in the "fine linen, clean and white," and, with her long-parted Husband restored to her embrace, she shall be exalted to the sovereignty of that very world where she has been treated as "the off-scouring of all things."

The hostility of the world and its prince to the Church of God is not new. It is the ancient feud between the two "seeds" (Gen. iii. 15), which, in successive forms, and with varying intensity, each age has evolved. Compromise or inconsistency may modify this warfare ; but ended it cannot be, save in the extinction of the one seed or the other. The world hopes to absorb the Church, and so to terminate the variance ; but this absorption is what the true Church so greatly dreads, for by it *she* loses and *her rival* gains everything. It is an absorption, the root of which is unbelief, and the development of which is, at the best, the form of godliness without its power.

SERMON XLV.

THE CHURCH'S WIDOWHOOD.

"And there was a widow in that city; and she came unto him, saying, Avenge me of mine adversary."—LUKE xviii. 3.

MOST unweariedly has Satan sought, age after age, to silence the widowed Church's cry, to muffle her voice, to seduce her into unfaithfulness, and to persuade her to part with her weeds of widowhood. That he has never *wholly* succeeded we know; for a remnant, at least, has always been found who abode faithful, though sometimes clothed in sackcloth, in addition to the widow's raiment, and sometimes with that sackcloth stained with blood. Yet too frequently has he succeeded in part,—to an extent which may well alarm us, and lead to self-questionings of the most searching kind. He succeeded in a measure with the church of Ephesus, so that her Lord was constrained to address her as one who had left her first love. He succeeded still more with Sardis, till only a few names were left which had not defiled their garments. Even more sadly did he succeed with Laodicea; bringing her into such a condition of evil that she was on the very edge of entire rejection; elating her with such thoughts of self-sufficiency and wealth as to make her wholly lose sight of her estate of lowly widowhood; decking her with the world's gay attire, and leading her to exchange the widow's cry for the world's song, "I am rich and increased in goods, and have need of nothing." But the full measure of his success is only seen in Babylon. In her, seduction has been triumphant, and not a vestige either of the widow's weeds or of the widow's cry can be found in her. The temptation which proved so unsuccessful in the Lord has succeeded in her,—the offer of the world's kingdoms. With these, Satan has bewitched and beguiled her. For these, she has forsaken her Lord, and espoused herself to the god of this world, who satiates her to her heart's content with the carnal abundance of his kingdom, so that she is no longer a widow, but a queen; no longer desolate, but "glorifying herself, and living deliciously;" no longer poorly or plainly clothed, but decked in purple, and pearls, and gold; no longer crying, in her helplessness, "Avenge me of mine adversary," but ruling over the nations, nay, giving them to drink of the golden cup of her uncleanness, nay, seducing even the kings of the earth to pay her suit and service, intoxicating them with the pleasures of her unlawful love.

Between the state of backsliding Ephesus and that of apostate Babylon, there is a mighty difference; and yet these churches reveal but different degrees of the same evil. Ephesus represents the beginning, Babylon the end, of the downward course, between which extremities there exist many stages and gradations; but the type of evil is, to a certain extent, the same in all. In every one of them we see Satan laying snares for the Church, beguiling her out of her widow's seclusion, making her dissatisfied with her poverty and weakness, persuading her to put off her weeds, and conform to the gay attire of the multitude around.

This, then, is one of the Church's special dangers. Such is Satan's object in assailing her. Such the small beginnings of apostasy, and such the fatal end! In ways most subtle, by degrees quite imperceptible, she is persuaded to leave her first love; and then, having done that, she is ready for any amount of backsliding.

Is it not thus that Satan is spreading his fascinations for the Church in our day? Fain would he draw her out of her seclusion into the gay whirl of earth. He spares no art to tempt her to act inconsistently with her widow's character, and to become unfaithful to her widow's vow. His object is to bring her down from her high standing as the Church of God, holy and beloved, separated unto Christ, and set on high by his redeeming power; to draw her off from that consecrated ground which her Lord had intended her to occupy, that she may mingle with the bustling crowds of the world's highway, or take her place in its assemblies of pleasure and revelry.

In carrying on his seductions, he makes use of various appliances. He begins with objects which are in themselves lawful ; he goes on with those which are suspicious and questionable ; and he ends with those which are positively sinful and pernicious.

He approaches the Church subtilely and with fair words, as an angel of light. How excellent and noble is science,—how fitted to exalt the soul, and to feed its immortal longings! Most true. Nor ought we ever to say one word to the disparagement or depreciation of science. But may it not be too absorbing? May it not displace higher things? May it not lead to a too exclusive cultivation of the understanding, and so nourish intellectual pride, and seduce the soul into the mere wisdom of this world? The Church is to be on her guard; not against science, but against the way in which science has been used to dazzle or bewilder the Church's eye, and so withdraw her affection and her gaze from the things above.

Or, again, he comes to her applauding the world's literature, and exhibiting it to her in all the fascinations of poetry and romance. Let us not discredit literature, or treat it all as alike unprofitable. But let us beware of its enchantments. Let us see that even in its lawful parts it does not come between us and the vision of the eternal kingdom, or lead us astray with the enticing words of man's wisdom. And as to those parts of it that appeal to the sentiment, or the passions, or the lusts of our nature, which are mere gratifications of our love of pleasure, such as the novel, or the idle song, or the loose opera ;—how can we touch, or taste, or handle ? What has a heaven-born soul to do with earthly vanities like these ? What has the widowed spouse of Christ, mourning her Lord's absence, and longing for his return, to do with scenes and sounds such as these, which feed the flesh, which eat out the very core of faith, which rekindle fires that should be for ever quenched, and refasten links that should be for ever broken ?

Or, farther, he comes to her with the more direct blandishments of pleasure as his snares. "What sin, what harm in the dance, or the theatre or the assembly ?" And how often is he at once responded to,—" Yes, what sin, what harm in these ? May a man not be a Christian and yet enjoy these ?" This would we say in reply. In primitive days no man would have thought of claiming the name of Christian who enjoyed them ; and if a man can think himself a Christian while enjoying these, he must have misunderstood the character of a follower of Christ ; he must have forgotten the Lord's own awful words,—" If any man will come after me, let him deny himself, and take up his cross, and follow me ;" and he must have set aside the apostle's solemn exhortation, " Love not the world, neither the things that are in the world : if any man love the world, the love of the Father is not in him." If any say, "This is an hard saying, who can hear it ?" we answer, Is it harder than that, " She that liveth in pleasure is dead while she liveth ?" Is it harder than that, " The friendship of the world is enmity to God ?" Is it harder than that, "Come out, and be ye separate, and touch not the unclean thing?" Is it harder than that, "Ye cannot drink the cup of the Lord and the cup of devils; ye cannot be partaker of the Lord's table, and the table of devils?"

Besides, what congeniality can one whose characteristic is that of widowhood, and orphanage, and strangership, find in such scenes as these? Laughter and revelling are for the whole-hearted and the sorrowless; how suit they the widow's weeds and the widow's cry? If the Church of God would mingle in such scenes, she must first renounce her widowhood; for how strange, how spectral, would be the entrance of widowhood, in the reality of grief, as well as in the outward garb of mourning, into such haunts of hollow mirth as the gay world presents! How startling, nay, how displeasing and disturbing, would be the sombre hue of the widow's raiment in that blazing hall of midnight,

> "That dazzling mass of artificial light
> That shews all things, but nothing as they are."

Into such uncongenialities, how is it possible for the Church of God to enter? With incongruities and inconsistencies like these, she can have no sympathy. If she understands her own character and calling, she must see that she has a peculiar path to pursue,—a path which cannot admit of any such compromise between the things of heaven and the things of earth.

She, like her Lord, is from above; the world, like its prince, is from beneath,—and how can there be an alliance between parties, whose interests, sympathies, hopes, joys, are so far asunder? How can the Church of God descend from the high eminence to which she has been lifted up, and tread again that enchanted ground which she professes to have forsaken for ever? Can she lose sight of her calling? Can she forget her widowhood? Can she see no crime in being unfaithful to her absent Lord, and unjust to the memory of one who has loved her so well? Can she think of imitating (even in spirit, or for a day) the apostate Church, Satan's harlot bride, and saying, "I sit as a queen, and am no widow, and shall see no sorrow?"

The god of this world is doing his utmost, in these last days, to ensnare the Church, to seduce her into worldliness, to draw down her eye from the heavenly glory, to silence her cry, to induce her to drop her widow's raiment, and if not altogether to identify herself with the world, at least to be less peculiar, less singular in her walk, less solemn in her testimony against the "fashion of this world," the "things that perish with the using," "the lust of the flesh, the lust of the eye, and the pride of life."

Shall he succeed? Shall his sophistry prevail? Shall his appeals to all that is best in the *natural man* be met with acquiescence on the part of the saints of God? Shall his arguments and wily flatteries, addressed so skilfully to our love of natural beauty, wisdom, goodness, truth, be yielded to, so that we shall give up our distinctiveness as the called of God, and the heirs of his kingdom? Shall he persuade us to be less strict, less holy, less heavenly, with less of the sorrowing widow in our deportment, and more of the crowned queen?

Shall we resist, or shall we yield? Shall we hold fast our profession, or shall we fling it aside? Shall we try to seize a portion here, or shall we be content to wait in faith, until the Lord return?

Surely this is a question for the age,—a question for the Church of God,—a question for every child of the kingdom. It is a question, too, for those who are still wholly of the earth : " Will ye cling to the earth; and what will that earth to which you cling do for you?" It is a question for those who think it possible to be both lovers of God and lovers of pleasure: " Will ye try to reconcile what is irreconcileable? Is not God enough without the world,—is not Christ enough without its pleasures?" It is a question for the anxious and the earnest: " Will ye not *decide*,—will ye waver, will ye halt, will ye try something less than an entire surrender of the whole man to God?" It is a question for the Christian : " Will you be less than your name implies,—less than a child of heaven, less than an heir of God, and a joint heir with Christ?" It is by *faith* you stand. It was the belief of God's free love, as manifested in the cross of his Son, that made you what you are; and if that faith has any meaning, it means that you are no longer of the world, that your treasure is above, that your inheritance is not here, and that you are waiting, in patient love and hope, amid weariness and buffeting and trouble, for the grace that is to be brought unto you at the revelation of Jesus Christ.

SERMON XLVI.

THE WORLD'S ORACLES.

"The idols have spoken vanity."—ZECH. x. 2.

THERE are not many who think for themselves; and even those who are reckoned to do so, depend for the materials of thinking upon what they hear, or see, or touch. In the things of God this must be so, much more than in others. It is in hearing him that we are furnished with materials for thinking rightly about him. "Faith cometh by hearing, and hearing by the word of God." God's place is to speak, and ours is to listen. He expects us to listen to him, for he has a right to speak; and we know that, if we do not, we are sure to think wrong concerning himself and his ways; concerning both good and evil.

But we do not like this. It is irksome to be always in the attitude of listeners; at least, of listeners to God. We prefer guessing, or speculating, or reasoning. Or, if we find that we must have recourse to some authority beyond ourselves, we betake ourselves to any pretender to wisdom,—and, above all, to any one who professes to be the representative of the invisible God, and to speak in his name. Hence the Gentiles resorted to their "oracles," and the apostate Jews to their "witchcrafts," and to private oracles, or household gods, called "Teraphim," set up in imitation of the great public oracle, the Urim and Thummim, through which God spoke to them in his holy place. It is to this that Zechariah refers, "The idols" (Teraphim) "have spoken vanity" (x. 2). They whom you consult as the depositories of divine wisdom, who pretend to guide you and to utter truth, have spoken vanity; they have cheated you with lies.

Such was Israel's history. They trusted in faithless oracles. They became the dupes of those to whom they had come for guidance in the day of perplexity. They had grieved away the voice that spoke to them by the jewelled breastplate, and they had betaken themselves to other voices that only misled and befooled them. Their Teraphim spoke vanity.

This has been man's history too, as well as Israel's. He has chosen another counsellor instead of God; it may be the Church, or reason, or public opinion. He has betaken himself to some oracle; he has listened to its utterances; it has cheated him with words of vanity; and its divinations have been as the treacherous staff, which not only breaks under the weight of the traveller, but pierces his hand as he leans on it.

Poor world! such is thy story. Misplaced confidence, disappointment, darkness; the blind following the blind, till one pit receives both the leader and the led!

The world's Teraphim have not been few; nor has their authority been either weak or transient. They have swayed millions of destinies; not always consciously, on the side either of the speaker or the listener, but still irresistibly. There is "public opinion," that mysterious oracle, whose shrine is nowhere, but the echoes of whose voice is everywhere. No Hindoo ever crouched before his idol with more of submissiveness than do men, calling themselves enlightened, cringe before the shadowy altar of this "unknown god,"—nay, of this Moloch, through whose fires has been made to pass many a tortured conscience that would fain have sided with God and with truth, but dared not, lest it should stand alone. But, besides this idol, or oracle, of public opinion, there is the standard of established custom,—schools of literature and philosophy, or theology; and there is what is called the spirit of the times. Nay, there is sometimes the idol of personal friendships, or of admired authors, or of revered teachers. What havoc do these often make of consciences! How they mislead and pervert! How subtilely do they work in drawing the confidence away from God, and in setting up other standards of truth and holiness than his word and law!

Then let us mark on what points these Teraphim mislead us. They misrepresent the real end and aim of life, assuring us that the glory of the God who made us cannot be that end, inasmuch as that is something quite transcendental, something altogether beyond our reach, or our reason, or our sympathies. They give doubtful, often delusive, answers to such questions as these, "What is truth? what is happiness? what is holiness?" In regard to these things, most certainly, the world's idols have spoken vanity. We can give no credit to their utterances. He who trusts himself to their guidance will go utterly astray. He will miss the very things he is seeking. He will not get hold of truth; he will come short of happiness; and, instead of holiness, he will become satisfied with some artificial standard of moral character which man has set up for himself.

But how is it thus? Why are men thus misled and befooled? *They have no confidence in God himself;* nor have they learned to say, "Let God be true, and every man a liar." They seek not the Holy Spirit, nor submit themselves to him as their Teacher. They look askance at the Bible, as if there were some danger in making too much of it, or as if it were only one out of the many standards by which we are to measure ourselves and our opinions; nay, as if, in these days, there was so much in the Bible of what is obsolete and unsuited to an age like this, that, were it not for some traditional reverence for that book, and admiration for its beauties, it might in a great measure be set aside. Besides, men do not like the teaching that they get from God and his word. It does not suit their tastes. They do not relish it at all. Hence they choose the prophets of smooth things, the "Teraphim" that utter lies and vanity. "These be thy gods, O Israel." These are the world's oracles. As for God, and his Spirit, and his book, they say, as the king of Israel did of Micaiah, " I hate him, for he doth not prophesy good concerning me, but evil" (1 Kings xxii. 8).

But *how* do these Teraphim speak their vanities? They do not need to do so by uttering gross error. Nay, it is seldom that they try this, though, undoubtedly, error is the real *terminus* at which they aim. But they mingle the true and the false together; so that the true is neutralized by the false, and the false is adorned and recommended by the true. The fair fragments of the latter hang like gems around the former, making it comely and attractive. With what seductive persuasiveness do these counsellors of the world, these oracles of the race, win the ear of men! They point to the great men who have pursued paths very far asunder from those who stickle so sternly for adherence to the naked word of God. They bid us listen to the world's philosophers and poets,—to Kant, to Goethe, or Coleridge, or Wordsworth. They ask us to take the experience of these mighty men of mind or song, and to abjure the narrowness and one-sidedness into which we shall otherwise be shrivelled up, if we become men of one book, even though that book should be the Bible,—men of one school, even though that school should be that of the apostle Paul.

And why do these oracles speak thus? They are fond of speaking, and they like to be listened to. It is a great thing to be consulted as an oracle, and to be quoted as an authority. They have no high or sure standard of their own, and hence they can only speak according to their own foolishness. "They know not, neither do they understand; they walk on in darkness." They "grope for the wall as the blind" (Isa. lix. 10); and they who set their trust on them must be content to spend their lives in doing the same.

The world has always had its oracles, its Teraphim, its *Dii minores et majores*. By them it has been guided in the strange career of separation from God, which the apostle calls "the course of this world" (Eph. ii. 2). They have helped to mould the world, and to make it what it is; and in its turn it has, in large measure, moulded them and made them what they are. For "the god of this world" is the god of these gods, the oracle of these oracles. "The spirit that worketh in the children of disobedience" (Eph. ii. 2), is the spirit which speaks through these oracles, and which is, by means of these servants of his, imbuing the world more thoroughly with his own falsehood and unholiness, conforming it more entirely, age after age, to his own image, and withdrawing it more widely from the living Jehovah, the God and Father of our Lord Jesus Christ.

Formerly, it was more as "the ruler of the darkness of this world" that Satan wrought and spoke;

now, it is more as an angel of light, into which he has transformed himself (2 Cor. xi. 14), that he may ensnare the more, nay, deceive, if it were possible, the very elect. Thus, that which God calls "a wonderful and horrible thing" has come to pass; "the prophets prophesy falsely, and the priests bear rule by their means; and my people love to have it so" (Jer. v. 30, 31). No wonder that he should ask, "What will ye do in the end thereof?"

It is as the angel of light that Satan is now the world's oracle, or rather, the inspirer of its oracles. He has changed his voice as well as his garb and aspect. He has hidden his grossness, and modified his language to suit the change. He has veiled his sensualism under the guise of poetry, and thrown the mantle of philosophy over the offensive nakedness of atheism. He is still an atheist with the scoffer; a wanton with the lewd; a blasphemer with the profane. For he changes not. But, to disgust as few as possible, and to entangle in his net the many who shrink from all open grossness, he has set up a more refined system of worldliness, of which the watchwords are, "Harmless amusements," "Innocent gaiety," "Intellectual feasts and healthful sports," and such like. Now, there are amusements that are harmless; but are these in the theatre or opera? There is gaiety that is innocent; but is this to be found in the ball-room, and in the giddy whirl of the waltz? There are sports which are healthful; but are these on the turf or in the ring? There are feasts of the intellect; but are these contained only in the light novel or the loose song? Are they to be found in the lecture-rooms of those who cleverly substitute philosophy for faith, reason for revelation, man's wisdom for God's; who prove to us that, though the Bible may contain the *thoughts* of God, it does not speak his *words;* who artfully would reason us into the belief that sin is not *guilt*, but only a *disease*, a mere moral epidemic; who maintain, with the philosophic Buddhist, that *incarnation*, not *death*, is the basis of divine reconciliation; that the tendencies of creaturehood are all upward, not downward; that forgiveness is not a thing needed by any one, seeing condemnation can have no place under the government of a God of love; who affirm that, though the love of God leads us to conclude the existence of a heaven, yet that his righteousness does not by any means infer the necessity either for a judgment or a hell.

As an angel of light, all his snares and sophistries partake, more or less, of light. He does not appeal directly to our lusts, but to our love of the beautiful and the bright. He does not take his stand upon our natural hatred of God, but upon our thirst for truth and knowledge. By such indirect methods he beguiles us as effectually into error and sin; nay, seduces us as surely into apostasy from God, as when he ensnared our first mother, under the promise of wisdom. "Ye shall be as God," he says still;—independent of all other beings and wills, thinking what you please, enjoying what you desire, and taking in the whole round of indulgences, physical and intellectual, at your will.

As an angel of light he instructs his oracles (as we see in the journalism of the age) to appeal to men's natural humanity, that so he may get them to substitute *this* for union through the blood of the covenant, and brotherhood in the Son of God. He instructs his oracles to address themselves to our intuitions of virtue and uprightness, that he may by these supplant holiness, and conformity to the image of "the Word made flesh." He instructs them to press home amendment of life and the relinquishment of all offensive evil, that he may utterly efface the idea of being "born again," of the necessity of "conversion," and of the Holy Spirit's indwelling fulness, as the one true source of all that God calls "religion." Thus he "blinds the minds of them which believe not lest the light of the glorious gospel of Christ, who is the image of God, should shine into them" (2 Cor. iv. 4).

Tutored by this angel of light these oracles of earth speak of the "majesty of mind profound;" or of "the splendid might of mind," in all the elation of intellectual pride. They speak loftily of "the world's vast lie," of "earth's falsehoods," of the age's "shams," all the while complacently congratulating themselves that they have found their way out of these unrealities. They think to dig through the husk into the kernel of all religions, and, out of their uncertain speculations, to construct a new theology. "Attempt the high," they say; "seek out the soul's bright path;"

> "Upon the summit of each mountain-thought
> Worship thou God."

They spurn the belief that this lapsed creation is wholly evil; exulting in its self-rectifying, self-regenerating power.

> "The universal solvent of disease
> Still bounds through nature's veins."

It is from Satan as an angel of light, and from his oracles as the reflections of that light, that we have most to dread. The disguises which he is putting on are fatally seductive. The lengths to which he goes, in pretended reverence for religion; the subtle skill which he has put forth in beautifying what is sensual, in refining what is carnal, in purifying what is gross;—the artful way in which he has mixed up the true and the false, the lawful and the unlawful, the certain and the uncertain, the earthly and the heavenly, the human and the divine; the marvellous cunning he has displayed in infusing a sort of religious element into what is meant to be the counteractive of religion; in throwing a religious hue over subjects and scenes, intended by him to withdraw the heart from God; the sophistry by which he has succeeded in substituting the beauties of Pantheism for the blasphemies of Atheism; the dexterity by which he has introduced love to the Creator's works, instead of love to the Creator himself, natural "earnestness" for the zeal of the renewed man, self-reliance for dependence upon the Almighty, sympathy with "nature" for fellowship with God; the successful subtlety with which he has confounded opinion with truth, speculativeness with honest inquiry, credulity with faith, misanthropy with separation from the world;—these things are truly fitted to alarm, inasmuch as they threaten the obliteration of every sacred landmark, and the final substitution of evil for good, and darkness for light.

The illumination coming from the Sun of righteousness is one thing, and that proceeding from Satan, as an angel of light, is quite another. Satan's object is to confound these two kinds of light, so that men may be misled, as by the gleam of a false beacon, which ensnares even a skilful pilot, and hurries the secure vessel suddenly upon the rock. One of our greatest dangers in these days, arises from this effort of the evil one. If he had set up his light in a wholly opposite quarter, and given it a colour like himself,—the lurid glare of hell,—men would not have been deceived. But he has imitated so nearly the hue of the true light, and placed it so near the heavenly lighthouse, that thousands mistake the beacon, and find themselves unexpectedly a wreck.

Thus it is that the idols have spoken, and do still speak, VANITY. They cheat men with a thousand falsities. They proclaim hopes that end in disappointment. They dupe the heedless, and then mock their miseries. They promise men liberty, while they themselves are the servants of corruption. They promise the bread of truth, and give only the husks of error. They promise joy, and defraud the unwary with the "pleasures of sin." They speak peace, when, instead of peace, there is wrath. They teach men to say, "I am rich, and increased in goods, and have need of nothing," when they are "poor, and miserable, and wretched, and blind, and naked." They tell men "To-morrow shall be as this day, and much more abundant," when time is on the edge of bankruptcy, and the world's great famine is at hand, when men's famished spirits shall ask for bread in vain; when earth shall plead for something to fill the craving void,—which should have been filled by God himself and his incarnate Son,—and there shall be nothing but the chaff, or the sand, or the air.

Shun the idols that speak vanity. Listen to no voice, however pleasant, save that which is entirely in harmony with God's. Take nothing for truth save what comes from him. Follow no light but that of him who says, "I am the Light of the world." Abjure every pleasure, every indulgence, of which Christ is not the alpha and the omega, or which would grieve that Holy Spirit of God, whereby we are sealed unto the day of redemption.

Men may say, Don't be singular, don't pretend to be wiser or better than others. Let us answer, without shrinking, "Let God be true, and every man a liar." Those who have listened to the oracles of earth have always been a multitude; while they who have listened to God have always been few. Let not this discourage us. We have but one voice to listen to, and it speaks articulately, so that we have no excuse either for hesitation or mistake. While others are listening to the idols who speak vanity, let us be intent on knowing what the Lord has spoken. Many may walk on in darkness; but it is written, "The wise shall understand" (Dan. xii. 10). Let others betake themselves to "the wizards that peep and mutter; should not a people seek unto their God?"

What though the oracles have spoken,—are they our gods? Are they the representatives of Him in whom are hid all the treasures of wisdom and knowledge? Do they speak according to the law and the testimony?

It is written, "The idols have spoken vanity." They have cheated their worshippers. They are doing so still. They give fair words, but that is all. The issue is disappointment and shame. Are you allowing yourselves thus to be cheated by Satan and his pretended wisdom,—by the world and its deceiving oracles? Are you the dupes of these idols, who, having once lured you into the snare, will only laugh at your calamity?

Be wise in time. For the day of these oracles is fast running to a close. "The idols he will utterly abolish." The vanities which they have spoken will be soon exposed. The hollowness of their promises will, ere long, be detected. Listen not to them, but to the faithful and true Witness,— to the words of the living God; to him who says, "Learn of me;" to him who utters no vanity, but who has the words of everlasting life,— the truth which fills, and satisfies, and gladdens,— yea, who is himself "the Way, the Truth, and the Life."

SERMON XLVII.

THE VAIN WISH.

"Let me die the death of the righteous, and let my last end be like his."—Num. xxiii. 10.

We must not lose sight of the *place* where these words were spoken. It was in the land of Moab, and amid the wild desolation of its bare grey hills. It was hard by the land of promise, but not in it; quite within sight of it, yet still with Jordan and the Dead Sea between. It was a land of enemies; a land of false worship; a land whose king hated Israel, and was searching everywhere for curses to launch at him. From this stranger-land, and from these hills, round which the exhalations from the sea of death are gathering, and over which the gloom of the shadow of death is resting, the prayer comes up, "Let me die the death of the righteous, and let my last end be like his."

Nor must we forget the *man* who spoke them. He is a Mesopotamian seer; a man who, though a worshipper of false gods, knows much of the one true God. He is one who wants to serve two masters, and to make the best of both worlds; and, while serving Moab's Baal, would like to be in favour with Israel's Jehovah. He knows enough of Jehovah to stand in awe of his displeasure, and enough of Jehovah's people to desire an inheritance among them. But, like Demas, he loves this present world, and he covets the wages of unrighteousness. He would like to lose nothing of the good either of this world or the next. He would like to pitch his tent among the goodly tabernacles of Israel; but then, he must come out from his own nation, and break with Moab; he must forego all Balak's rewards, and give up honour, wealth, reputation, friends; and he cannot make up his mind to this. He would like religion, if it were not so dear. He would fain have a home both in Israel and Moab, and be both Baal's and Jehovah's prophet; but, since he cannot thus unite heaven and earth just now, he starts the thought, But might I enjoy them in succession; Moab just now, Israel afterwards? Might I not serve Baal just now, and Jehovah hereafter? Might I not go on living as heretofore, but make a change at *death?* This is the thought that is working its way through these words, " Let me die the death of the righteous." He sees that the death of the righteous is the best, whatever his life may be, and from the gloomy depths of a "divided heart" he sends up this bitter cry.

But it is with the *wish* or *prayer* itself that we have specially to do. (1.) What does it mean? (2.) What state of feeling does it indicate?

I. *What does it mean?* He knew that he must die, and that, after death, he must live for ever.

He had seen men die; he had seen the men of Aram, and Midian, and Moab die; but it was without hope; and he had seen the mourners go about the streets for them, but they sorrowed as those who had no hope. He would not die *their* death. He had seen, or at least heard of, other deaths, for he evidently knew much of Israel and Israel's history. He had heard of the deaths of Abraham, and Isaac, and Jacob, in other days; and, it may be, he had heard of Aaron's death on Mount Hor, just a short time before; and he knew how the righteous die. "Let me, then, die *their* death." Dimly, and from afar, he had read the joyful truth, afterwards brought nearer and into fuller light,— "Blessed are the dead that die in the Lord."

But the words mean more than this; for he speaks not merely of death, but of something beyond death, —the last end of the righteous. This is no repetition of the other. There is a parallelism indeed, but it is an ascending one; this second part containing more than the first; and by "last end" the seer meant *resurrection*,—a truth far more widely known, at least among the nations in any way linked with the patriarchs and patriarchal traditions, than is generally admitted. Balaam's prayer was, "Let me share the death of the righteous; and let me share his resurrection too." How full and comprehensive! There is no vagueness about the object of the wish, whatever there may be about the feelings or actings of him who uttered it. It is a prayer for us to join in; and, though once the prayer of an unbeliever, it may well be the prayer of a believing man.

II. *What state of feeling does it indicate?* It was not in *pretended* earnestness nor idle flippancy that these words were uttered. They were sincere. The Syrian prophet felt what he was saying. Compelled by the almighty Spirit to look into Israel's future, and utter glorious things concerning it, he was roused up to desire such a future for himself, to covet such a glory and such an immortality as awaited Israel when the Star of Jacob should arise, bringing morning, and gladness, and an incorruptible inheritance. Sick at heart, and weary of the hollowness of his own heathenism, and all that it could give him, he cries aloud, from the depths of a dissatisfied heart, "Let me die the death of the righteous." Disappointed and sorrowful, he sees the eternal brightness in the distance, with all its attraction, and beauty, and unchangeableness, and in the bitterness of his spirit he cries out, "Would God that I were there!" The feeling soon passes off, but while it lasts it is real. But, with all its reality, it leads to nothing. It leaves him where it found him, amid the mountains of Moab, as earthly, as covetous, as carnal as before. He would fain have the death of the righteous, but he sees nothing desirable in his life. He would fain have Israel's inheritance, but he has no wish to be a worshipper of Israel's God.

Balaam's wish is a very common one, both in its nature and in its fruitlessness. Sometimes it is a mere passing wish, called up by vexation and weariness ; at other times it is a deep-breathed prayer ; but, in both cases, it is too often inneffective, leading to nothing. Men, young as well as old, get tired of life, sick of the world and its vanities. They see that it has nothing for them after all ; and that, even if it had, none of its pleasures can last. When it has done all it can, it still leaves them with a troubled conscience, an aching head, and an empty heart. It makes promises, but cannot keep them ; it gives gifts to its lovers, but they perish with the using ; it strews roses in the path of its admirers, but this is only to cover its hideousness ; it prepares its revellings and banquetings, but these are to intoxicate and poison ; it spreads out its thrones and pomps, its costly gems and pearls, its gold and silver, its purple and scarlet, its gaiety and splendour ; but these fill up nothing : they bind up no wounds, they knit no broken ties, they staunch no bleeding hearts, they heal no blighted affection ; they leave sorrow still sorrow, and pain still pain, and tears still tears, and death still death, and the grave still the scene of farewells, and the dwelling of corruption. Is it wonderful, then, that the vexed spirit should at times fling all such earthly mockeries aside, and groan out the fervent prayer of the Syrian seer, "Let me die the death of the righteous ?" Have you not often done so ? And have you not added, "O that I had wings like a dove ; then should I fly away, and be at rest ?"

In too many cases, this is transient and sentimental. It leads to no action, no result. It vanishes like a bright rainbow from a dark cloud, and there is no change. Is it to be so with you? You *hope* to enter heaven; you *wish* for a happy death at last; but will wishes save you? Will wishes pluck out death's sting, or conquer the grave, or make you partaker of the resurrection of the just? You can't wish yourself into heaven, or out of hell. Your wishes will do nothing for you, either here or hereafter. If hungry, a wish won't give you bread; or, if thirsty, a wish wont quench your thirst; or, if suffering, a wish wont soothe your pain; or, if dying, a wish won't bring back health into your pale cheek and faded eye.

Yet, a wish may be a good beginning. All fruit begins with buds and blossoms; and though these often come to nought, yet sometimes they end in much. And, therefore, I would reason with you; I would plead with you. That *wish* may be the beginning of your eternal life. It may lead to much; Oh, let it lead you on! Do not trust to it, as if it made you safe and right; yet do not despise it, as if it were nothing. It may be like the angel that came to Lot to lead him out of Sodom: be not, therefore, forgetful to entertain this stranger; for you may be entertaining an angel unawares. Yield to it, and let it lead you on. Let it lead you out of the world. Let it lead you out of self. Let it lead you to the cross. Let it lead you to the blood of sprinkling, the fountain opened for sin and for uncleanness. Let it lead you straight, and without delay, just as you are, to Christ Jesus himself, and to God, the Father of our Lord Jesus Christ. Let it lead you up to the mercy-seat, where the blood speaks pardon, and the High Priest waits to bless. Let it do all this *now*.

Do not suffer that wish, however faint, to die away. It is the touch of the Spirit within you. It is the voice of Christ, saying, " Come unto me." It is the call of the Father, yearning over his prodigal, and beseeching him to be reconciled and blest. But a prayer like this, pointing both at death and resurrection, specially speaks of him who is the resurrection and the life. Go to *him* with your longings after the death and resurrection of the righteous. Go to him with that weary spirit, he will give it rest ; with that empty heart, he will fill it ; with that aching head, he will soothe it ; with that troubled mind, he will calm it ; with that faded eye, he will brighten it. He will give you " beauty for ashes, the oil of joy for mourning." Go to him with your sorrow, he will turn it into joy. Go to him with your death, he will transform it into life. Go to him with your sins, he will forgive them frankly. Go to him with your stony heart, he will take it out of you, and give you the heart of flesh. Go to him with your chains, he will snap them asunder. Go to him with your hunger, he will feed you ; with your thirst, he will give you drink ; with every burden, and care, and weakness, he will remove them all.

Oh, do not rest in a wish, a prayer, however good. That will not save you. Balaam went as far as that, Demas went farther, Judas farther still; yet they were lost. Be not like these. Quarrel with sin at once. Break with the world at once. Linger no longer on the mountains of Moab or the plains of Midian. Enter Israel's land. Pitch your tents in the midst of the beloved nation. Say with Ruth, when she left Moab, "Whither thou goest, I will go; and where thou lodgest I will lodge: thy people shall be my people, and thy God my God. Where thou diest, will I die, and there will I be buried: the Lord do so to me, and more also, if aught but death part thee and me."

You know that you must die. Do not dismiss that subject with a wish or a hurried prayer. Do not treat it sentimentally, and sing, "O for the death of those that die like daylight in the west!" Do not trifle away its solemnity, or say with the French infidel (Mirabeau), "Let me die to the sound of delicious music!" Look at death full in the face. Take up Balaam's prayer. It is a good one; only let be carried out. Die in Jesus, and you die well. "Blessed are the dead that die in the Lord." But the dying in Jesus must be begun by the living in Jesus. Only this will do. Live in him, and it will not be hard to die.

SERMON XLVIII.

THE MORTAL AND THE IMMORTAL.

"Neither can they die any more."—LUKE xx. 36.

OURS is a dying world; and immortality has no place upon this earth. That which is deathless is beyond these hills. Mortality is here; immortality is yonder! Mortality is below; immortality is above. "Neither can they die any more," is the prediction of something future, not the announcement of anything either present or past. At every moment one of the sons of Adam passes from this life; and each swing of the pendulum is the death-warrant of some child of time. "Death," "death," is the sound of its dismal vibration. "Death," "death," it says, unceasingly, as it oscillates to and fro. The gate of death stands ever open, as if it had neither locks nor bars. The river of death flows sullenly past our dwellings; and continually we hear the splash and the cry of one, and another, and another, as they are flung into the rushing torrent, and carried down to the sea of eternity.

Earth is full of death-beds. The groan of pain is heard everywhere,—in cottage or castle, in prince's palace or peasant's hut. The tear of parting is seen falling everywhere; rich and poor, good and evil, are called to weep over the departure of beloved kindred, husband or wife, or child, or friend. Who can bind the strong man that he shall not lay his hand upon us or our beloved ones? Who can say to sickness, Thou shalt not touch my frame; or to pain, Thou shalt not come nigh; or to death, Thou shalt not enter here? Who can light up the dimmed eye, or recolour the faded cheek, or reinvigorate the icy hand, or bid the sealed lip open, or the stiffened tongue speak once more the words of warm affection? Who can enter the death-chamber, and speak the "Talitha Cumi" of resurrection? Who can look into the coffin, and say, Young man, arise? Who can go into the tomb, and say, Lazarus, come forth?

The voice of death is heard everywhere. Not from the bier alone, nor the funeral procession, nor the dark vault, nor the heaving churchyard. Death springs up all around. Each season speaks of death. The dropping spring-blossom; the scorched leaf of summer; the ripe sheaf of autumn; the bare black winter mould,—all tell of death. The wild storm, with its thick clouds and hurrying shadows; the sharp lightning, bent on smiting; the dark torrent, ravaging field and vale; the cold sea-wave; the ebbing tide; the crumbling rock; the up-torn tree,—all speak of dissolution and corruption. Earth numbers its grave-yards by hundreds of thousands; and the sea covers the dust of uncounted millions, who, coffined and uncoffined, have gone down into its unknown darkness.

Death reigns over earth and sea; city and village are his. Into every house this last enemy has entered, in spite of man's desperate efforts to keep him out. There is no family without some empty seat or crib; no fireside without a blank; no circle out of which some brightness has not departed. There is no garden without some faded rose; no forest without some sere leaf; no tree without some shattered bough; no harp without some broken string.

In Adam all die. He is the head of death, and we its mortal members. There is no exemption from this necessity; there is no discharge in this war. The old man dies; but the young also; the grey and the golden head are laid in the same cold clay. The sinner dies; so also does the saint; the common earth from which they sprang receives them both. The fool dies; so also does the wise. The poor man dies; so also does the rich. "All flesh is grass."

The first Adam died; so also died the second Adam, who is the Lord from heaven. But there is a difference. The first Adam died, and, therefore, we die. The second Adam died, and therefore, we live; for the last Adam was made a quickening spirit; and this is the pledge of final victory over death and the tomb. Thus, the grave is the cradle of life; night is the womb of day; and sunset has become sunrise to our shaded and sorrowful earth. Yet, this is not yet realised. We are still under the reign of death, and this is the hour and the power of darkness. The day of the destruction of death, and the unlocking of sepulchres is not yet. It will come in due time. Meanwhile we have to look on death; for our dwelling is in a world of death,—a land of graves.

If, then, we would get beyond death's circle and shadow, we must look above. Death is here, but life is yonder! Corruption is here, incorruption is yonder. The fading is here, the blooming is yonder. We must take the wings of the morning and fly away to the region of the unsorrowing and the undying; where "that which is sown in weakness shall be raised in power, and death be swallowed up in victory."

It is not that God loves death, or desires to see the extension of its gloomy reign. It was not because he loved it that he let it loose upon the world at first; nor, after so many ages, has he begun to love it now, or to become familiar with it, or to look with indifference upon the ills which attend it,—the sorrow, the weeping, the pain, the desolation, the breaking in pieces of the great temple of humanity, and the undoing of all that divine handiwork which at first he pronounced so very good. No. But sin has entered; and law, unchangeable, remorseless, righteous law, demands the execution of the lawful sentence, "In the day thou eatest thereof, thou shalt surely die;" "dust thou art, and to dust thou shalt return." Man has only himself to blame for a mortal body and a ruined earth. God hates death, and all that death has done, as truly as he hates sin. He abhors the grave and its corruption.

He did not make man to be the prey of worms, nor create earth to be either a sepulchre or a hell. The eye weeps, yet God did not make it to weep, but to sparkle with gladness; and the lips utter sorrow, yet God did not make them to speak aught but praise and joy. So man dies; but God made him not to die, but to live. Earth is a vast grave-yard; yet God made it a paradise of life. His soul loathes the corruption of mortality, with which our world is overspread. He abhors death, and will, ere long, arise and avenge himself upon it for the ravages of six thousand years. No stronger language of abhorrence could be used, no more solemn purpose of divine vengeance could be indicated than the following,—"I will ransom them from the power of the grave; I will redeem them from death; O death, I will be thy plagues; O grave, I will be thy destruction: repentance shall be hid from mine eyes" (Hos. xiii. 14).

We look forward to the day of incorruption; but not so earnestly nor so sincerely as God himself. It is on resurrection that his heart is set; and not an hour longer than is absolutely needful shall that glorious consummation be delayed. The Church desires it; this body groans for it; all creation longs for it; but God still more than all. His object is not to perpetuate, but to terminate the reign of death; through death to destroy him that has the power of death. His purpose is to abolish death, to bind Satan, and to give his saints glorified bodies, and introduce the new heavens and new earth, wherein dwelleth righteousness. All heaven above is interested in resurrection. It is a thing such as angels have never seen, save in the case of the risen Son of God, the gate of whose rocky sepulchre they descended to open. They long for the resurrection-glory, as truly as they join in the joy over one sinner that repenteth.

Blessed words are these : "Neither can they die any more." It is not simply, Neither *shall* they die any more, but neither *can* they die any more. Death, which is now a law, an inevitable necessity, shall then be an *impossibility*. Blessed impossibility! Neither *can* they die any more! Oh, the security which these words give! Oh, the comfort, the unutterable gladness which they diffuse through the soul! Neither *can* they die any more! Death and the grave are cast into the lake of fire. They who are partakers of the first resurrection and of the world to come, are made for ever immortal. They *live* for ever. They *cannot* die. They have put on incorruption. They are clothed with the immortality of the Son of God; for as the Head is immortal, so shall the members be. Ah, this is victory over death! This is the triumph of life! It is more than resurrection ; for it is resurrection, with the security that death can never again approach them throughout eternity.

All things connected with that new resurrection-state shall be immortal, too. Their inheritance is unfading. Their city, the new Jerusalem, shall never crumble down. Their paradise is as much beyond the power of decay as it is beyond the reach of a second serpent-tempter. Their crowns are all imperishable; and the white raiment in which they shine shall never need cleansing or renewal. No failing of eyesight; no wrinkles on their brow; no hollowness in their cheeks; no grey hairs upon their heads; no weariness of limbs; nor languor of spirit; nor drying up of their rivers of pleasure. The evil days shall never come nor the years draw nigh when they shall say, We have no pleasure in them. The keepers of the house shall never tremble, nor the strong men bow themselves, nor the grinders cease, nor they who look out of the windows be darkened. No fears shall be in the way, nor shall the almond-tree flourish, nor the grasshopper become a burden, nor shall desire fail, nor shall the mourners go about the streets. The silver cord shall not be loosed, nor the golden bowl be broken, nor the pitcher be broken at the fountain, nor the wheel at the cistern. One generation shall not pass away, nor another come. There shall be a time to be born, but not a time to die; a time to plant, but no time to pluck up that which is planted; a time to heal, but no time to kill; a time to build, but no time to break down; a time to laugh, but no time to weep; a time to dance, but no time to mourn; a time to get, but no time to lose; a time to love, but no time to hate; a time of peace, but no time of war. Never again shall it be said, The days of darkness are coming; for the sun shall no more go down, neither for brightness shall their moon withdraw itself, for the Lord shall be their everlasting light, and the days of their mourning shall be ended. Then shall the wise man's maxim be out of date for ever, "The day of death is better than the day of birth;" and never more shall his lament over a fading world be heard, "Vanity of vanities, all is vanity." Here they sing,

> Ah! I shall soon be dying,
> Time swiftly glides away.

But then their song is only of life, for they know that they *cannot* die any more. Here they say, as one, feeling his mortality, has plaintively sung,

> Go and dig my grave to day,
> Homeward doth my journey tend;
> And I lay my staff away
> Here, where all things earthly end;
> And I lay my weary head
> In the only painless bed.

But there they shall sing, not their death-dirge but their resurrection-song, with resurrection-voice, in the glorious resurrection-land, "where they shall hunger no more, neither thirst any more ; but where the Lamb shall lead them to the living fountains of waters, and God shall wipe away all tears from their eyes."

SERMON XLIX.

LONGINGS FOR THE LAND.

"And I besought the Lord at that time, saying, O Lord God, thou hast begun to shew thy servant thy greatness, and thy mighty hand: for what God is there in heaven or in earth, that can do according to thy works and according to thy might? I pray thee, let me go over, and see the good land that is beyond Jordan, that goodly mountain, and Lebanon. But the Lord was wroth with me for your sakes, and would not hear me: and the Lord said unto me, Let it suffice thee; speak no more unto me of this matter. Get thee up into the top of Pisgah, and lift up thine eyes westward, and northward, and southward, and eastward, and behold it with thine eyes: for thou shalt not go over this Jordan. But charge Joshua, and encourage him, and strengthen him: for he shall go over before this people, and he shall cause them to inherit the land which thou shalt see. So we abode in the valley over against Beth-peor."—DEUT. iii. 23–29.

THE *scene* here lies in "the valley over against Beth-peor," at the base of the hills of Moab, that long grey ridge of barren mountains that overshadows the Dead Sea and the plain of Jordan. The land is as inhospitable as the people, and no doubt Israel was glad at the prospect of leaving it behind.

The *time* is the end of the forty years' sojourn in the desert. The tribes are just about to pass over into Canaan. The land lies before them, with but a few miles of rugged country and the Jordan between. Some weeks, perhaps less, will bring them over.

Their desert warfare, and toil, and travel are done. They have, as it were, come up to the gate of Eden, and have nothing to do but to go in and exchange labour for rest, barrenness for fruitfulness, mountains of bare rock, and plains of scorching sand, for fresh fields and vineyards, and rich plains, and hills waving with terraces of olive to the summit.

This nearness to the long-looked-for land stirs up the spirit of Moses, and he resolves to make one effort more to be allowed to enter. Entrance into it had been his hope from the day he left Egypt. The land flowing with milk and honey had been constantly before his eyes. And though God had intimated to him that, on account of his speaking unadvisedly with his lips at Meribah Kadesh, he was not to enter the land; yet now, when placed within sight of it, the longing to enter it rises up within him in all its force, and he resolves to attempt, once again, to obtain entrance, if that, perchance, he may be permitted to set foot in it before he die.

Let us note, then, the following points in this narrative :—

I. *Moses's desire to enter.*—(1.) It was strong and deep; the strongest and deepest desire of his soul in regard to anything earthly. Is our longing for the heavenly Canaan as vehement as his for the earthly? (2.) It was a holy desire. There was nothing carnal in it; nothing of the flesh or of self. It was the desire of a holy man for a share in the fulfilment of the divine promise. (3.) It was a patriotic desire. Canaan was his true fatherland, though he had never dwelt in it. It was the home of his fathers, and the inheritance of his children, the land in which Israel's hopes were wrapped up. As a patriot, Moses could not but long to enter in. (4.) It was a natural desire. Though brought up in ease and luxury, for now eighty years he had been a dweller in tents in the wilderness, a man without a home. How natural that he should be weary of the desert, and long for a resting-place! (5.) It was a desire connected with the welfare of his nation. Israel was to be blest in that land of blessing, and he desired to see his nation settled in the Lord's land. (6.) It was a desire connected with the glory of God. He knew that God was about to choose a place wherein to set his name, and to shew his glory. He had once before pleaded, " Shew me thy glory ;" and what could be more desirable in his eyes than that he should see the manifestation of this glory, and witness the mighty power of God in the land which he knew was to be the centre and stage of all these? Moses's desire, then, seems a reasonable, proper, and true-hearted desire. We greatly sympathise with the old man of *six score* in the feelings here expressed; we would kneel down beside him, and plead with God that he would not deny the request of his aged servant. It is but a small request ; and how blessed for the old man, like Simeon, to get the fulfilment of his lifetime's longings before he die! It was not, indeed, for salvation he was pleading : all that was settled long ago between him and his God ; but as the saved man, as a son and heir, he was asking for a nearer sight of this part of his inheritance,— asking to set his *mortal* foot upon a land which, in resurrection, he knew he would, in days to come, tread with *immortal* foot, and gaze upon with immortal eye. He was now within sight both of the earthly and the heavenly Canaan ; the upper and the nether glory were both before his eyes ; he longed to depart, and to be with Christ, which is far better ; but still, with all the heavenly full in view, and ready to be entered on, he still desired the vision of the earthly; he still pleaded, "I pray thee, let me go over and see the good land that is beyond Jordan, that goodly mountain, and Lebanon."

There was nothing wrong, or carnal, or low in this desire to look upon the earthly. That which is earthly is not necessarily carnal, and that which is material may be as spiritual as that which is immaterial. There may be a carnal view of things heavenly, as truly as there is a spiritual view of things earthly. The former is that which unbelief always takes, the latter is that which faith realises. It is not spirituality to abuse the body, to despise matter, to soar above the clouds. True spirituality is that which accepts material things as those which God created and pronounced good; which loves to visit them, and gaze on them in faith, as manifestations of the glory of the invisible God; as helps to the understanding of the great mystery of godliness, "God manifest in the flesh."

II. *His arguments* (ver. 24).—The first part of his argument is, "Thou hast shewed me the beginning, wilt not thou shew me the end?" It is natural, even in man's works, when we have seen the beginning, to desire to see the end; and to expect that he who has shewn us the one, will shew us the other. Moses feels as if he would be tantalized, almost mocked, by not seeing the end. He argues that God's willingness to shew him the beginning, is a pledge of his willingness to shew him all. We may all use this argument. Thou, who hast forgiven me past sin, wilt thou not forgive all present and all future sin? "Being confident of this very thing, that he who hath begun a good work in you, will perform it until the day of Christ" (Phil. i. 6). The second part of his argument is, that, to stop here, would leave so much undiscovered of his greatness and mighty hand, that, for the sake of the glory to be unfolded, and the power to be revealed, he might expect to be allowed to enter. So great is the undiscovered glory of God, and so desirous is God to reveal it to us, that we may use this argument with him respecting anything we desire. The third argument looks at the very little already seen,—only a glimpse. Moses pleads this *little*, and, because of it, asks to enter Canaan. He had seen much of God's power, yet he speaks as if it were little; not as if undervaluing the past, but still feeling as if it were comparatively nothing. So, all that we have tasted hitherto is small. It is in the ages to come that he is to shew the exceeding riches of his grace; and hence we may call the past a little thing, and use it as an argument with God. We might, perhaps, shrink from this, were it not that we call to mind his unspeakable gift; and, measuring other gifts with this, we may speak of them as small. We may argue, the blessings we have received are large, when we consider ourselves and our demerit; but, when measured with that gift which has purchased everything for us, and which is the pledge of all, they are as nothing. Let not the greatness of the blessings sought discourage us; rather let us deal with them as Moses did, and, pointing to their greatness, make that greatness our plea. It is a light thing with God to give us anything or everything. Let us ask, and let us expect the best gifts,—knowing that he will do for us exceeding abundantly, above all we ask or think.

III. *God's answer.*—It is not what we should have expected. It falls heavily on us, and it must have fallen still more heavily on the old man's ear. It sounds stern to us. Yet it is the answer of wisdom and love. Three things are recorded here. (1.) *The anger.* God was angry at Moses, or rather, he had been so; and the reasons for it were as strong now as at the first. Israel had provoked Moses, and Moses had provoked God. Israel's conduct had roused Moses to speak and act unadvisedly, so that he dishonoured God before all Israel. This public act of sin cannot be passed over, even in Moses; for, if God passed over offences in Moses when he was visiting them on the people, what would be said? This great dishonour done to God by Moses, though at the close of a long life of consistent service, must be publicly condemned. This is the anger spoken of. Moses is not to be cut off with the rebels, nor to have a grave in the wilderness; but some notice must be taken of his sin. God will by no means clear the guilty. (2.) *The refusal.* The anger leads to refusal of the petition. Often had the petition been presented and refused; now it is presented and refused for the last time. "He would not hear me!" Strange words these respecting God and his treatment of the prayer of a saint,—"He would not hear me!" Oh, with what feelings of abasement must Moses have listened to this last refusal! Such a refusal from One who had hitherto denied him nothing, from One who had so freely forgiven all his iniquities! How solemnly would he feel, in that hour, the necessity of such a testimony against the sins of his saints! How bitterly did that refusal call his sin to remembrance! (3.) *The prohibition.* "Let it suffice thee; speak no more unto me of this matter." This is the final closing of the whole question, the sealing of Moses's lips. He had, doubtless, often spoken to God on the subject; but now he is forbidden even to speak of it again.

There is something severe in this check; yet there is something very parental. It shews the intimate terms on which God was pleased to be with Moses; so that, when His child grew too importunate, He lays his hand upon his lips, with, Hush, speak no more on that subject. God is not a man that he should lie. His purpose must stand. But Oh, what an idea of the efficacy of prayer must Moses have had, when he thought by it to change the purpose of God! This was more than moving mountains. And how much God must delight in importunity, when he lets it go so far, and only checks it at the last with a rebuke so gracious and gentle!

IV. *God's condescending grace.*—Entrance is denied, but a full vision of the land is granted (ver. 27). He strains his purpose (if one may speak so) as far as possible, without breaking it. The actual request is denied, but something as like it, and as near to it, as might be, is accorded. He takes him to the top of Pisgah, one of the highest of the mountains of Moab, and from it he shews him the whole land. Looking westward, he sees Jerusalem, and Bethlehem, and Bethel, with the terraced hills of Benjamin and Ephraim stretching away in the grey distance, to the great sea. Northward, he sees the wooded vale of Jordan, with its forests of palms and pomegranates,—the fruitful heights of Galilee and Gilead, up to the snowy peaks of Lebanon, and "that goodly mountain," Hermon.

Southward, he sees the wooded hills of Judah, with the vineyards of Eshcol, and the olive heights of Kirjath-Arba in the distance, and perhaps the rising table-lands around Beersheba. Eastward, he sees the forests and pastures of Ammon, already, in part, under the dominion of Israel. The whole compass of the land he is permitted to gaze upon, that he may have a taste of Israel's long-promised inheritance. And Oh, with what intensity of gaze and yearning of spirit must he have viewed that fair expanse of scene!

Thus far grace condescends, shewing us to what lengths God can go, in answering prayer, even when a purpose of his own stands in the way. How rich must have been that taste of grace to Moses, after the refusal he had received! How deep his sense of the parental tenderness, the loving condescension, indicated in this! The denial of the request seems only to furnish a new opportunity for a manifestation of love, tenderer and more indulgent, than could have been given by the granting of the prayer. What an indulged and favoured child does Moses seem, even in this very scene of apparent sternness! O love that passeth knowledge! O condescension of God, to what depths of indulgent tenderness wilt thou not stoop!

Take these three closing lessons.

1. *What one sin can do.*—One sin cost Adam Paradise; one sin costs Moses Canaan. In the case of Moses it is the more startling, because it is

a forgiven sin, and he is a forgiven sinner. His sin is forgiven, yet it leaves a stain behind it; it traces a testimony to its unutterable evil on the person of the sinner. It could not cost him the heavenly inheritance; the everlasting covenant and God's electing love had secured that unconditionally and indefeasibly. But it costs him the earthly; for God must give public testimony against a sin publicly committed. O saint, give heed to thy ways! Thy inconsistencies may cost thee dear. They cannot close the kingdom on you; the blood that bought you has bought the kingdom for you: but they may bring you down to a lower level; they may dim the lustre of your raiment; they may take out some of the gems of your diadem. O man of God, beware of sin. Keep thyself pure. Walk and speak circumspectly. Follow the Lord fully.

2. *What God's inflexibility is.*—He cannot change. He cannot call that no sin which is sin; nor that a small sin which is a great sin; nor that a private sin which was a public sin. His purpose is not the easy, pliable, changeable thing which ours is. He is the God only wise, only righteous, only mighty, and is, therefore, above all such vacillations. He is without variableness or shadow of turning; the same yesterday, to-day, and for ever. O saint, remember that thou hast to do with a holy and unchangeable God! O sinner, think that thou hast also to do with him, and that this inflexibility is, as yet, all against thee! He will not alter

either his law or his gospel to suit you. You must take them as they are, or perish for ever! It is true that he who believeth shall be saved; it is as true that he who believeth not shall be damned!

3. *What the grace of God is.*—Many waters cannot quench it, nor the floods drown it. To what lengths it will go, in order to pardon a sinner or to bless a saint! Believer, be strong in the grace that is in Christ Jesus! Unbelieving man, take refuge now in that rich grace which is still held out to thee, for the forgiveness of all thy sins, and for the bestowment of blessings, and joys, and hopes; which will make thee richer than Israel with his earthly Canaan; gladder than Moses with his bright vision of the land flowing with milk and honey!

SERMON L.

CHRIST AND THE NEW CREATION.

"If any man (one) be in Christ, he is a new creature (there is a new creation to him); old things are passed away; behold, all things are become new."—2 Cor. v. 17.

It is usual to make this affirmation of the apostle refer merely to the change of nature which takes place in conversion. For then the renewal of man's whole being is effected; the "inner man" undergoes a total transformation; the old man passes away, and the new man comes in his place. In all parts of being we experience a change, save in these "vile bodies," whose renewal is not to be looked for till the appearing of the Lord.

That the words include and imply all this there can be no doubt. For all that is excellent in the matter of restoration must begin with the individual man, and must begin, too, with the innermost region of the individual man. Hence it is written, "Except a man be born again he cannot see the kingdom of God," intimating that all true connection with the coming kingdom must begin with personal renewal.

"In Christ," "a new creature," how much do these words imply! How complete the inward transformation which they describe! What condemnation do they pronounce upon the shallow, meagre religion so common among us, making us feel that hardly any description of its professors could be more exaggerated or unreal than that of being "in Christ," and "new creatures." Take yon member of the Church. He wears the garb and bears the name of Christ. He is a fair average specimen of a large class. He has the reputation of being a Christian; yet he is fond of the world; he grasps at its gold; he loves its fashionable gaiety; he reads its novels; he frequents its haunts of amusement; he enjoys its company; he relishes its foolish talking and jesting;—is he "a new creature," is he "in Christ Jesus?" Is it possible that, with so much worldliness, so much selfishness, so much self-indulgence, so much pleasing of the flesh, he can have been "begotten again," whatever his profession may be?

"In Christ!" How mighty the expression! How singular, yet how exact the description! "In Christ," then, out of the world. "In Christ," then, out of self! "In Christ," then, no more in the flesh, no more in sin, no more in vanity, no more in darkness, no more in the crooked paths of the god of this world. "A new creature!"—then, from the very root of being, upward throughout all its branches, a marvellous change has taken place, a change which nothing can fitly describe, save the creating of all things out of nothing at the beginning, or the new-creating of this corrupted world into a glorious earth and heaven, when the Lord returns to take possession of it as his kingdom for ever. "A new creature!"—then old feelings, old habits, old tastes, old hopes, old joys, old sorrows, old haunts, old companionships,—all are gone! Old things have passed away, all things have become new. Christ in us, and we in Christ,—how thorough and profound the change must have been! "Christ formed in us," nay, "in us the hope of glory;" and we created in Christ unto good works after the very likeness of incarnate Godhead,—how inconceivably glorious the renewal,—the transfiguration wrought in us,—for nothing short of transfiguration is it, considered even in its general and most common aspect.

But the expression is a peculiar one, and worthy of our careful notice. It is not, "If any man be a new creature, he is in Christ Jesus; as if the being in Christ were merely a result of his being a new creature; but it is, "If any man be in Christ, he is a new creature;" implying that it is his inbeing in Christ that makes him a new creature, and that this newness of being springs from his being in Christ. It is the soil of paradise alone that can produce the trees of righteousness, so it is our being "rooted in Christ" that gives birth and growth to the new creation. It is not the tree that makes the soil, but the soil the tree. What would even the vine, or the fig, or the pomegranate, be, if planted on the bare rock, or the salt, grey sand? Let us then mark the words,—"If any man be in Christ, he is a new creature." It is his grafting into Christ that has made him what he is. Christ himself is the soil in which the Holy Spirit plants, with his own hand, the trees that grow up and flourish in the courts of our God.

But the words are even more peculiar than our translation shews. Literally rendered, they give this sense, "If any man be in Christ, *there is a new creation*,"—that is, a new creation is the result; a creation not less perfect or majestic than that which the prophet announces, "Behold, I create new heavens and a new earth;" or than that which Christ himself proclaims, when it is said, "He that sat upon the throne said, Behold, I make all things new." Thus, then, in the case of the man that is in Christ Jesus, there is "a new creation,"—a new creation within, a new creation without,—a new creation already in part accomplished, but waiting its blessed consummation when the great Creator returns in glory to complete his handiwork within and without, in soul and in body, in heaven and in earth.

Let us look, then, at this new creation, first, as it is within us; and secondly, as it is without us.

I. *The new creation within.*—This I do not confine to the mere renewing of our moral nature. It seems to take a wider range.

(1.) *First of all, it points to our new standing before God.* If I be a new creature in Christ, then I stand before God, not in myself, but in Christ He sees no longer me, but only him in whom I am,—

him who represents me, Christ Jesus, my substitute and surety. In believing, I have become so identified with the Son of his love, that the favour with which he regards him passes over to me, and rests, like the sunshine of the new heavens, upon me. In Christ, and through Christ, I have acquired a new standing before the Father. I am "accepted in the beloved." My old standing, viz., that of distance, and disfavour, and condemnation, is wholly removed, and I am brought into one of nearness, and acceptance, and pardon: I am made to occupy a new footing, just as if my old one had never been. Old guilt, heavy as the mountain, vanishes; old dread, gloomy as midnight, passes off; old suspicion, dark as hell, gives place to the joyful confidence arising from forgiveness and reconciliation, and the complete blotting out of sin. All things are made new. I have changed my standing before God; and that simply in consequence of that oneness between me and Christ, which has been established, through my believing the record given concerning him. I come to him on a new footing, for I am "in Christ," and in me there has been a new creation.

(2.) *It points to our new relationship to God.* If I am a new creature, then I no longer bear the same relationship to God. My old connection has been dissolved, and a new one established. I was an alien once, I am now a son; and as a son, have the privilege of closest fellowship. Every vestige of estrangement between us is gone. At every point, instead of barriers rising up to separate and repel, there are links, knitting us together in happiest, closest union. Enmity is gone on my part, displeasure on his. He calls me son, I call him Father. Paternal love comes down on his part, filial love goes up on mine. The most entire mutual confidence has been established between us. No more a stranger and a foreigner, I am become a fellow-citizen with the saints, and of the household of God, every cloud being withdrawn that could cast a single shadow upon the simple gladness of our happy intercourse. There has been truly a new creation; "old things have passed away, all things have become new." Our new relationship is for eternity. He is eternally my Father; and I am eternally his son.

(3.) *It points to the spiritual renewal of the whole inner man.* In this respect the new creation has done wonders indeed. It has not only broken my chains, and given me the liberty of the heavenly adoption, but it has altered the whole frame and bent of my being, so that, as formerly, by the law of my old nature, I sought the things beneath, so now, by the necessity of my new nature, I seek the things above. Sin has become hateful, holiness supremely attractive. The flesh has lost its power, the Spirit has gotten dominion. The vision has been purged, so that now I see everything as with a new eye; the evil, with an eye that loathes it; the good, with an eye that loves it. I approach everything with new feelings, new tastes, new sympathies and antipathies. I behold everything in a new light, and from a new position and point of view. Myself, this world, the world to come, God and Christ, and the everlasting joys,—all these are to me now what they have never been before. My whole inner man has changed respecting them. There has been a new creation.

Oh, the unimaginable blessedness of those on whom this new creation has taken place. Oh, the unutterable, the endless misery of those on whom no change has passed, in whom old things still remain, and who shall be left for ever to the dominion of that old nature, in which there is the love of sin and the hatred of Christ, and the enmity to God, and all that can fill the soul with woe and darkness; all that can create a hell to man or devil,—a a hell within and a hell without; a hell, with its consuming fire and its everlasting curse; a hell, with its despair and darkness, and incurable remorse; a hell, with all the memories of quickened conscience, and the stings of its undying worm; a hell, with its separation from heaven and all holy beings; a hell, with its weeping, and wailing, and gnashing of teeth!

II. *We speak, in the second place, of the new creation without.* What we have already said regarding the new creation is certainly contained in the apostle's words; but it does not exhaust them. There is more behind; and in reading the passage in its whole connection, we are made to feel as if its special reference were to the new creation without,—the new creation which we look for at the coming of the Lord. In this, the words find their complete fulfilment. This only exhausts or fills up the expression, "There is a new creation." This only rightly satisfies the description, "Old things are passed away; behold, all things are become new."

And this is truly the manner of Scripture. It makes use of an expression whose vast compass includes a great range of kindred objects. It takes up a figure which will apply to the whole of a particular process, or series of steps, and which, according to the circumstances, we may use to denote the beginning or the end, the first small unfolding or the perfect consummation, of which that first unfolding was the germ, or root, or seed. Thus the word "redemption" is used; sometimes referring to the first step of that process,—the plucking us out of the prison of the strong one,—and sometimes to the glorious summing-up, in the resurrection of the body and the installation into the kingdom. In like manner " salvation " is used, so that in one place we are said to be already saved, in believing; at another time, we are said to be waiting for a salvation which the mighty Saviour is to bestow on us when he "appears the second time, without sin, unto salvation." Thus the new creation comprehends everything which that word can denote,—the renewal of the inner man at conversion, the restoration of the outer man at the resurrection of the just, the introduction into that kingdom of glory which is to consist of "new heavens and a new earth." The apostle's words would thus signify, not merely that if any man be in Christ he is made new within, but if any man be in Christ he is made an inheritor of the new creation, an heir of God, and a joint-heir with Christ Jesus. There has been a new creation within, and its counterpart, the new creation without, is as certainly his inheritance. The one is the beginning and earnest of the other. The indwelling Spirit, who is the author of the new creation, is the earnest of the inheritance, until the redemption of the purchased possession, and by him we are sealed unto the day of redemption.

But how is it, then, that the apostle speaks of this new creation as past already, whereas it is yet to come? For the same reason, and in the same way, that he speaks of our "having received a kingdom," whereas the kingdom is yet future; of our being made kings and priests, whereas our kingship and priesthood are not yet realised; of our having "come to mount Zion, to the city of the living God, the heavenly Jerusalem," whereas we are only on our way to these; of our being seated with Christ in heavenly places, whereas we are still sojourners on earth. In these passages we are represented as actually having that, which will, ere long, be ours; we are spoken of as actually in the midst of scenes, which are shortly to compass us about. We are said and supposed to be where *faith* places us,—faith, which " is the substance of things hoped for, the evidence of things not seen." So powerful and so intense is the anticipation of faith, that what is future becomes present, nay, past ; what is invisible becomes visible, what is far off becomes nigh.

In the passage before us, then, the apostle at once carries us forward into the midst of promised glory. If we are in Christ, then are we not only where he is just now, at the Father's right hand, but where he shall be hereafter, when he comes to make all things new. To be in Christ is to be in the midst of that new creation, which is to come forth from the ruins of these old heavens and this worn-out earth. If any be in Christ, then to him the new creation has come,—" Old things are passed away ; behold, all things are become new." He is not so much one dwelling in this valley of tears, or even one looking from the hills of Moab, to survey the land of his inheritance ; he is like one who has already reached his glorious home,— who sees around him the perfections of the new creation,—to whom old things have passed away, and all things have been made new, and who is looking back upon this land of the storm and the curse, as one who has escaped its evils, and on the wings of a dove has found his way to the city of peace, and laid himself down upon the banks of the pure river, clear as crystal, proceeding out of the throne of God and of the Lamb. Thus faith is taught to anticipate the glory, and to dwell in the midst of it, as if it had actually arrived; so that if any man be in Christ, to him the new creation has already come; "Old things are passed away; behold, all things are become new."

If these things be so, then how differently, from from what we too often do, should we read such chapters as the two closing ones of Revelation. It is not imagination, dwelling upon pictures, as some speak; it is faith conducting us into the very midst of the reality. It is not a prying curiosity, craving after excitement, that incites us to conjecture or speculation as to what we shall be hereafter; it is faith leading us into the many mansions, and bidding us dwell there even now. It is not visions or dreams, giving us pictures of the unreal; it is faith transporting us at once into the midst of the real, so that in reading God's revelation respecting the new creation, we feel as if we were more truly and sensibly surrounded by its unseen glories than by all that we here touch, and taste, and hear, and see.

If these things be so, then what manner of persons ought we to be in all holy conversation and godliness? For our dwellings are not now outside the courts of God, or merely within view of a far-off glory. They are within the sanctuary, nay, within the holy of holies. Beside the mercy-seat, within the veil, under the very brightness of Jehovah's presence,—there faith places us; there we pitch our tents; there we spend our days. And surely, by beholding this glory, not afar off, but nigh, we ought to be changed into the same image from glory to glory, even as by the Spirit of the Lord.

To be in Christ Jesus! How much may be expected from us, in all holiness, and truth, and conformity to the will of God. To be seated with him in heavenly places, partakers of his love and throne,—what ought this elevation to do for us, in bringing us into the resemblance of him at whose side we are seated! To see and feel ourselves so surrounded with the purity and glory of the new creation, as that the new heavens and earth seem nearer us, and more closely in contact with us, than this present evil world,—what a purifying influence ought such a thought to exert upon us! What manner of persons ought we to be in all holy conversation and godliness? How entire should be the separation between us and a world such as this,—a world whose influences are all unholy, whose tendencies are all downward, and whose friendship is enmity with God. If we be in Christ, then its old things have passed away, passed out of sight, and are to us among the things that were, but now are not. If we be in Christ, then the new things of "the world to come" have taken their room, and are to us the great realities which occupy both eye and ear. What, then, have we to do with sin, with the flesh, with the vanities of so vain a life as the men of earth are leading? Our "conversation," our "citizenship," is in heaven. How consistent, then, ought we to be, how watchful, how circumspect in word deed, and that men may know how completely we have broken our connection with this present evil world. Our relationship to the new creation, "the inheritance of the saints in light," is close and sure! How thoroughly conformed to this "world to come" ought we to be!

Again, if these things be so, how little ought we to be moved by the tribulations that attend us. Offences will come, sorrows will come, burdens, cares, annoyances, thorns in the flesh, will come. We shall be tempted; we shall suffer; we shall be shot at by the archers; we shall groan, being burdened; we shall be weary and faint, and sometimes heavy-hearted. But let us not be shaken. Let none of these things move us, or occasion aught of dismay and darkness, as if all were going wrong with us. Let us call to mind the new creation into which we have been introduced. Let us look around us on its glories, and go upon our way rejoicing. Why should we be cast down with the changes of the changing earth, seeing the unchangeable is already ours? Why should we be fretted, and vexed, and tossed too and fro, when old things have passed away, and all things have become new? Why should we sigh, and weep, and bow down the head, seeing the lines have fallen unto us in such pleasant places, and so goodly a heritage is ours?

SERMON LI.

APOSTOLIC SIGHS.

"I would to God ye did reign, that we also might reign with you."—
1 Cor. iv. 8.

This is one of the very few passages in which the apostle gives vent to his feelings as a suffering and injured man. Through no less than six verses here (8-13), there runs the utterance of a solemn sorrow,—we might almost call it melancholy,—at the contemplation of his present lot as an apostle of the Lord.

His life had many a bitterness. Danger, weariness, contempt, persecution, hunger, thirst, nakedness, buffeting, reviling, stoning, bonds;—these were its chief earthly ingredients; and had there not been something heavenly, compensating for all these, he would have been, of all men, most miserable. He *felt* the sorrow; for conversion had not lifted him out of the region of human feeling; yet, he seldom refers to it; and when he does, it is more with triumph than with sadness; as when he says, " I reckon that the sufferings of this present time are not worthy to be compared with the glory that shall be revealed in us" (Rom. viii. 18.)

Here his reference to his sorrows has more in it

of sadness than elsewhere. Yet he has not repented of his course; he is not ashamed of his apostleship; he is willing to drink even a bitterer cup than he has yet tasted. The sadness that thus comes is altogether natural, and shews how truly the apostle was a *man;* a man of like passions with ourselves. We get a passing insight into the noble soul, and learn how profoundly he felt the evils, that, like the waves of the storm, beat upon him without ceasing; and how oftentimes his heart was like to break, even in the midst of the joy unspeakable and full of glory,

He does not draw back, nor refuse to pay the cost of apostleship. He accepts the present honour and the coming glory, with all their conditions and penalties. For the joy set before him he endures the shame. But he feels the agony; and Oh, with what a tone of serene, yet shaded feeling do we hear him speak these words, " I think that God hath set forth us the apostles last, as it were appointed to death; for we are made a spectacle unto the world, and to angels, and to men. We are fools for Christ's sake, but ye are wise in Christ; we are weak, but ye are strong; ye are honourable, but we are despised. Even unto this present hour we both hunger, and thirst, and are naked, and are buffeted, and have no certain dwelling-place; and labour, working with our own hands; being reviled, we bless; being persecuted, we suffer it; being defamed, we entreat; we are made as the filth of the world, and are the offscouring of all things unto this day."

With some, I fear, there is more than the apostle's sorrow. They do not, perhaps, repent having taken up the cross ; but they shrink sometimes from what it has brought upon them. They counted on a little, but it has come to much. They gladly took up the cross, but they had not ascertained its weight and its sharpness. They were prepared for some bitterness ; but not for all this gall and wormwood. They made ready for battle, but the fight has proved sorer and longer than they dreamed of. They were not unwilling to bear shame for his name ; but the reproach has proved heavier than they can bear. They knew that they were to meet resistance from the world ; —but not all this enmity, this malignity, this misrepresentation. They did not refuse sacrifice and suffering ; but the poverty, the disappointment, and the all but broken heart, have gone beyond their calculations. The wounds are deeper, the fiery darts are sharper, the furnace is hotter, the road is rougher, the hill is higher, the stream is deeper, than they had thought.

They do not wish they had not become Christians ; but they hardly know what to do, nor which way to turn. They submit, but they do not count it all joy. They have the sadness of the apostle, without his exulting gladness. His was but half a sorrow, because of the joy ; theirs is but half a joy, because of the sorrow. In such a case, they need to be put in mind of the apostolic hope, by which the primitive Church was sustained, lest Satan should get an advantage over them, or lest they be weary and faint in their minds.

There is another class of Christians, however, of whom Paul here more especially speaks. They are the easy-minded and self-satisfied, who think themselves full and rich. They have not been emptied from vessel to vessel, and so they have settled on their lees. They are not Laodiceans, but very near them; they are not foolish virgins, but very like them. They would not think of following the world; but they do not like the idea of confronting and condemning it. They would rather be saved from the ill-will and scorn which separation from its vanities and gaieties is sure to produce; all the while enjoying Christianity at their firesides, and congratulating themselves on the prudence by means of which they have succeeded in avoiding the reproach, without relinquishing their profession. They would rather not expose themselves to too much shame, for over-zeal, or over-decision, or over-boldness in the cause of Christ. A little compromise with the world, they think, does no harm. A proper enjoyment of its harmless amusements, they are persuaded, is of great benefit to themselves, and of wonderful use in conciliating worldly men, and smoothing away their prejudices. They look with no small dislike upon the outspoken fervour of fearless single-eyed disciples, to whom Christ is everything, and the world nothing;

nay, they join with the scoffer in reviling these men as excited enthusiasts; professing themselves the best of Christians all the while, and announcing that the religion they admire is unostentatious and undemonstrative, modest and retiring; nay, they grow warm in denouncing zeal for Christ, and never fail to add that these over-zealous Christians do more harm than good. Of such it is that the apostle writes these words of solemn rebuke,—"Now ye are full, now ye are rich, ye have reigned as kings without us." And it is in reference to their conduct that he adds these other words of sorrowful irony,—"I would to God ye did reign, that we also might reign with you;" I would it were what you seem to think, the time of the kingdom; I would that the day of reigning were come, that we might be delivered from these calamities; but, alas for us, that day has not yet broken; we are not in the kingdom yet, but only suffering the tribulation on the way to it.

Let us now ascertain the exact teaching of these words.

I. *There is a reign for us.*—We are made kings and priests unto God, in virtue of our oneness with him who is our King and Priest as well as God's King and Priest. The Church is a royal priesthood, a noble band of Melchisedecs, each one of which can say even now, "We have received the kingdom that cannot be moved." In unison with the host above, we sing not only, "Thou hast redeemed us by thy blood," but, "We shall reign on the earth." It doth not yet appear what we shall be,—for the disguise of mortality is on us,—but we know that the crown of life, the crown of righteousness, is in store for us, and that, if we suffer, we shall also reign. Not safety merely, nor blessedness, nor glory, but a kingdom, a sceptre, a throne. The world's reign is now; the Church's reign is coming. Satan is now earth's prince; Christ will soon be king.

II. *That reign will end our tribulation.* There is first the suffering, and then the glory. The dawn of the glory is the dispersion of the clouds, and the stilling of the storm. For that glory comes from the presence of the glorious one; and in his presence there can be no mourning, and no darkness. It is *his* reign, as well as *ours;* and into his kingdom nothing that defileth or darkeneth shall enter. Were that era still the time of his *absence*, we could not be assured of its unmingled brightness; but it is the day of his *presence*, and that is the assurance to us of its sorrowless splendour. There shall be no night there, for the sun goes not down. There shall be no more curse, for the Blessed One is there. The winter is past; the rain is over and gone; the clouds return no more. Not the kingdom only, but the King, has come; and with him all his saints. The last battle is over; the usurper dethroned and bound; mortality is swallowed up of life; the days of mourning are ended; the tears are wiped away. The marriage of the Lamb is come; the Bride and the Bridegroom have met; the New Jerusalem has descended; Solomon and Pharaoh's daughter are upon its throne. We shall hear no longer of a church militant and a church triumphant; no more of a "divided Christ," or a "divided Church;" part weeping, part rejoicing; some above, some below; souls in heaven, bodies in the grave; Christ's redeemed members scattered everywhere. All this is over. Separation, distance, death, toil, weariness, sighing,—all have fled away. The year of the redeemed is come. Their reproach is ended; their reigning is begun.

III. *We are to look and long for that reign.*—When the apostle says, "I would to God that ye did reign, that we also might reign with you," he meant to say, "Oh that that day were come which ye seem to think has arrived already; then should we and you rejoice and triumph together." He saw nothing on this side of that reign but reproach and tribulation. Streaks of sunlight there might be, but not the day. Hours of rest might relieve the lifetime's weariness, but "the rest that remaineth" was awaiting the arrival of the King.

In prosperous days the Church has forgotten these things; becoming contented with the imperfect and the mortal; ceasing to sigh for the incorruptible and the undefiled. Hence she cannot be trusted with ease. This has always been to her a peril and a snare. In gracious wisdom God has made her path rough and her cup bitter ; that she may not take her ease, nor tarry by the way ; but set her affection on things above.

In telling us of the kingdom, God meant us to think much of it, to desire it, to count all earth a shadow when compared to it. Our eyes are to be upward, eastward, watching for the day. Our "hearts' desire and prayer" is to be for the hastening of the kingdom. For the Church's sake, as well as for our own, we are to plead for its arrival. This is our hope ; and there is none like it ! These are our prospects, and what is there here that can come between them and us ! It is not sentimentalism, nor fanaticism, nor fancy, to desire the kingdom. It is simple faith ; that faith which is the substance of things hoped for. Love, too, constrains us to these longings. Yes, love ; love to the king compels us ; for while the expectation of glory to ourselves is no mean nor feeble motive ; yet, above and beyond this, there is personal attachment to the Lord himself ; — true-hearted loyalty which quickens within us the vehement longing that he should be glorified !

SERMON LII.

THE CHURCH'S AMEN.

"He which testifieth these things saith, Surely I come quickly: Amen. Even so, come, Lord Jesus. The grace of our Lord Jesus Christ be with you all. Amen."—REV. xxii. 20, 21.

It is "the true Witness" that speaks here. He speaks from heaven; and not to his apostles merely, nor to the seven Asian churches, nor to the saints of his own age; but to *us* in these last times.

This is the final burden of the Church's great prophet; and these last words of his are heard, not in Jerusalem or its temple, by crowds of listeners in the old land of prophets; but in a Gentile island afar off, amid desolate silence; as if to intimate that the glory had departed from Israel, and that the sure word of prophecy, though still issuing from Jewish lips, must no longer be spoken in Israel's land. The voice which we hear is that of "one crying in the wilderness;" and speaking, across the waves of the Ægean, to the distant nations of earth, and to the ages yet to come.

Yes; the Speaker is the "Faithful Witness," the "Amen," the first-begotten of the dead, the Alpha and the Omega;—He of the "golden girdle" (i. 13); and the "golden candlesticks" (i. 12); and the "seven stars" (i. 16); and the "flaming eyes"

(i. 14); whose "voice is as the sound of many waters" (i. 15). It is He, indeed, "the root and the offspring of David, the bright and morning star!"

It is of the last things that he speaks; and these concern us more deeply, as the ages roll by. The time has been long; longer than the church believed in early days; but the lapse of so many ages is to us the best assurance, that the time of tarrying is drawing to a close; that the night is far spent, and the day at hand.

There are five *last* things here which form the contents of this final burden: the last testimony; the last prophecy; the last prayer; the last blessing; the last Amen.

I. *The last testimony.*—The whole Bible is the testimony; for in it Christ is both the teacher and the lesson, the witness and the testimony. But the Revelation is his *last* testimony; and the marvellous words of the latter part of this chapter are more especially so. Let the Church listen; let the world give heed.

> Oh, but they say the tongues of dying men
> Enforce attention, like deep harmony.

And these are more than the words of dying men. They are Christ's last words from the heaven of heavens; fraught with infinite significance; breathing both love and terror, like the very "trump of God." Terrible is the warning, "He that is unjust, let him be unjust still;" yet winning is the grace, "Whosoever will, let him take of the water of life freely." Glorious is the proclamation, "I am the root and the offspring of David, the bright and morning star;" yet blessed the attitude in which it seeks to place us, "The Spirit and the bride say, Come; and let him that heareth say, Come." Truly this final testimony is the fullest, the most startling of all. It sounds like the voice of the last trumpet.

II. *The last prophecy.*—" Surely I come quickly." Brief but distinct is this announcement; and it comes from his own lips. He heralds himself and his kingdom. He puts the trumpet to his own mouth to sound abroad this last message, "I come!" I came, and I come! I who came, and departed, am coming again. Yes, I myself! Not certain great events, whether terrible or glorious; not revolutions merely, or wars, or the overthrow of kingdoms, or famines, or pestilences; but I myself in person! Not the latter-day brightness only, nor the spread of truth, nor the restoration of Israel, nor the conversion of the world; but I myself in person! Ah, yes; this is the one mighty event which fills up the vast future of the world's history, and makes all other things to seem as nothing. "I come *quickly.*" Here is something more. He will lose no time; nor delay a moment longer than is absolutely necessary. He will not be slack concerning his promise (2 Pet. iii. 9); he will come, and not tarry (Heb. x. 37.) A faithless church shall not be able to say, "My Lord delayeth his coming" (Luke xii. 45); nor a world of mockers to ask, "Where is the promise of his coming" (2 Pet. iii. 4)? Yes; "*Surely* I come quickly." Appearances may indicate no such thing; the world's sky may be cloudless, and its sea smooth; men may have assured themselves of prosperous days, and be saying, "Peace and safety;" yet *surely* he cometh! As a snare, as a thief, as lightning, he cometh! He, the very Christ, the risen Saviour, Jesus of Nazareth,—he cometh! In his own glory, in his Father's glory, with his mighty angels, in the clouds of heaven, King and Judge, Conqueror and Avenger, Redresser of wrongs, Opener of prison-doors, Binder of Satan, Renewer of creation, Bridegroom of his Church, Star of Jacob, Sun of Righteousness, Owner of the golden sceptre, Wielder of the iron rod, Wearer of the crowns of earth,—he cometh!

III. *The last prayer.*—"Amen. Even so come, Lord Jesus;" or, as the words more literally run, "Yes, surely, come, Lord Jesus;" for the words the apostle here uses, in his response, are the same as those used by Christ in his announcement; as if he caught up the Master's words and echoed them. Thus gladly and fervently does the Church respond to the promise; as one who felt the blank created by the Lord's absence, and welcomed with her whole heart the intimation of his return; for she is her beloved's and her beloved is hers; his desire is toward her, and hers is toward him. This is the summing up of her petitions, as was the seventy-second Psalm the filling up of all David's prayers (Ps. lxxii. 20). Are *our* hearts, like hers, thus beating toward the Beloved One? Is this the burden of *our* prayers? Or, at least, does this petition always form a part of them? Alas! Is not this the petition most commonly left out? Is not the Lord's advent the thing but seldom prayed for? We plead for the coming of the kingdom, but not for the arrival of the King. Yet this, more than ever in these last days, ought to be the first and last of the Church's prayers; for all that she desires for herself, for the world, and for her Lord himself, is comprised in this. It was the beloved disciple that first burst forth with this eager response, " Amen. Even so, come, Lord Jesus." The words came from the inmost soul of him who had, sixty years before, leaned on the Master's bosom. Sad because of the long absence, wearied with exile, tired with persecution, sore at heart because of the backsliding in the Churches, overwhelmed with the terrific announcements he had just been the instrument of uttering in his island-prison, he quickly took up the glad promise, and responded, " Even so, come, Lord Jesus." It ought to be so with us. We have many things to try us, and to make us long for the arrival of the Lord. We have this vile body to weigh us down. We have fightings without and fears within. We have sin and error and defection in the Church.

We have abounding iniquity in the world. We have dear ones that have been laid to sleep by Jesus, in the grave, to await resurrection and reunion. Shall not these things, enforced by personal attachment to the Lord himself, prompt the unceasing petition, "Even so, come, Lord Jesus?"

IV. *The last blessing.*—"The grace of our Lord Jesus Christ be with you all." Thus the Holy Spirit shuts up the volume; and the beloved disciple sends out this as his last salutation to the saints; as if he could ask nothing greater for the Church on earth than the communication of the free-love of him to whom he here gives his full designation, *Lord Jesus Christ.* It was on this free-love that we took our stand when first we received the Father's testimony to the beloved Son; and it is our belief of this free-love that makes us what we are, and separates us from a world to whom this free-love is nothing;—"we have known and believed the love that God hath to us." A small point of difference this may seem to many; but in God's estimation everything;—the belief or disbelief of the free-love of Father, Son, and Holy Ghost. It is on this free-love that we rest; it is out of this fountain that our enjoyment flows; and it is under the shadow of this pillar-cloud that we pass through the wilderness to the city of habitation. Let no evil heart of unbelief separate us from this grace, or make it seem less precious and divine. This is the pure river, clear as crystal, proceeding from the throne of God and of the Lamb. He that drinks is refreshed for evermore. What then can an apostle, knowing, as John did, the contents of this vessel of grace, desire more for the saints, than the continued possession of the Master's grace. It is this that, upon its calm current, carries into the soul all joy and strength, all health and consolation; and he who will allow these heavenly waters thus to pervade him will lack nothing. Earthly, human love, is of all things here the most fitted to gladden; how much more, then, that which is heavenly and divine! It is food, and water, and wine, and medicine; it is light, and air, and liberty, and refreshment; and what more can we desire, for the best beloved of our hearts, than this free-love of God; or what larger prayer can we breathe out towards them than this, "The grace of our Lord Jesus Christ be with you?"

V. *The last amen.*—This is not an amen to this chapter only, or this book only; but to the whole Bible; of which the burden, from Genesis to Revelation, is Jesus Christ, the seed of the woman. It is an amen to the prayer for the grace of Christ; it is an amen to the sigh for the Lord's appearing. It is an amen to the prophetic announcement of all the glorious and all the terrible things written in this book. It is the concentrated utterance of the Church's longings; her glad response to all that **God has spoken**; the subscription of her name to her belief in all that the Holy Spirit has written; the summing up of her unutterable groan. How much does this amen comprise! Faith, hope, and love are in it; and, with these, such a boundless satisfaction of spirit as can only get vent to itself in that one brief word, which sums up all the aspirations of its joy, "Amen and amen!"

As a golden clasp, it draws together and fastens into one the now finished parts of the heavenly volume; reminding us of its verity and perfection, its fulness and its accuracy, as the record not only of the thoughts, but the words of him who is himself the Word, the Truth, the divine Amen. As God's seal, it vouches for the infallible certainty of Scripture; as man's seal, it expresses his acquiescence in that revelation, as well as his confidence in its teachings of wisdom, as the unchangeable and the true.

We, too, in this last age, add our *Amen*, as did David when he said, "The prayers of David the son of Jesse are ended." Ours is, indeed, but a fragment of the universal amen of heaven and earth, one note of the Church's triumphant utterance in the day when all shall be fulfilled that God has written from the beginning. Still, we speak it, as the setting of our seal to the truthfulness of that Holy Spirit by whom holy men of old spake as they were moved. Yes; we add our Amen;—solemn, yet joyful; retrospective, yet also prospective; the outbreathing of prayer, yet of hope as well; in the assurance, that what we read is no volume of speculation or opinion, still less of cunningly devised fables; but the book of truth,—fixed, authentic, divine,—the one genuine book of unmingled truth which an untrue world contains.

THE END.

www.ingramcontent.com/pod-product-compliance
Lightning Source LLC
Chambersburg PA
CBHW051849300426
44117CB00006B/317